FOLLOWING THE DRUMS

FOLLOWING THE DRUMS

AFRICAN AMERICAN
FIFE AND DRUM MUSIC
IN TENNESSEE

JOHN M. SHAW

UNIVERSITY PRESS OF MISSISSIPPI / JACKSON

The University Press of Mississippi is the scholarly publishing agency of the Mississippi Institutions of Higher Learning: Alcorn State University, Delta State University, Jackson State University, Mississippi State University, Mississippi University for Women, Mississippi Valley State University, University of Mississippi, and University of Southern Mississippi.

www.upress.state.ms.us

The University Press of Mississippi is a member of the Association of University Presses.

In this book, some quoted material contains racial slurs for African Americans. While those words have been retained in elided form, this is in no way an endorsement of the use of such slurs outside a scholarly context.

First printing 2022
∞

Library of Congress Cataloging-in-Publication Data

Names: Shaw, John M., (John Michael) 1967– author.
Title: Following the drums : African American fife and drum music in Tennessee / John M. Shaw.
Other titles: American made music series.
Description: Jackson : University Press of Mississippi, 2022. | Series: American made music series | Includes bibliographical references and index.
Identifiers: LCCN 2021060227 (print) | LCCN 2021060228 (ebook) | ISBN 978-1-4968-3954-1 (hardback) | ISBN 978-1-4968-3955-8 (trade paperback) | ISBN 978-1-4968-3957-2 (epub) | ISBN 978-1-4968-3956-5 (epub) | ISBN 978-1-4968-3959-6 (pdf) | ISBN 978-1-4968-3958-9 (pdf)
Subjects: LCSH: Fife and drum corps—Tennessee—History. | Fife and drum corps music—Tennessee—History and criticism. | African American musicians—Tennessee—Interviews. | African Americans—Music—History and criticism. | Music and race—United States—History.
Classification: LCC ML1311.T3 S53 2022 (print) | LCC ML1311.T3 (ebook) | DDC 784.8/309768—dc23
LC record available at https://lccn.loc.gov/2021060227
LC ebook record available at https://lccn.loc.gov/2021060228

British Library Cataloging-in-Publication Data available

"I used to follow the drums, but I've gotten too young for that now . . ."
—CAROLYN HULETTE, SENATOBIA, MISSISSIPPI, AUGUST 2018

CONTENTS

FOREWORD

One afternoon in the summer of 1984, when I was still a student at Bartlett High School, I was sitting on the front porch of my friend Jessie Yancey's house in the Oak Grove community east of Bartlett. There was a distant sound of drums booming, and I asked Jessie what it was. "There's a tribe back in those woods," he replied, with his characteristic sense of dry humor. Nothing more was said about it that afternoon, but years later, I recalled the incident with a friend who had been there that day, and he said that what we heard was the result of something going on at "a lodge." There was a white Masonic lodge at Ellendale, and I had thought that perhaps this was what my friend meant, but I have come to believe that I was possibly hearing the last of Black fife and drum activity in the Bartlett area. There were chapters of the Independent Pallbearers Society, or IPB, at both Oak Grove and Brunswick, and a chapter of the Social Benevolent Society at Fullview Missionary Baptist Church in Ellendale. The tradition of these organizations was to beat drums to announce the death of a member, and sometimes at the funerals of members as well.

More particularly, this present work resulted from a investigation I initiated to determine if Fayette County, a historically Black county in West Tennessee, had a fife and drum or blues culture similar to that of Marshall County, Mississippi, the county just below it in the Mississippi Hill Country. Ultimately, I learned that it did, but a by-product of the search was a reference to a Bartlett fife and drum band, the United Sons and Daughters of Zion No. 9 Band, an ensemble that was led by the Bartlett bluesman Lum Guffin, and that had been recorded (perhaps in 1973) by the Swedish blues researcher Bengt Olsson.

That info led to a comprehensive search for Black fife and drum music in Tennessee, and thanks to advances in technology such as the online digitization of newspapers—which in turn has made them searchable by keyword—it is now possible to find historic references to Black fife and drum bands and events, as well as the social and benevolent societies that hired and sponsored them. This sound of fife and drum was in fact among the earliest secular forms of Black music after the Civil War, and it became a soundtrack of Black America during Reconstruction. It can now be stated conclusively that Black fife and drum music was ubiquitous in Tennessee during the years of Reconstruction, and although it was later clandestine and out of the public eye, it continued well into the early 1980s. As the generation that can recall the phenomenon of Black fife and drum bands at picnics is passing away, it is hoped that this work will commemorate and document a forgotten aspect of Tennessee's Black history and music history.

ACKNOWLEDGMENTS

This research would not have been possible without a large amount of assistance from many generous people. Thanks first of all to Dr. David Evans, my mentor, who started me down the road to traditional blues research, and who made me want to be an ethnomusicologist in the first place. Thanks to Dr. Kenneth Kreitner for patiently dealing with me as I pursue the study of popular music rather than classical music. Thanks to Kesha Burton and T. Dewayne Moore for inspiration. Thanks to Carl Vermilyea for his support of fife and drum research. Thanks to the Reverend Arthur Becton, who gave me important information about drummers, picnics, and the Social Benevolent Society No. 4 in Ellendale. Thanks to Roy Brewer, president of the Independent Pallbearers No. 6 of Brunswick, who agreed to be interviewed about the Brunswick Picnic and the fife and drum bands that played. Thanks to Errol Harmon, president of the Independent Pallbearers No. 9 of Capleville, his mother Elizabeth Harmon, and his aunt Sandra Stepton, who all gave valuable information about their chapter's fife and drum band and its picnics. Thanks to Annie Humphrey for filling in the gaps about her father's fife and drum band in the Fredonia community of Fayette County. Thanks to John Edwards and Myles Wilson, who both gave great background information about their respective counties, and John Marshall and Ted Maclin, who both gave great background history on the area around Mason, Braden, and Keeling, Tennessee, where fife and drum activity was rampant. Thanks to Murphy Thomas, who did his best to put me in contact with people who could remember fife and drum picnics in the Collierville/Mount Pisgah/Fisherville area. Thanks to David Katznelson, whose reissue of Bengt Olsson recordings made this research happen. Thanks to Bobby Merriwether, my friend and the grandson of Lum Guffin, as well as the members of the Guffin family, for their assistance and insight into Lum's music and life. Thanks to Robert Gordon and Suzette Moser, who graciously allowed me access to Bengt Olsson's unpublished manuscript about blues in West Tennessee, which yielded more important and helpful information. Thanks to the staff of the University of Memphis Libraries, the Memphis Public Library, and the Tennessee State Library and

Archives for their assistance. Thanks to Stephan Michelson, Giambattista Marcucci, Steve James, and Tav Falco for their assistance regarding Lum Guffin. Thanks to the late Bengt Olsson, whose research first revealed that there were fife and drum bands in Tennessee. And, finally, all thanks to God, without Whom nothing is possible.

A NOTE ON SOURCES

In writing this book on Black fife and drum music, it has been necessary to use some sources, including newspapers from older times, that use extremely offensive language with regard to race. After much deliberation, I have made the decision to quote the articles as written, rather than bowdlerizing the material, well aware that many will find the quotes offensive. For one thing, the articles are a product of their time, and since this book is at least in part about how white Southerners reacted to Black fife and drum bands, the racist language used by Southern white newspapers is certainly germane to the topic. Furthermore, I think it is important that we see starkly how the white Southern press during Reconstruction stoked the fires of racial hatred. If the editors claimed they were reflecting the opinions of their readers, it is of course just as true that they were shaping them too. It is possible that there still would have been trouble between the races even if the newspapers had been more reasonable and reasoned in their approach to the subject of race, but I am fairly certain that there would not have been as much trouble as there was. Would white Southerners have believed they were better than the best Black man if their morning paper had not told them so day after day? Finally, it also has to be noted that some of the most offensive articles also give some of the most useful information—the inscriptions carried on banners in Black parades, the tunes a Black fife and drum band played on the Memphis riverfront, the uniforms a Black benevolent society wore in a parade, and the like. Throwing out such articles because of the use of offensive language would impoverish our available information in many ways. It is certainly not my intent to offend unnecessarily, and I hope the reader will understand my reasoning.

It is also true that in the nineteenth century, there were fewer conventions of spelling and punctuation. Different reporters and editors spelled words differently, or used punctuation differently. I have also decided to quote articles verbatim—spelling, punctuation, or grammatical errors are generally not corrected in quoted articles. An exception might be a missing word I have added in brackets where the article as written makes no sense without doing so.

FOLLOWING THE DRUMS

INTRODUCTION

Black Fife and Drum Music and Previous Scholarship

Despite a seemingly fair amount of scholarly interest in Black fife and drum music since Alan Lomax first encountered such a group near Sledge, Mississippi, in 1942,[1] there have been few scholarly writings of any length on the subject. No books exist that deal solely with the topic, nor do any dissertations. Black fife and drum music, as found in the Mississippi Hill Country today, is a predominantly rural form of instrumental music, usually played at picnics. The band generally consists of a musician blowing a fife (often called a "fice" by older residents), a snare drum (often called a "kettle"), and a bass drum (which may be called a "drum" or a "big drum"). Most fife and drum bands consist of at least three musicians, although bands can be larger, or occasionally smaller, such as one fifer and one drummer. Sometimes the fife is omitted and the drummers play alone. Most commonly, the fifes are folk-made instruments of bamboo cane, although occasionally wood or metal fifes are seen. While the drums might also have been homemade at one time, all modern bands use manufactured drums. The genre today is primarily found only among the Turner/Thomas and Hurt families in Tate and Panola Counties in Mississippi. Although scholars and journalists tend to use the term "fife and drum band" or occasionally "fife and drum corps," it is more common to hear local residents refer to "the drums," a "drum band," or "drum and fife," all of which seem to emphasize the importance of the drums.

Three master's theses have been written about Black fife and drum music, and without exception, they all address the phenomenon as it is found in the Mississippi Hill Country, primarily centered around the Rising Star Fife and Drum Band as run by Othar Turner and his granddaughter Sharde Thomas.[2] Lauren Joiner's "'Stuff You Gotta Watch': The Effect of Anglo-American Scholarship on North Mississippi Blues Fife and Drum" was the first of these to appear, in August 2009.[3] Although Joiner gives a detailed account of the genre's origins and its similarities to some forms of African music, her primary focus is on the ways that interaction with

3

ethnomusicologists and blues researchers changed the music and its environment. Carl Vermilyea's "The Otha Turner Family Picnic: Occupying Musical and Social Space in-between Saturday Night and Sunday Morning" appeared in May 2011 and was primarily concerned with a particular Hill Country fife and drum event.[4] As such, although it yields a lot of interesting information about the genre in general, its primary focus is on Otha Turner's annual picnic and the Rising Star Fife and Drum Band in the Gravel Springs community near Senatobia, Mississippi. Later that same year, Canadian researcher Kathleen Danser's "Representations of African-American Fife and Drum Music in North Mississippi" appeared, basically a devastating review of the ways that films and recordings of the genre, controlled by outsiders, tended to emphasize an "exotic" or "primitive" framework for this music.[5] It is noteworthy that all of these works deal exclusively with the fife and drum phenomenon as it is found in Mississippi; only one of them, Vermilyea, mentions Tennessee, and that only in the discographical information at the end of the thesis.[6]

One dissertation, the masterly work of Dr. Sylvester Oliver of Holly Springs, touches on Black fife and drum music. His "African-American Musical Traditions in Northeast Mississippi" is an attempt to investigate Black music in an entire region, although the primary emphasis is on Marshall County, and as such, the work examines far more than just fife and drum music. Like the theses mentioned above, it deals only with the phenomenon as found in Mississippi.[7]

One scholarly article seems to deal strictly with fife and drum—Dr. David Evans's "Black Fife and Drum in Mississippi," which originally appeared in the *Mississippi Folklife Register* in 1972.[8] As its title suggests, it is primarily concerned with the tradition as found in the Mississippi Hill Country, although Evans mentions Bengt Olsson's research in Fayette County, Tennessee, regarding a fife and drum band,[9] and also George Mitchell's discovery of such a band in the Waverly Hall community in Georgia. Peculiarly, given the fair amount of awareness of the genre, Evans's 1972 article still remains one of the best articles on Black fife and drum music, even after forty-seven years.

Although no books deal strictly with fife and drum music in the Black community, quite a few deal with the subject at least in passing. Perhaps the very first to do so was the amazing *Drums and Shadows: Survival Studies among the Georgia Coastal Negroes*, a Georgia Writers Project book of the Works Project Administration that appeared in 1940, two years before Alan Lomax encountered Sid Hemphill's band near Sledge, Mississippi.[10] At a time when the general scholarly consensus was that the process of slavery had largely stripped African Americans of any African retentions, the team of ethnographers and writers that interviewed Black Georgians in the Sea Islands found many folk beliefs and practices of West African origin, including an emphasis on drums. While at least some of the drums and practices mentioned seemed to be more African or Caribbean in nature, the mention of "kettle drums" and "bass drums," their use to send messages, for funerals, and in connection with secret lodges and societies all resemble practices in Tennessee.

In the early 1970s, a couple of general books about Black music appeared that mentioned Black fife and drum music in a very general sense: Eileen Southern's *The Music of Black Americans* and John Storm Roberts's *Black Music of Two Worlds*.[11] In both of these works, only the briefest mention of the genre is made, with Roberts noting the occurrence of fife and drum ensembles in the Caribbean and West Africa as well, which he attributes to European influence.

The bulk of the remaining books that mention fife and drum do so in the context of the Mississippi Hill Country, and most of them specifically in reference to Napoleon Strickland, Sid Hemphill, or Othar Turner and the Rising Star Fife and Drum Band. These include works by George Mitchell, William Ferris, and Alan Lomax.[12]

More recently, a couple of books that are primarily composed of photographs have also featured Black fife and drum music, chiefly in Mississippi. These include George Mitchell's *Mississippi Hill Country 1967* and Michael Ford's *North Mississippi Homeplace*.[13]

Mississippi fife and drum music was also well documented in two recorded albums—*Afro-American Folk Music from Tate and Panola Counties, Mississippi* and *Traveling through the Jungle*,[14] both of which feature liner notes from Dr. David Evans—and in a film that Evans helped produce with William Ferris and Judy Peiser: *Gravel Springs Fife and Drum*, which documents Otha Turner's music at L. P. Buford's picnic near Senatobia.[15]

As can be seen, very little research exists on Black fife and drum activity outside of Mississippi, and there is almost none on the phenomenon as it occurred in Tennessee. The exceptions are an unpublished revision by Bengt Olsson of his seminal work *Memphis Blues*, which he left incomplete at his death in 2008, and a 1974 project by Mark and Judy Mikolas in conjunction with Bill Barth and Bengt Olsson to interview and film fife and drum musicians in the rural areas near Mason, Tennessee. The original publication of Olsson's book, although a groundbreaking achievement in its own right, did not mention Black fife and drum music at all.[16] On the other hand, the unpublished revision has a whole chapter devoted to the subject of Black fife and drum music in Tennessee, particularly the Broad-nax Brothers, the Fredonia Fife and Drum Band, and the United Sons and Daughters of Zion Chapter No. 9 Band of Bartlett, Tennessee, led by the blues musician Lum Guffin.[17] This material, some of which appeared earlier in the liner notes to the compact disc *On the Road Again* on the Flyright label, constitutes nearly all previous scholarship on Black fife and drum music in Tennessee.[18] Without Bengt Olsson's recordings and writings, we might have little to go on. The Mikolas project, which was at times somewhat confusingly referred to as "Memphis fife and drum," was under the auspices of the Super 8 Film Company of New York, owned by Mark Mikolas and Gunter Hoos, and it resulted in five hours of Super 8 film footage and fifteen hours of interview tapes.[19] Lack of funding forced the Mikolases to sideline that project in favor of a film about Cleo Williamson, a female blues musician from Simsboro, Arkansas, which was entitled *Tell the Angels*. The fife and drum materials were donated to the Center for Southern Folklore in Memphis but seem to have disappeared.

One of the difficulties with all of the existing research about Black fife and drum bands is a lack of discussion of its past, or of its context. How and why did these bands form? Who hired them? What role did this music play in the Black communities where it occurred? Were the bands independent organizations, or were they affiliated with other organizations? It is my intent to demonstrate that African Americans, newly emancipated from slavery at the dawn of Reconstruction, chose Black fife and drum music as a representation of a developing self-image as Black Americans. That fact explains the music's widespread application in that era, as well as the responses of white Southerners to it. It may also explain its decline after the so-called Redemption period of Southern politics, or at least its retreat to a more clandestine and rural existence.

Chapter 1

"TO DRUM FOR THE FUN OF THE THING"

African American Drumming and Fife and Drum Music before and during the Civil War, 1776–1865

As other researchers have pointed out, the beginnings and subsequent history of Black fife and drum music are not well documented, to say the least. The general assumption is that its beginnings are the result of the similarity between certain flute and drum ensembles in West Africa and the early American military tradition of fifers and drummers. Eileen Southern associated the emergence of Black fifers and drummers with their contact with the military traditions in colonial America: "Militia Day, also known as Training or Muster Day, never failed to attract a large gathering of bystanders, including slaves. More than likely, many a black fifer "picked up" the skill of playing his instrument on these occasions. In the early years, all servants, including "Negars" and Indians, were compelled to undergo military training. Every company has at least one fifer (or trumpeter) and one drummer."[1] Her views of a connection between early Black drumming in colonial or state militias and later fife and drum bands have been generally repeated by most scholars on the subject since, including Evans, Joiner, Lomax, and Vermilyea. But Lauren Joiner, who has written arguably the most in-depth attempt to account for the early origins of fife and drum music, also describes points of similarity with West African musical traditions: "In addition to these colonial roots, it is important to note that ensembles featuring different kinds of transverse flutes and drums existed in African traditional music. Paul Oliver recorded such a group of Mamprusi tribesmen in Ghana in the early 1970s for a recording entitled *Savannah Syncopators*. In other areas of Northern Ghana, similar ensembles still exist today such as jongo, a festival music native to the Kasena region."[2]

Outside of the military tradition, Southern has documented how colonial and state authorities in the South took steps to forbid drums and drumming among people of African descent, particularly after the use of drums in revolts such as the Stono Rebellion in South Carolina.[3] However, the rules do not seem to have been strictly enforced in matters related to the military or the militia, as Paul Alan Cimbala noted in his excellent thesis on slave musicians: "Slave musicians were also on hand for their masters' militia musters and parades. Since colonial times there had been a tradition of black musicians providing tuneful cadence for Southern cavaliers. Colonel Patton of North Carolina, for example, enlisted his slave as a drummer during the Revolution, and in the June 30, 1822 issue of the Baton Rouge Republic the owner of a runaway identified his slave as a former army drummer who had served in the War of 1812."[4] Cimbala goes on to list many antebellum references to Black fifers and drummers in the South and, in a footnote, links this antebellum practice to the later Georgia fife and drum tradition, although he also notes the differences between them.[5]

In summary, it would seem that the military fife and drum tradition created a perfect storm. Here was an American musical tradition involving instruments that were extremely importance in many West African cultures; and this music was being used to accompany marching, another activity found in certain African rituals. As a result, Black musicians were eager to play fifes and drums, while white military commanders believed that Blacks excelled at these tasks.

EARLY NEWSPAPER ACCOUNTS OF BLACK DRUMMERS

Perhaps somewhat surprisingly, Black drummers were almost always mentioned in early American newspapers, even in the South, in conjunction with military activities. One of the earliest accounts was from a Natchez newspaper called the *Mississippi Free Trader*, reprinting an article from the *New Orleans Delta*, regarding a drummer from the "Legion" named Dave Doody.[6] While the "Legion" is not otherwise identified, a later article from Marysville, Ohio, regarding a New Orleans parade in 1856 commemorating the Battle of New Orleans in the War of 1812 mentions the "Louisiana Legion" as well as a well-known Black drummer who had participated in the battle: "Leading one of the military bands was the great negro drummer Jordan—the same Jordan who beat the American Army to arms on the plain of Chalamette [*sic*] on that eventful day when English veterans turned their backs to the rifles of the militias of the south and west."[7] But a most remarkable article from an Alabama newspaper, the *Tuskegee Republican*, suggests that there were already emerging differences in white and Black drumming styles, and that at least initially, white Southerners enjoyed seeing and hearing Black drummers:

Last Saturday, we had the heaviest rain in this place that we have had for a month or six weeks, in consequence of which the regimental muster, that we were to have had, did not come off; but instead of it the negro drummer gave us a regular beat on his drum, which, for our part, we think infinitely superior to any muster we ever saw; and we think it would not be a bad plan, if the next Legislature would so alter and modify the law, as to have regular drumming on stated occasions, instead of the very irregular mustering that our officers regularly order. We don't see but what it would answer just as good a purpose in the way of making soldiers of our citizens and giving them, besides, a taste for music and the fine arts, and costing nobody nothing; as we have no doubt plenty of negroes can be got to beat the drum just for the fun of the thing.[8]

The perception seems to have been that Blacks enjoyed drumming and were good at it. Certainly many Black military drummers were almost famous. An 1858 article in the Nashville *Republican Banner* lamented the passing of "Old Bob," a Revolutionary War drummer who had been present at the battles of Eutaw Springs, Guilford Court House, and Brandywine. He was said to have been 107 years old when he died in Elbert County, Georgia.[9] The movement of troops at the dawn of the Civil War brought more mention of legendary Black drummers, such as this account from the *Mississippi Free Trader* of Natchez:

The Mobile Advertiser, announcing the arrival in that city of the Greensboro Artillery Guards, has the following notice of a somewhat noted character: Their negro drummer must be mentioned, for he is almost as well known in the State as any white man. This sable votary of the "red planet Mars" is the identical "Old Lun" who "beat the hide" for Gen. Sam Duffy through the Creek wars and did the same for the Greensboro volunteers through the Mexican war. Like Old Jordan of New Orleans, who beat the reveille behind the breastworks of Chalmette, on the 8th of January 1815, and is now enlivening the state garrison at Fort Pike with his rat-tat-too, Old Lun is eager as a boy to be in any "fun," as he calls "fighting," that may be going on.[10]

Most of the earliest accounts seem to be of military drumming, without much mention of fife, but at the beginning of the Civil War, there begin to be mentions of both fifers and drummers, with specific tunes occasionally mentioned. From this account in a Virginia newspaper of a Black fife and drum band playing for the departure of Confederate troops in Jackson, Mississippi, it not only appears that the Confederate units often had Black musicians, but also that these musicians were not above a subtle musical dig at the whites: "For awhile the scene was very affecting, lovers and sweethearts took a long, fond kiss, reminding us of poor Jeannette and Jeannot, but just as our feelings were so wrought up, the negro drummers and fifers cruelly but ignorantly struck up something like 'Jim Crack Corn, I don't care,' which of course soon dampened all our tender sympathies and emotions. These negroes seemed to have their sable sweethearts also mourn for them, for we observed that they were trying to shed a tear over the departure of their Dandy Jims."[11]

Thus, it is apparent that there is significant evidence for the use of Black fifers and drummers in Southern local and state militias, as well as in units of the Confederate army. What we can take away from these accounts is that Blacks in the South certainly had access to fifes and drums during the antebellum period.

EARLY ACCOUNTS OF BLACK DRUMMERS AND FIFE AND DRUM MUSIC IN TENNESSEE

There are also accounts of Black drummers and fife and drum bands in the state of Tennessee, although the earliest dates associated with the phenomenon seem to occur in much later articles, in which residents are recalling the early history of their communities. Perhaps the earliest reference to at least a Black encounter with fife and drum music is in Murfreesboro and Rutherford County, from a *Daily News-Journal* article that sadly is somewhat vague about times and dates:

> The first Guinea negroes brought to Rutherford County were put up and sold on the public square. They were bought by Thomas O. Butler and Dr. John M. Watson. The negroes were christened Boson and Jenny. No matter how they were occupied, when a fife and drum began making martial music these negroes would quit their work and follow in the wake of the musicians until the music ceased. The first negroes direct from darkest Africa were bought by James Earthman, the great-grandfather of the present family of that name in this city.[12]

The lack of hard-and-fast dates in the article reduces its usefulness, but we can peg some dates with research into the names it mentions. From a page on Ancestry.com, we can see that James Earthman was born in Orange County, North Carolina, in 1780, and died in Rutherford County, Tennessee, in 1830, so the events in question probably had to predate 1830.[13] Also online is a gravestone reference for Dr. John McLaren Watson, who was born in 1798 in North Carolina and died in 1866 in Rutherford County, Tennessee.[14] Other dates of importance would be the founding of Rutherford County in 1803 and the suppression of the African slave trade by Congress in 1807. It seems likely that these incidents could be placed in the later years of the decade between 1810 and 1820 or so, although of course this must be a conjecture.

Similarly, from an 1887 article in the *Clarksville Leaf-Chronicle* comes an account of an early Black bass drummer and fifer in the 1840s:

Sometime in the forties an Irish gentleman, William White, and his family arrived here on a trading boat. He rented a two-story frame house then standing on the present location of Elder's Opera House, and opened business with about a dray load of merchandise. . . . Mr. White had a negro in his employ, known to all, at that time, as January Bradley, the bass drummer of the age.[15] He was a large-boned, broad-shouldered man, about six feet five inches high, and we believe he was as near in glory when beating his favorite musical instrument, as he ever got when leaving "these mundane shores." January had, as an assistant, a colored man named Henry Rivers, who made the welkin ring with the fife. They were very important adjuncts to the military companies of that day. Henry Rivers was a worthy citizen, and lived until a few years ago. He said, and it was currently believed just prior to his death that he was a centenarian.[16]

The first reference to Black drummers in Memphis is in connection with a large parade of Memphis fire companies downtown in 1859. This is also of interest, as it is one of the few antebellum references to such drummers outside of a military context:

The president of the day of the No. 5, Invincible Fire Company was Samuel Richards, Marshal, J. B. Gotti; their uniform was red shirts, black pants, and firemen's hats. The hosemen, or Shelby Reds, made a very fancy appearance; they wore red pants stuck in long boots, white shirts, and jockey caps; they had the name "Shelby Reds" on the blue tops of their boots. The engine, Invincible, was drawn by four black horses furnished by D. F. Wright. The hose carriage, Telegraph, was tastefully decked with wreaths and flowers, and followed by negro drummers and a banner.[17]

A year later, in 1860, the *Clarksville Chronicle* duly recorded the first mention of Black drummers in connection with political activity, a rally of the fading Whig Party, which it derisively referred to as the "Whangdoo-dles": "Well the day came: Last Saturday morning was ushered in brightly and cheerfully, and nature seemed compassionately disposed for once to favor even the evil-doers. Everything about town, however, bore the customary aspect of summer quiet. Once in a while, the far-off boom of a single little cannon perhaps was heard, and a couple of solitary looking darkies beat a doleful rub-a-dub out of two drums. This certainly looked discouraging."[18]

With the beginning of the Civil War, we encounter a reference to the arrival of prisoners in Nashville, turned over to a home guard that had Black drummers: "The Gazette states that a number of prisoners, who arrived in this city on the 19th, were delivered over to a company of Home Guards, and marching up the street, the negro drummers struck up the tune of the ever-popular 'Dixie.' That was the 'unkindest cut of all.'"[19]

Quite apart from being another reference to Black drummers serving in the Confederate army, or the mention of a specific tune, is the fact that this article might explain the tendency of Blacks in rural fife and drum communities to mention only the drums, despite the presence of a fife. In the article above, only drummers are mentioned, yet we are told that they "struck up the tune of the ever-popular 'Dixie.'" If only drums were playing, one tune would more or less sound like another, so the wording of the article implies the presence of a fife. This would suggest that the fife was seen more as an adjunct to the drums, and in fact that seems to be the view today in north Mississippi, where Black fife and drum music still exists.

Oddly, for those fighting a war to retain Black slavery, the Confederate veterans seemed to recall their Black drummers and fifers fondly, from the perspective of thirty or so years after the fact. When a Clarksville National Guard unit challenged a Confederate veterans' group to a military drill competition, the Confederates' response lamented their inability to obtain their old fifer and drummer, one of whom had died in 1885, and the other presumably either enfeebled by old age or deceased:

To the Confederate soldiers of Forbes Bivouac: I am in receipt of a challenge from the Clarksville City Guards offering to drill a company, composed of members of our organization, the drill to take place early in September, the prize to be a flag. . . . .It is to be hoped that the patriotism that impelled you to rise up in arms thirty-four years ago is still alive, but we have not Uncle Henry Rieves and Zack Slaughter, with their drum and fife to excite you to enthusiasm. . . . C. H. Bailey, President, Forbes Bivouac.[20]

From the 1880 census records at GenealogyBank.com, we learn that Zack Slaughter, the bass drummer, was born in Kentucky in 1825 and was living in Clarksville. We have no mention of him in newspapers prior to 1868, when he was being vilified as a particularly violent adherent of the Radical Republicans. Complained the *Nashville Union and American*, with regard to politically inspired violence, "An equal amount of this savage ferocity is shown in the attempt of Zack Slaughter (colored) to murder Frank Green (colored), for no other offense than he was for Col. Buck for Congress."[21] More detail was given on the incident in the rival *Republican Banner*: "Monday night Zack Slaughter shot at another colored man named Frank Green on the Public Square. We understand that the adherents of Arnell have been giving Slaughter whiskey for some time past to keep him in the Arnell harness, and under its influence, he attempted to kill Green, with whom he was talking about the different candidates."[22] The court sentenced Slaughter to six months in prison in 1869, but in 1870, the *Leaf-Chronicle* records Slaughter as trying to form a "Colored Fire Company" in Clarksville, which the paper saw as a "good move," one to which the citizens should give encouragement.[23] In 1876, he was charged with assault with intent to murder, in an incident not recorded elsewhere, but was acquitted.[24] The *Leaf-Chronicle* duly reported Slaughter's death in 1885, by which time his vehemence in support of the Republicans had either been forgotten or pardoned: "Zack Slaughter, an old and worthy colored man of this place died last Sunday. Many of those who were young men during the stirring times of '61 remember the rattle of Zach's kettle drum as it called the men to the political gatherings and military rallies of those days."[25]

The reference to the snare drum as a kettle drum in his obituary is consistent with the practice in rural Black communities, where the term "kettle" is still encountered. Slaughter's fifer, Henry Rieves or Henry Rivers, cut a far lower profile, and almost nothing about him appears in the newspapers of the day, although uncertainty over his name may also be a factor. A few real estate transactions involving a Henry Rivers appear in the pages of the Clarksville papers, but it is not clear whether this is the Black fifer in question. No man with either name appears in census records for Montgomery County, but a Black man named "Henry Rieves" is listed in the 1880 census records from Madison County, Tennessee, quite a distance from Clarksville. His occupation is listed as "preacher" and he was born in 1830, so this could be the fife player mentioned. As he appears in no other census, we can surmise that he died between 1880 and 1900.[26]

After the first year of the Civil War, references to Black fifers and drummers almost disappear from the newspapers. The reasons for this are not readily apparent, as the onset of war would likely have made this phenomenon more common rather than less. However, it would seem that the rigors of war, its disruptions of the mails and the presses, military censorship, and perhaps even the scarcity of paper and ink caused papers to limit their publications to only the most essential news. Aside from constant advertising from stores and factories in Nashville doing a booming business in drums and fifes, newspapers in Tennessee were silent about fife and drum bands until after Nashville had fallen to the Union.

In 1863, Black fife and drum music made a reappearance in the pages of the *Nashville Daily Union*, when military governor Andrew Johnson, a pro-Union Democrat, sought volunteers to help build the Northwestern Railroad, a road crucial to Union military operations:

> A more noble example of devotion to the public service was never witnessed than occurred in this city yesterday. It was on the part of the hated and oppressed negro. Gov. Johnson found it necessary to impress men to complete the Northwestern Railroad, a work of the very first importance, and necessary to the military operations of the government. Yesterday morning as we understand it, a deputation of colored men waited on the Governor, and offered to raise volunteers from among themselves for that work. He accepted the proposition; and soon, with fife and drum, they were marching the streets with a banner, on one side of which was inscribed "Volunteers for the Northwestern Railroad," and the reverse the Goddess of Liberty holding the flag of the Union, with the words "The Union must be preserved." We understand 230 volunteered during the afternoon and evening.[27]

In this incident, we see perhaps the beginnings of a pattern that would persist through the Reconstruction period. The use of Black fife and drum bands as a method of advertising or calling attention to a rally, event, activity, or product,[28] the use of it with banners in processions, the use of it in connection with political activity, and the use of it perhaps as a way of calling attention to the newfound status of Black people as free and equal citizens. A couple of days later, the same newspaper noted "Uncle Sam's colored recruits" with "banners, drums and fifes," and pointed out the demoralizing effect of this phenomenon on the Confederate soldiers and their supporters.[29]

In the wake of the Emancipation Proclamation, Black fife and drum music was now appearing on both sides of the war, and this development may well have played a role in the genre becoming the defining soundtrack of Black self-assertion during the Reconstruction period that followed.

Chapter 2

"THE INEVITABLE FIFE AND DRUM"

Fife and Drum Music, Benevolent Societies, and Black Political Organizing in Tennessee During Reconstruction, 1866–71

On New Year's Day, 1866, the *Memphis Daily Appeal* newspaper gave an account of Black celebrations in the streets of Memphis. Although the writer seemed to believe they were celebrating the New Year, it was not uncommon for African Americans to celebrate Emancipation on January 1, due to it being the day that the Emancipation Proclamation was declared to be in effect in the rebellious states: "In the early part of the day, the 'Sons of Ham' and the 'S. B.'s' society, composed of negroes formed into procession, and paraded in a quiet and orderly manner many of the principal streets."[1]

Given that the paper referred to the procession as "quiet," it is likely that there was no music in it, but already the Black community of Memphis was beginning to assert its right to the use of public social space as free citizens. Of note is the reference to the Sons of Ham and the SBs (the Social Benevolent Society), the two earliest Black benevolent societies to appear in Memphis, having been founded in the 1850s before the end of slavery.

Emancipation brought hope and joy to Americans of African descent, but it also brought new troubles and difficulties. Blacks had to establish communities, burial grounds, religious institutions, educational institutions, and social and benevolent organizations with very little help from the federal government, their former masters, or outsiders. In an interview, Roy Brewer, then the president of the Independent Pallbearers Society No. 6 at Brunswick, Tennessee, in Shelby County,[2] described the process as it was told to him by older members:

> They was coming off the plantations. They didn't have much of nothing, no more than what the masters gave them. They were in slavery at that time, but the old master seeked out to give them something they could go on. He gave them . . . he started them off as a church where they was going to sing and they were singing up under a burlove. At

that particular time back then, people didn't have nowhere to bury
. . . their dead, so he gave them a cemetery. The cemetery started off
as Grisham Cemetery. The old master's name was Griffin. Mr. Griffin
gave them two acres of land for a cemetery, to have different ones to
bury in . . . .a burlove is an Indian hut.[3]

Brian Daniel Page, in his excellent dissertation on Blacks in post–Civil
War Memphis, agrees with Brewer, stating that "neighborhoods typically
developed around black churches" and that "these congregations began as a
brush arbor."[4] The choice of such arbors and groves for places of worship may
have reflected simple necessity, as no buildings were available, but they may
have also indicated a desire for seclusion from the dominant white society, or
even a residual African sensibility regarding the sacredness of groves. Phelemo Olifile Marumo, in a paper comparing Christian and African Traditional
Religion views of the environment, quotes S. Awuah-Nyamekye regarding
sacred groves among the West African Akan people,[5] and throughout the
Southern United States the word *Grove* occurs frequently in the names
of Black churches, particularly Baptist churches. During Reconstruction,
the groves and arbors gave way to buildings, and soon, schools appeared
beside the buildings, as the Freedmen's Bureau and Northern missionary
societies encouraged Black churches to donate land for schools. Throughout West Tennessee, many Black schools shared names with churches and
were generally located directly beside them. Once the newly forming Black
communities had churches, cemeteries, and schools, then benevolent or
burial societies began to be formed. The absence of life insurance made such
societies an absolute necessity to Black people in the Reconstruction South,
and the activities of these societies actually played a big role in the development, spread, and continuance of Black fife and drum music.[6] While such
Black societies were largely rendered irrelevant by the availability of health
and life insurance, they survive in the city of New Orleans as social aid and
pleasure clubs, and also in a few rural areas across the South.

"MORE MUSIC THAN FORCE":
BLACK FIFE AND DRUM MUSIC IN TENNESSEE, 1866

The first explicit mention in a Tennessee newspaper of Black fife and drum
activity during Reconstruction comes from Nashville in March 1866, when
the *Nashville Union* noted "three half-starved looking darkies parading
the streets with a drum, a fife and a 'banner,' on which were several 'Brien

mottoes.'"[7] Judge Brien was a candidate for office in Nashville at the time, so this is the first account of the use of fife and drum music for a political rally in Tennessee after the Civil War. Although the franchise had not yet been extended to African Americans in Tennessee, political activities would come to account for a considerable amount of the fife and drum activity that was visible to the white newspapers, and the resulting association between Black political ambition and fife and drum music may have accounted for the growing hostility toward the genre of music among white Southerners. The article also highlights a trend that would become all too common during Reconstruction, a tendency on the part of white Southern papers to use sarcasm and ridicule as weapons against the Black community. The growing assertiveness of African Americans annoyed white Southerners, and their carrying themselves with dignity as free and equal citizens was more than Southern editors seemingly could bear. Often the most vile epithets and slurs were used in print against Black Tennesseans, particularly when they were engaged in musical or political activity.

Whether Black organizations such as the Sons of Ham could hold public events in public social space in Southern cities like Memphis was not always clear in the earliest days of freedom. As such, the Sons of Ham, when desiring to celebrate the June 6, 1866, anniversary of the capture of Memphis by Union troops in 1862, wrote a letter to the mayor of Memphis, John Park, asking for clarification of the situation:

MEMPHIS, TENN. May 24, 1866
   To the Hon. John Park, Mayor of Memphis:
   The colored benevolent society, known as the Sons of Ham, wish to have a celebration on the 6th day of June, in a quiet and orderly manner, providing they can obtain the consent of the city authorities. They do not wish to take any steps against the wishes of the citizens of Memphis. They respectfully ask your approval of this note, and, if agreeable, the presence and protection of your police on that day. We are, in behalf of the society, very respectfully, your obedient servants,
   SOLOMON MOORE, President.
   J. H. SAILOR, Secretary.
   MOSES HERRON, Marshal.
   The Mayor returned this with the following endorsement; The Sons of "Ham" and all other sons can do just as they please, provided they do not break civil law.
   May 24, 1866.
   JOHN PARK, Mayor.[8]

The mayor's laissez-faire response must have been encouraging to Black Memphians with regard to accessing the public streets, squares, and parks on festive occasions. Certainly, the presence of a "Marshal" among the listed officers of the Sons of Ham indicated the importance of parades and processions in these early Black organizations. On June 6, the *Public Ledger* mentioned that the Sons of Ham were commemorating the capture of Memphis with a "grand picnic . . . at a shady grove on the Charleston railroad, a short distance from the city. The speakers are Gen. Fisk of the Bureau and a Memphian named W. H. Fitch Jr."[9] Oddly, only the *Nashville Union and American* carried an after-the-event report, describing the public procession with a "negro band":

CELEBRATION BY THE SONS OF HAM—Yesterday being the anniversary of the capture of Memphis by United States naval forces in 1862, was celebrated by a procession and other jollifications, by the "Sons of Ham" so-called, who passed up Main to Madison street, and from thence—we do not know or inquire, where—to enjoy certain pleasures, which we have no doubt were appropriate and edifying, to themselves at least. We saw a negro band followed by about twenty or twenty-five individuals of various shades of complexion, from canary yellow to ebony black, and this constituted the procession—so-called![10]

The nature of the "negro band" in question is not described, but it could well have been a fife and drum band. How the early Black bands got instruments at the end of the Civil War has been a matter of some conjecture. The sale of discarded brass instruments from the army through Southern secondhand stores has been posited,[11] and there are also recurring stories in African American history and folklore about instruments, particularly drums, having been given to Blacks by the departing Union soldiers at the end of the Civil War.[12]

Accounts of the Fourth of July 1866 in Memphis did not mention any drums or fifes,[13] but rumors of fighting at a Black picnic at Fort Gillem near Nashville prompted an account of the incident in the *Nashville Union and American* that mentioned drums: "The bloody affray that was stated to have occurred at this place on the Fourth, amounts to nothing. Some of the 5th cavalry got on a bender, and paid the negro picnic a visit. While there, one of them knocked a drum from a seat, belonging to one of the negroes. The latter deeming it an insult to their exercise, assembled and drove the soldiers from the ground. There was no shooting done, and no one hurt."[14]

Throughout Reconstruction, we encounter accounts in which interference with drummers or vandalism of drums is taken as an insult. The drummers were extremely protective of their instruments, perhaps a habit learned in the army, or else because of the expense or difficulty of replacement should they be damaged or lost. In the same issue of the same newspaper, the Black Fourth of July festivities in Pulaski, Tennessee, were mentioned: "Independence Day in Pulaski was celebrated alone by the colored population.[15] A small procession marched across the square several times to the music of a fife and drum, and under the folds of a curious flag."[16] Everything about this incident is interesting. The practice of celebrating the national holiday on the public square in Pulaski, with the military instruments of fife and drum, was a decidedly provocative act. Black citizens of Giles County were clearly indicating that they were full citizens with rights equal to those of whites, and that they had the right to occupy the public space at the center of town. Of further interest is the "curious flag" mentioned. While we might assume that such a celebration would be under the flag of the United States, it would seem from the description that it was not. Was this a banner representing a burial or benevolent society?

The next day's *Union and American* brought a similar description from Winchester and Decherd, in Franklin County, Tennessee, of a Fourth of July celebration there: "The Fourth passed off quietly here, without any demonstration whatever. We understand our colored friends assembled in large numbers at Decherd, and made quite a display—men, women and children marching and countermarching over the hot fields, at the sound of the drum, led by two or three gentlemen with red ribbons around their shoulders."[17] Judging from the description of the leaders and the decorations with ribbons, it is likely that this commemoration was organized by a benevolent society.

On August 6, 1866, the State Colored Convention opened in Nashville at a church called Caper's Chapel. After electing a committee of delegates from each of the state's three grand divisions (West, Middle, and East), the assembled representatives heard several speeches from Black leaders of the state of Tennessee, before an interruption was occasioned by the attempt of a Black fife and drum band to march into the convention:

> Some confusion was created in the Convention by some half-dozen discharged colored soldiers, with fife and drum, marching up to the door of the church in a menacing manner, as though they desired a difficulty. They were uniformed and armed—had their swords drawn. A member of the Convention was sent out to remonstrate with them,

as the music disturbed the speaker. It did but little good. Mr. LEVERE remarked that there was more music than force in the little squad that was attempting to disturb the meeting. Their conduct was severely censured.[18]

When the Convention reconvened in the afternoon, the squad of soldiers and their fife and drum band again tried to disrupt the proceedings. The convention voted on a formal censure of the disrupters, and when this resolution was taken outside and read to them, they marched away to West Nashville with no further protest. The reason for the intrusion was never explained.

In September, the *Republican Banner* reported the funeral of the president of the Sons of Relief, a Black burial society: "The Nashville Order of the Sons of Relief, a colored organization, turned out with drum and fife yesterday, to attend the funeral of their president, William Miller."[19]

So, as early as the first year of Reconstruction in Tennessee, we can see that Black fife and drum music was used for political rallies; for parades and processions in celebration of national holidays; for days of importance to the race, such as Emancipation Day; for picnics and other festive occasions; for demonstrations and protests, such as the attempt to march into the State Colored Convention; and for funerals, particularly the funerals of society members. In short, fife and drum music was a feature of a wide array of Black public events. What also is noteworthy is what we do not see in that first year, namely any newspaper complaints about Black fife and drum music. Observers seemed to view it with more curiosity than alarm.

"REMEMBER FORT PILLOW WHEN YOU CAST YOUR VOTE": BLACK FIFE AND DRUM MUSIC IN TENNESSEE, 1867

As the new year of 1867 opened, the *Memphis Daily Appeal*, in its "River News," noted a Black unit of soldiers onboard the boat *Julia*, and could not resist the opportunity to make them the object of ridicule: "The Julia passed up on Sunday. She had a jig-a-dier-brindle, a reegiment [sic] of the troops who 'fought nobly,' a fife and several kettle drums aboard. Whar the troops were gwine, we did not learn, but evidently not to drive 'Max' outen the country.[20] We suggest they be sent back here as a 'starter' for a bureau 'reconstruction' and that Ryland of the St. Louis Democrat, be appointed 'head scenter.'"[21]

Although Black fife and drum music was not nearly as common in East Tennessee (owing primarily to the rather small numbers of Black residents), the area was a Republican stronghold, and a "colored convention" in the town of Jonesborough in April 1867 involved a fife and drum procession, as well as a series of resolutions, one of which was expressing gratitude for the actions of the state legislature in extending the franchise to Blacks.[22]

With African American Tennesseans now able to vote, the Conservative Party, as the ex-Confederates called themselves, enlisted Black advocates and tried to convince the new Black voters to support their former masters, with little success. One such rally, in Columbia, ended up becoming a rally for the Radical Republican opposition, as *Brownlow's Knoxville Whig* gleefully reported:

> After the speaking came the demonstration which showed up the farce of the Conservative meeting. Some one cried out "Three cheers for Brownlow and Arnell," which were given with a will. Joe Williams then proposed a vote, the result of which all but two of the freedmen ranged themselves on the side of Brownlow and Arnell. The meeting then dispersed, and, procuring a large American flag, fifes and drums, the freedmen formed into procession, cheering for Brownlow and Arnell, and in good military style, marching up and down the streets over two hours, rending the air with their shouts for the Radical party, Brownlow, Arnell and Congress.Every time the procession passed the Bureau office, from which depended an American flag, the color bearer dipped his colors, amid the cheers of the freedmen, the colored women waving their pocket-handkerchiefs from the sidewalks.[23]

The Black fife and drum bands became indispensable features of Radical political conventions and gatherings, as a letter writer from Lewisburg in Marshall County noted in May of 1867: "The Radicals had what they called a grand mass meeting and convention, but it proved to be a farce so far as mass was concerned. Rob't Wiley, the notorious Radical leader in this county, came in town about ten o'clock this morning, followed by about forty colored men and women. The men marched in double file with fife and drum, and muskets at a shoulder, accompanied by only two white men, besides Wiley, the commander in chief."[24]

By June, the *Republican Banner* could speak of the "inevitable fife and drum" in connection with an ill-fated attempt to have a Radical rally in the town of Edgefield, now known as East Nashville. Although the organizers had not secured a building, they had made sure to secure a fife and drum band![25] In July, the first serious riot involving a fife and drum band occurred in the town of Franklin, in Williamson County, when Black members of the

Loyal League, a Republican organization, took offense at a speech made by Joe Williams, a Black Conservative:

> In about fifteen minutes, the drums, fifes and banners were brought out, the long roll sounded, and everybody turned their eyes for a moment to the center of the square, where the musicians stood. Part of the crowd immediately started away, and in a little while commenced forming as if for a procession, taking their cue from the whites and setting up yells for Brownlow. . . . The drums continued beating, and as Williams had ceased speaking, all the members of the League gathered at one point, and formed in columns for marching, displaying their banners conspicuously. These banners bore the inscriptions: "Treason Must Be Made Odious, and Traitors Punished;" "My Policy Played Out;" "Remember Fort Pillow When You Cast Your Vote;" "The Radicals Build, The Conservatives Burn our Schoolhouses and Churches;" "Andy Can't Control Congress;" "Vote The Radical Ticket."[26]

The events of Franklin ended in tragedy, with the shooting death of one Michael Cody and the wounding of a large number of Black members of the League. The rival *Republican Banner* gave a similar account of the events in Franklin but emphasized more the fife and drum band: "The colored Loyal League had been parading during the day with drum and fife, and carrying banners with various inscriptions, including such as the following. Remember Fort Pillow when you go to the polls. And this—The Radicals build School Houses and the Conservatives burn them. After the speaking they reformed and paraded the principal streets for an hour or more and came to the Public Square, marching and counter-marching, and finally started off to League Headquarters, where processions were usually disbanded."[27] The Black Conservative speaker Joe Williams was also quoted in the paper, and he mentioned the fife and drum band as well:

> There was no disorder at all. I was about to close my remarks when a white man, named Bliss, who was in the crowd, and had for some time seemed extremely impatient, went to the leader of the League, and told him to have the long roll beaten. This request was at first refused, but Bliss became very excited and insisted. The drum was then beaten and the League set up a yell and fell into ranks as if the movement had been previously arranged. . . . In about a quarter of an hour, we heard the fife and drums, and we went out to see what was

the matter. The League marched up to opposite our headquarters and halted. Immediately the firing commenced, but owing to the darkness I could not see which party fired first.[28]

The Republican commissioner of registration for Williamson County gave a different account of events leading up to the Franklin tragedy:

> At the close of the meeting this afternoon, the colored Union League marched through the streets and fired a salute in the Square. This caused considerable excitement and was followed by angry words and threats. In order to allay the excitement and prevent any further demonstration, the League marched out of town just before dark, where they were addressed by Hon. W. Y. Elliott, candidate for State Senate, and myself, at the conclusion of which they voted in accordance with our advice to march quietly back to the Square and disperse. They accordingly marched back in good order; and just as they arrived at the Square, from best information I can obtain, a pistol was fired from a crowd of persons assembled near the courthouse, followed by two volleys from the same direction. This was instantly answered by the members of the League, who at once dispersed. Both pistols and muskets were used.[29]

An account in *Brownlow's Knoxville Whig* gave some background on things that had gone on prior to the riot in Franklin, including threats made against the Loyal League by Black Conservatives, leading to the League arming itself with weapons. The sheriff of Williamson County had also denied the League the right to carry their drums or banners into the county courthouse on the occasion of a Republican rally.[30]

On July 18, 1867, the *Nashville Union* published the official report of General Carlin of the Freedmen's Bureau on the Franklin riot, which placed the blame in part on Conservative outrage at the drumming and drilling of the Loyal League:

> The colored league had recently procured drums and a fife, and had been marching about the outskirts of the town after supper for several nights, without disturbing anyone. On different occasions, they were interrupted by colored Conservatives (Dick Crutcher and A. J. Gadsey passing through their columns while marching, firing shots, etc.). . . . There is no doubt that the Conservatives viewed the marching and displays of the league as a military demonstration, and feared that

it might result in strife. Imprudent remarks and foolish boasts were made by individuals of both parties, and each had come to regard the other with a jealous eye.[31]

With the release of Captain Michael Walsh's report in the *Republican Banner* of July 23, 1867, it began to become clear that the fife and drum band may have actually been the factor that provoked the Franklin riot: "On Thursday, prior to the riot, Edward Crutcher said: 'This beating of drums by these God damned n----rs and their marching up and down must bring on a riot. The people won't stand it. They depend on old Brownlow to give the law, but I will give three feet and that before Saturday night. You'll see what I tell you. The n----r is not able to fight the white man, and I hate to see him mobbed, but it will be done.'"[32] Ultimately, the use of fife and drum in procession, along with provocative banners, was enough to offend and outrage the ex-Confederates. At least in part, this was due to the association of fife and drum music with military action in the minds of white people. That fife and drum could have other meanings in the Black community was not understood by whites. To them, the Black community parading with fife and drum music was an act of menace that had to be met with force.

With the Franklin riot and similar events in the background, the *Republican Banner* on July 14 reported on the departure of five recruits for "Sumner's company" from the depot in Nashville, led by a drum and fife and "accompanied by an admiring crowd of freedmen."[33] "Sumner" was Captain James H. Sumner, a Black tavern owner in Nashville whom Governor Brownlow had commissioned as a captain in the State Guard, the militia unit that the legislature had created to protect the voting rights of freedmen and Unionists.[34] The laws enfranchising Blacks and disfranchising ex-Confederates were deeply unpopular with many white Tennesseans, and their disapproval soon gave way to outright terrorism and insurrection. The State Guard was intended to combat this, and Black Tennesseans cheered at seeing some of their own march off under a Black captain to do battle with the Ku Klux Klan.

Even when Radical political meetings did not exactly come off as planned, they generally featured fife and drum music:

> Slade Town was to have been brilliantly illuminated with tallow candles, and the citizens of that quiet suburban villa were to hear the gospel according to Radical teachings. A torchlight procession was planned to dazzle the eyes of the crowd. The drum and fife squeaked out their discordant notes along Church Street. One solitary torch,

made by culling holes in an old cigar box and covering them with colored paper threw its sickly rays over the face of the gallant drummer, who was evidently not "the drummer boy of Shiloh." Between High and Vine on the opposite side of the street, might be seen a solitary torch-bearer who came forth to reinforce his solitary friend. The two united and walking at the head of the column, composed of drummer, fifer and a half-dozen little juveniles, made such a grand pyrotechnic display as the denizens of Church Street have not seen for many a night.[35]

In December, on the Memphis riverfront, a labor meeting of Black stevedores featured a fife and drum band, marking perhaps the first time that this music was seen in connection with labor organizing and activity. The *Daily Memphis Avalanche* gave the details with some distaste: "The negro stevedores and deckhands held a caucus yesterday on the landing. Speeches were made and a procession, headed with drum and fife, marched up and down the levee to collect material with which the leaders intended to pack the negro convention last night. Negroes that had been in the city twenty-four hours were selected for voters. 'Sich' is life."[36]

On the same day, the *Public Ledger* expressed alarm at the beating of drums among Blacks, suggesting editorially that it meant insurrection: "As the negroes are beating their drums pretty heavily, we should like to know what it all means. Is the poor white man, whose latch-string, however humble, is always out, and whose heart warms with hospitality and glows with intelligence and courage, to be deprived of rights, privileges and property, and kept under the instrumentality of the negro? And how long? Shall the poor white man have no rest from alarms in his sanctuary for his wife and children? And how long is it proposed to continue this state of things?"[37] The occasion for the *Ledger*'s editorial was apparently the beginning of widespread drilling and fife and drum activities by Blacks in South Memphis, probably under the auspices of a benevolent society or the Union League. But in the minds of whites, all such Black drilling and drumming were political acts, and provocative ones at that. The *Avalanche* gave a more detailed account of the drumming, calling it an "intolerable nuisance":

The people of South Memphis are at the present time sorely afflicted with an intolerable nuisance, which comes upon them nightly about ten o'clock, and lasts until between two and three each morning. Crowds of noisy, drunken negroes, led by drums and fifes, nightly parade up and down the principal streets in that locality, making night hideous with their everlasting clamor. We have no objection to political meetings or to processions, but when they become matters of nightly occurrence, they are apt to become a bore and a nuisance, and should be abated. Money all over town is scarce, except in the hands of those controlling the colored leagues, who spend it with a lavish hand in furtherance of their electioneering schemes; and the quantity of tanglefoot whisky demolished nightly is the fruitful source of all this annoyance, as but few of the enthusiastic Africans could be persuaded to go home as long as there was any prospect of another drink. Will the authorities take some steps to at least alleviate this nuisance?[38]

The *Appeal* complained of "a band of two or three of the basest sort of drums" that played daily on the river landing,[39] on the same day that the *Avalanche* complained about a Black procession organized by Dr. P. D. Beecher, a Radical political leader:

Quite a crowd of negroes paraded the streets yesterday, under the Beecher banner, preceded by the fife and drum, calling together the Beecherites, to attend a meeting on South Street.[40] These enthusiastic voters monopolized the whole sidewalk, to the annoyance and discomfort of all the passers. When it was not considered disgraceful to participate in a political procession, it was usual for such bodies to take the middle of the street, so as not to inconvenience the public. The middle of the street was good enough for white men, but negroes must have the sidewalk.[41]

Again, Black fife and drum music was linked in the white community not only with Black political activity, but also with Black insolence and arrogance. The *Ledger* continued to rail against fife and drum music, while giving interesting descriptions that sound remarkably like Alan Lomax's later field recordings, at least with regard to the "panther screams" and "yells":

We may get accustomed, but not partial, to the fife and drum in times of peace. It is a standing menace. If white persons should parade our streets with colors flying and drums beating, and make the still hours of night hideous, with drunken orgies, demoniac yells, and insane boasts of being freemen in the sense of unlimited license, mingling devilish threats and panther screams with the strains of martial din, alarming the old, the feeble, the nervous and the timid, while good men sleep, we should say they were disturbers of the public and private peace, and that if there was any authority of government in the city it was a duty to make arrests. And when the blacks are doing this thing, night after night, through all the city, we insist that the same duty exists, and that it shall be performed. If one portion of the people is permitted to play hell and raise the devil day and night, so should be the other. And, if the police functionaries are so in the interest or fear of Little Beecher and his squad, that they will not suppress these disorders, it is time to organize a force which can and will.[42]

There was soon evidence that Conservative appeals were having some impact on Black voters, and Conservatives were not above employing the fife and drum either, as it seemed to get results in the Black community: "Negrodom is now apparently divided in Memphis, and Conservatism has renewed hopes of help from the blackamoor. Forty or fifty ragged Africans, with a drum and fife, and a transparency inscribed 'FITCH AND JUS-TICE,'[43] straggled through our streets last Christmas morning. The dusky clients of BEECHER make night hideous with their ululations."[44] But the annoyance of Conservatives in the white community was beginning to boil over. Frustration with the seeming inability or unwillingness of the civil authorities to deal with what Conservatives considered the nuisance of Black demonstrations and fife and drum parades led to the formation of secret, paramilitary forces like the Pale Faces and the Ku Klux Klan. A fife and drum procession in Columbia, Tennessee, during the Christmas season led to an appearance of Klansmen when Blacks refused to disperse after being asked to do so by a policeman:

A large number of negroes gathered in Columbia last Wednesday, from all portions of Maury County, and, as is now their invariable custom, formed themselves in procession about ten o'clock A.M. and with drum and fife proceeded to march around the public square and principal streets. A policeman, by the orders of the mayor, waited upon them, and in a quiet and respectful manner, requested them not to beat their drums on the square, and to cease beating them on the streets when there were horses and vehicles, as it was likely to frighten the animals and might cause some person to be injured.[45] This they emphatically refused to do and evinced a disposition to show fight; whereupon the policeman ordered them to disperse, with the alternative of arrest if they did not do so. They obeyed, but collected in front of the Bureau and League headquarters, threatening to return and do as they pleased. At this point of the proceedings, two men on horseback, disguised and dressed in red, made their appearance up South Main Street. Soon the cry was raised and passed from mouth to mouth, "The Kuklux are coming!" The "pale faces" all wore a pleasing expression, while the dark-skins looked dejected and began dispersing. The two horsemen stopped for a few moments, then turned to put spurs to their horses and were soon lost to sight. Rumors became rife that in about two hours, three hundred of the "unknown" would be in the city. Time wore on, but nothing more was seen of the Kuklux. The negroes had, in the meantime, commenced leaving, only about fifty remaining, who marched up the street two or three hundred yards, stopped, held another consultation and dispersed. So ended a complication that at one time wore every aspect of becoming a bloody and terrible riot. Determination was fixed upon the countenance of every citizen to resist the malcontents to the bitter end, had they attempted to bully the civil authorities.[46]

Thus, we see in 1867 fife and drum bands becoming more and more visible at Black events and gatherings, to the point that newspaper accounts called it "inevitable" and the parades "their invariable custom." But we also see a growing backlash from white Tennesseans against this music, primarily because of its association with Black assertiveness and militancy, Black political activity, and the hated Radical party, as well as its tendency to keep people awake at night and frighten horses. Nevertheless, Blacks defiantly used fife and drum music to assert their right to assemble in public squares and public streets across Tennessee.

"WHY THIS RATTLE OF SPIRIT-STIRRING DRUM?": BLACK FIFE AND DRUM MUSIC IN TENNESSEE, 1868

As New Year's Day dawned in Memphis, 1868, the city was in the throes of a municipal election campaign, with rallies being held for numerous candidates. At least one demonstration involving fife and drum music on behalf of Dr. P. D. Beecher led to an arrest after a young boy threw snowballs at a Black snare drummer.[47]

Electioneering was going on in Nashville as well, as the *Nashville Union* reported the next day, describing in great detail a Black Radical meeting at the markethouse, with the editorial opinion that music was of great importance in Black estimates of the several candidates:

The meetings last night were miniature repetitions of the affair on the 21st ult. They can be no more described than it could be. The negroes were on hand in force, the official aspirants and their drummers having been engaged throughout the entire day in getting them together. Tuthill brought his artillery to the markethouse, and Peabody brought his base drums and brass band to the courthouse. . . . The markethouse was soon full, while a throng meantime had swelled in front of the markethouse, and Tuthill was satisfied that he had the crowd. But Peabody was up to snuff; he knew the powers of music, and while Tuthill was planting his batteries, he was marshaling his forces with sounding drums and hewgags and fifes and fiddles.[48] That band was a master piece of strategy. It played "the girl I left behind me," and then struck up a highland jig. This was conclusive to the negroes that Peabody was "qualified," and they filled the courthouse. Tuthill had no music. But he had plenty of backers who did the hip huzzaing, and whistled "listen to the mocking bird," with wonderful effect.[49]

Indeed, political rallies and other activities related to campaigns were some of the most conspicuous activities at which Black fife and drum music was seen in public. Other newspaper accounts referred to possible private lodge or society functions at which drums were heard from a distance, but the newspapers of course did not send reporters into these private events. Occasionally, fife and drum music was used on election days as well, to march prospective Black voters to the polls. When it occurred, it often led to outrage on the part of white residents, at least in part because under the laws of 1866, they were largely denied the vote for having supported the Confederacy. Thus the *Home Journal* of Winchester, Tennessee, in Franklin County vented whites' outrage:

Didn't we see it last Saturday in Winchester?—how the poor negroes went up like "dumb cattle driven," and voted the way their yankee masters said. Then they got the drum and fife, and headed by two infamous black scoundrels, with their swords unsheathed, and another pumpkin-colored individual carrying a loaded gun in the rear, they marched forth to beat up more votes, for there was beginning to be a little fear on the part of the white leaders in the election farce, that the Regular Republican Black-and-Tan Loyal-League ticket of bummers, mixed with home-made bought-ups, would not be elected entirely. And of course the old lodge was to be resorted to. Fife and drum, and military display work wonders with the negroes.

On they came, and a lively tune was commenced. The unnecessary military display was about to cause horses and teams to run away, and seeing, as some saw, that there was no earthly use in God's world for so much disturbance when everything and everybody was perfectly quiet—seeing, as some saw, that the negro demonstration was intended to insult white men who were quiet under the heavy yoke already placed upon their necks, "all of a sudden" the rank and file of these disturbers of peace were brought to a halt, and order was restored, at the sacrifice of a little pleasure to the poor duped negroes who are thus drilled to insult white people too honorable and too decent to admit negro equality.[50]

The editor twice indicated that the white people of the town saw Black fifing and drumming as an "insult" to white citizens. But the matter did not end there, after an anonymous letter was written to the editor of the *Nashville Press and Times* describing the day's events in stark detail as an attempt at wholesale slaughter of the Blacks who had come to vote:

At the election for county officers on the first Saturday of the month, the Union men of this county went to the polls unarmed and desirous of doing all in their power to show fair play, and by example prove to rebels that we were anxious simply to do what the law guarantees to us; we found the law-abiding town of Winchester full of armed rebels; and when the unarmed colored men had formed a procession with their fife and drum, without arms, or without giving any insult or behaving boisterously, a rebel rushed out from their lines, already formed of armed men, and cut the head out of the base drum, and at once the rebel line drawn up opposite the Court House drew their pistols, and the windows over their heads opened, revealing armed men, ready and prepared to slaughter the unarmed crowd.[51]

The outraged *Home Journal* editor responded, conceding at least the incident with the bass drum, while denying nearly everything else:

The extract says the rebels cut the head out of the drum. We will acknowledge one of our citizens did, if report be true, cut the drum, and Capt. Davenport, the Commissioner of Registration, told us it was right. He farther said he had ordered the negroes to go home. And right here let me ask why these negroes brought out their fife and drum. Was it not intended to insult and brow-beat the disfranchised men who are too honorable to act the hypocrite in order to get to vote! . . . Look at the ring leaders of the brave n----r procession that comes forth at a little Sheriff's election to insult our peaceable citizens. Two of them—Harry Jones and John Kenser—one the drummer and the other the fifer—one of them with a sword he carries to the Loyal League meetings—both these negroes are now in our jail under a charge of arson, trying to burn the negro church in our town. Harry has been turned out of his church twice, the other we know and can prove to be a notorious thief, for he was in our employ for two months or more—these negroes were the head-men, the ring leaders, and with fife and drum were scaring horses and teams. And why? Did any disfranchised man try to vote?[52]

The *Republican Banner* in Nashville soon vented its frustration with fife and drum music, asking if perhaps the Radicals could "spare us a little in the fife and drum nuisance this summer. . . . Why this rattle of the spirit-stirring drum and plaintive shriek of the ear-piercing fife?"[53]

As the Fourth of July approached, the *Memphis Post*, a local Republican paper that often carried news of the Black community, gave an announcement about an elaborate parade and picnic to be sponsored by the United Sons of Ham. It is unclear whether the "bands of music" were fife and drum bands or brass bands, but the announcement also features the first mention of a benevolent society called the Pole Bearers Association, which would prove to be very important in connection to Black fife and drum music in Shelby County.[54] Accounts of the affair were fairly muted. The *Avalanche* stated: "Africa was out in force yesterday. He paraded the streets early in the morning, and afternoon planted his delicate hoofs on nearly all the vacant ground between the head of Vance Street and the city limits. He was there with his family and his sweetheart, and had a good time of it dancing, eating, drinking, talking and going it with a general looseness."[55]

The congressional campaign in Tennessee led to more fife and drum rallies aimed at Black voters, and more complaints from the *Republican Banner*, railing at white Republican "trash" for having stirred up the Black community in this way:

It would seem bad enough for the radical candidates for Congress in this District who are so presumptuous as to consider themselves the most eligible persons to represent the people of Davidson in the National Legislature, to offer for that position, much less to subject the public to the incessant annoyance of drums and fifes, and the gathering together of the black people into noisy and excited meetings in public places almost every night. We have been blessed with rattling drums and screaming fifes for a week or more, with any number of turbulent, boisterous and excited convocations of negroes on street corners and the in the Court-house and Market House.[56]

The prevailing hatred and rage boiled over when a rally for congressional candidate William F. Prosser was organized by Blacks in South Nashville. As the *Nashville Union* griped with its usual irritability, the "Prosser drums" had brought together all the "lazy, sneaking negro loafers and pimps" in the area to the rally. As Silas F. Allen began to address the crowd, a group of small white boys began heckling nearby, and when J. P. Rexford took the rostrum, a rock was thrown at him, apparently from the direction of the boys, which led to people in the mostly Black crowd throwing rocks and firing pistols at the boys and into nearby homes. Whites returned fire, and the Black crowd ran in different directions, with the politicians seeking cover in nearby houses.[57] The rival *Republican Banner* gave a fairly differing account of the incident, mentioning that the neighborhood where the incident occurred was called Slatetown, and having evidently talked with the Black bass drummer:

Between nine and ten o'clock last night, a negro arrived in the city from Slatetown, having come from that place in double-quick time and wringing wet from perspiration, brought highly exaggerated reports of a big fight, which he alleged had taken place on the corner of Carroll Street and the Lebanon Pike. He stated that he heard the firing of the shots and had immediately thereafter set out for the city to arouse the police and to send them to the rescue.

A force of police was sent out, but it appears from information received at eleven o'clock, that the battle continued but a few moments, and upon their arrival upon the field no trace had been left on either side as to what direction the combatants had taken.

It is stated by the police that a Prosser meeting had assembled on the corner of the thoroughfares mentioned. Prosser had delivered himself of a buncombe speech, and had been followed by the notorious Captain Rexford. That while the latter was in the midst of his harangue, three successive shots were fired into the crowd, followed by forty others, some of which they allege, were fired from the windows and doors of houses in the direct neighborhood of the meeting. Whether any of these shots were exchanged was not ascertained.

So soon as the first three shots echoed through the ambient air the large crowd scattered in every direction and the most ludicrous confusion ensued. Rexford, Allen, Prosser, Sparling and others quickly removed themselves away with the fancy crowd, which was now rushing pell-mell down the various avenues of egress toward the city. No one was wounded, though several narrow escapes are reported. A woman residing near the spot is said to have fainted. The negro who pounded the bass drum stated that at the first shot, he slung that musical instrument over his shoulder and attempted to get away with it, but before he had attained any distance a bullet cut the string, which let it fall with a ghostly cavernous sound on the earth, and the bullet whistled a warning scream behind his shoulders. He did not stop to pick up the "spirit-stirring" drum, and did not go back for it until some time after the panic had subsided. He also stated that he and his company had been stoned on South Market Street in the afternoon, and that he had been "informed" that the meeting would be broken up at night.

No spectral cavalcade with masques appeared, and there were no Kuklux "around." The persons who shot into the crowd were not known. It is not certain that any shots were fired into it at all. The drummer stated that the Prosserites would hold a meeting at the same place to-night, and that they would be prepared to meet any contingency which might arise. He himself would have a pistoloric, which he boasted was as long as his drum stick, and when "she went it 'ud jess make the 'yearth tremble." This is all the particulars of the screaming farce that we have been able to glean up to the hour of going to press.[58]

Despite the *Banner*'s skepticism, something most certainly had to have occurred, because a drummer would not normally have left his bass drum behind except in the most dire of circumstances. The drummer's bold predictions about the next night's rally notwithstanding, it evidently was relocated to the Public Square of Nashville for security reasons. The *Republican Banner* noted the use of fife and drum and also mentioned a "band" that played "Hail, Columbia, Happy Land," but it is unclear whether the fife and drum band and the latter band were in fact the same entity.[59]

Most Southern newspapers of the Conservative ilk were given to racist epithets and ridicule directed at the freedmen, but the *Memphis Daily Appeal* was an extreme case in that regard, regularly hurling abuse at Black Memphians. On the other hand, they often gave quaint details, such as the instrumentation of bands, the tunes played, or the attire of Black society members in parades. Their description of a Black political gathering on the bluff was typical:

Yesterday evening, as twilight's shades were lengthening into night, a little while after old Sol had sunk to rest in the wilds of Arkansas, a band of music consisting of a big buck n----r and a base drum, another with a fife and a third with a clarionet, mounted the pile of lumber near the tanks on the bluff, and commenced playing "Meet me by moonlight alone."[60] It was not long before it had attracted around it a crowd of loafing steamboat darkies, deck hands, mackerels, and wharf rats of every color and description, who were anxious to know what the music betokened. Their inquiries, addressed to the three sable worthies constituting the band, could elicit nothing but a grunt. Mystery has a charm about it, and in this instance it worked as it always does, and caused the crowd, unable to find out anything definite, to go surmising; and all sorts of rumors were soon rife. All at once, a little shirt-tail darky came tearing through the crowd, and rushing up to the drummer shouted, "Dey's a comin'!" "Who? Who?" asked the crowd eagerly. "Whar he?" gasped the drummer, and wiping his face with his coat-tail, again asked, "Whar he?" "Aigh!" yelled the little nig, and pointing with his finger at something which was approaching from the direction of Madison street, with a slow and majestic tread, said, "dar dey!" "Free cheers for da honorable Barbour Lewis!" then yelled the drummer, and began banging the bass drum with frightful energy. "Free cheers for da honorable Ginral Smiff!" yelled the fifer, and commenced to blow with redoubled shrillness. "Free cheers for Capt. Ham Carter!" roared the clarionet man, and then all three commenced to play "See, the conquering hero comes." The crowd of n----rs, loafers and scalawags that had gathered by this time, was quite numerous, and hearing the names of the three great champions of one wing of the scalawag party approach, set up a most tremendous cheering and yelling; amid which the "something," dimly seen through the mists of the night, arrived close enough to let the crowd see that it was—it *was*—the immortal Gen. Smiff, the immortaler Barbour Lewis, and the immortalest Capt. Carter—the trio of Moseses that are to lead the Smith wing of the "bust up party" into the land of promise. They were received with open arms, and mounted the woodpile—the band playing "N----r in the Woodpile" and the crowd cheering.[61]

A week later, the *Appeal* editorially advised white residents to defy the law against carrying weapons, claiming that Black residents were armed and that the authorities were doing nothing to disarm them. They particularly took offense at a speech of Barbour Lewis with regard to weapons:

Mr. Barber Lewis said to the negroes of this city on Monday night: The Avalanche and APPEAL say you are armed and drilled. I say they are mistaken. The charge is an unpardonable slander. Have any of you known or heard of any colored men or other Republicans armed or drilled? (Cries of "no," "no," "never.") It is all a lie. We are men of peace. Four thousand of you, all of you, every man of you, pronounce the charge false, false.

Mr. Barber Lewis is very ready to tell people they lie. We want this question of veracity settled. We do not know, but we believe that he uttered a willful and deliberate falsehood; because we have, again and again, been assured, by persons of the highest character, and even by ladies, that in more than one place on the outer edge of the city, the negroes were drilling, to the music of the drum and fife, almost nightly. We shall be glad to know that such is not the case, but in the meantime, as we do believe our informants, and do not believe the denial, we repeat our advice to every Conservative to arm, that he may be able to defend himself. We repeat that the law against carrying concealed weapons is null and void; that it is not enforced to the disarming of any negro; that it is unjust and unequal in its operation; that we are under no obligations to obey it, and should be the stupidest fools to do so.

Let us know, now, whether the negroes are drilling or not. We want proof. We publish nothing as a fact that we have not good reasons to be so. We believe that it is true. We have ourself heard the drum and fife, out beyond the Memphis and Charleston Railroad depot, until nearly one in the morning, and seen negroes coming up Adams street afterwards. Mr. Lewis' denial does not change our belief. In the meantime arm! and organize! if you would not be massacred like helpless children. If we would have peace, it must be known that we are prepared to defend ourselves.[62]

To white people, fife and drum was military music. People employed it for use in military drills and preparing for war. If they heard it, they believed that a military unit was coming, or that some sort of skirmish or fight was imminent. But Black people used fife and drum for all kinds of things—parades and processions, funerals, political rallies, and picnics. And many of the descriptions given, even by those who complained, regarding the boisterous yells and shouts of participants, alleged drunkenness and noted the late hour to which these events continued. This suggests that they were not in fact military drills, at least in the sense that white residents feared. There is some evidence that benevolent societies did in fact do a sort of ceremonial drilling with wooden sticks or poles, but nothing would require them to be armed, as the *Appeal* claimed. White fears and biases were leading them to see threats where none existed.

In August of 1868, the *Public Ledger*, a newspaper not given to much praise of Black Memphians, gave a brief notice about something called Wardlow's Conservative Band: "Bob Wardlow wishes us to call the attention of his Conservative friends to the fact that he is prepared to furnish music throughout the campaign, either with his drum corps or full cornet band. He is also prepared with his string band to furnish music for balls and parties. All orders left at Ned Adams' barber shop, on Main street, near Jefferson, will reach him, and receive prompt attention. Those wishing to patronize a staunch colored Conservative will not forget Bob when requiring anything in the musical line."[63] Whether the "drum corps" also included a fife was not made clear by the brief report, but a further notice in the *Avalanche* on August 13 might suggest that it did, for it read, "Robert Wardlow offers the services of his Field, Marshal and String Band. Headquarters at the barber shop, No. 357 Main street."[64] Generally in that day a "field band" was another way of referring to a fife and drum band, although the notice is still somewhat ambiguous, as the comma between "Field" and "Marshal" may have in fact been a printer's error. What is evident is that Wardlow was a hustling musical entrepreneur, the first well-known Black bandleader in Memphis, and one of the first Black Democrats.

Robert Wardlow cut a wide and colorful swath across Memphis during the two years he was in the public eye. He first appears in the *Memphis Avalanche* in March of 1866, charged with murder in the shooting death of a man named Ike Campbell at Ferguson Hall on the corner of Hernando and Beale Streets.[65] This case twisted slowly through a legal labyrinth for more than a year. Wardlow had originally been released on bail, but was eventually rearrested by the Freedmen's Bureau, which ran a special set of courts for Blacks at the time, on the premise that Blacks could not get justice in ordinary civil courts in the South.[66] His case was apparently relinquished by the Bureau and returned to the courts of Shelby County, and he was evidently released again, because in September of 1866 he was charged with receiving stolen goods from a juvenile thief named Samuel Prager, who had stolen items from Prager's mother. Wardlow was fined fifty dollars and released.[67] His trial on the original murder charge came in November, and he was convicted and sentenced to nine years of imprisonment.[68] Although he applied for a new trial, in December the *Ledger* reported that Wardlow had been turned over to Sheriff Winters for transportation to the penitentiary in Nashville.[69]

Wardlow reappears in April of 1867, when the first hearing toward his retrial was held,[70] and while his case worked its way through the courts with him apparently released on bond, he also began his first forays into politics, rising to speak at a Conservative party meeting at the courthouse, presumably the same building where he was on trial:

> Alderman Smith introduced, in a neat speech, Mr. Robert Wardlow, a colored citizen, who proceeded to address the meeting, expressing the diffidence he experienced in the novel attitude in which he found himself. He explained the good feeling that had existed between his old master and himself. He referred to the invitations he had received to visit several secret leagues, but he did not like the nature of the invitations. He loved his liberty, and was willing to fight for it. He had served under the flag that waved over the liberty of the slave. He admired Mr. Lincoln, but he wanted to know what he meant by his offer to the southern people to lay down their arms and take their negroes back. He appealed to any colored soldier, if there were any present, whether he ever obtained justice in the United States army. On the subject of the franchise, they give us only enough to get us in trouble, and save themselves. What is the franchise worth if we can't live till the day of election? The ignorant colored men think it is their duty to be the enemy of southern men; but they are not all so. A liberal northern man, who has patriotic feeling, no longer feels like an enemy. He referred to the reliance the colored man might safely feel, that he would be well treated by those among whom he had been raised, and who were ready at all times to sustain him in any virtuous and correct action.[71]

The rival *Ledger* added the information that Wardlow was in fact chosen as one of the Black delegates to the state Democratic convention in Nashville.[72]

Up to this point, no mention had been made of Robert Wardlow having anything to do with music, but in June of 1867 "Wardlow's brass band" marched with a group of two hundred Black citizens to serenade Justice Creighton, a local Conservative official, which must have been somewhat awkward for Wardlow, as Creighton had presided over his first trial and sentenced him to nine years in the penitentiary.[73] A week later, Wardlow was finally acquitted by the jury on the charges of having murdered Ike Campbell. The state's only witness claimed that Wardlow had told him that he killed the victim in self-defense, but no eyewitnesses were available, two having died and the others having left the city.[74] To the *Appeal's* notice of Wardlow's acquittal, the *Avalanche* added the information that he was the leader of Wardlow's band.[75] By the end of July that year, he and his band were holding forth at a resort hotel in the mineral spring town of Iuka, Mississippi.[76] When the festive Christmas season came, Wardlow bought an advertisement in the *Memphis Avalanche* offering his services: "MUSIC FOR BALLS OR PARTIES ROBERT WARDLOW, 13 Jefferson Street CAN furnish good Music for Balls, Parties, etc., at short notice. Any number of musicians playing either string or brass instruments will be on hand. Orders can be left at the Barber Shop, 13 Jefferson street, or at 345 1/2 Main street."[77]

Throughout his musical career, Wardlow tended to run his business out of barbershops. Whether he was in fact a barber, or whether these were simply convenient Black-owned spaces in which to operate, is not clear. *Halpin's Memphis Directory* for 1867–68 does not show a barbershop at 13 Jefferson, but it does show Reuben Morrison's barbershop at 19 Jefferson and further states that it was a Black establishment. This could be the place in question. Because city directories in that day did not have a street directory with a list of addresses, businesses, and residences for each street, what the Main Street address entailed is lost to us.

By February of 1868, Wardlow was referring to his band as Bob Wardlow's Conservative Band. Electioneering was in full swing, and at a time when most Blacks supported the Radical party, Wardlow undoubtedly wanted to remind white Conservatives of his political point of view.[78] Still, gigs must have been somewhat hard to come by, for in May, he was again advertising his services in the *Avalanche*:

We are requested by the irrepressible, the true and reliable Robert Wardlow, to announce that his band is offered to the patronage of the public. It is composed of brass and stringed instruments, and is made up of the finest performers in the city. They will play either for parties in this city, or make a permanent engagement at any convenient watering place.[79] Orders left at Ned Adam's barbour [sic] shop on Maine [sic] street, between Union and Gayoso, will be promptly attended to.[80]

As "Conservative" Blacks in Memphis were not easy to come by, the Memphis newspapers generally gave Wardlow favorable coverage, but not always. His fairly brutal beating of a woman was noted by the *Appeal*, with an odd humor that showed little regard for the unfortunate female victim:

> Robert Wardlow, the leader of the negro brass band, gave Laura Bradford, a scrumptious, saucy looking wench, a most tremendous trouncing, which she no doubt richly deserved. But Robert let his angry passions so far get the better of him, as to pull out a pistol and threaten to blow the "top of Laura's head plum off," which Laura did not relish at all, and making her escape, had him arrested and carried before "Squire Walton, who, to cool his ardor, sent Robert to the Criminal Court under bonds of $1000. He also put him under $500 bonds to keep the peace."[81]

But if the white Conservatives and Democrats were aware of Wardlow's legal troubles, it did not seem to affect their demand for his services, for the month of August was the height of the election campaign, and it found Wardlow's band occupied almost every day at some rally or event. Soon they were not merely in Memphis, but at Wythe Depot (Arlington) in Shelby County and LaGrange in Fayette County as well. All of it must have taken a toll, for on Sunday, August 23, the *Memphis Avalanche* gave a funeral notice for Wardlow: "The friends of the late ROBERT WARDLOW are invited to attend his funeral this afternoon at four o'clock, from his residence, No. 158 Linden street."[82] Elsewhere in the paper, more details of his life and death were given:

> Mr. Robert Wardlow, the leader of Wardlow's well-known brass band, died at 6 o'clock yesterday afternoon at his residence, on Linden street, of congestive chills.[83] The deceased has been before the public five or six years, and was highly respected by all who knew him, white and black, for his honesty, faithfulness to principle and fidelity to his friends. At the time of his death, he was about thirty-five years old. His demise will be a painful surprise to many people. He had been in bad health for some time, but no one dreamed that his end was so near. Mr. Wardlow was the first colored Democrat ever known in Memphis, and he stood by his principles in the face of persecution and peculiarly trying circumstances.[84]

The next day, the *Appeal* gave an account of the funeral, at which the band he had led for so long performed: "The funeral of Robert Wardlow, who died on Saturday evening from a congestive chill, was well attended yesterday, his remains being followed to their last resting place by a large number of citizens, white and colored, headed by the band of which he was the leader. Deceased was about the first colored Democrat in Memphis, and lived to see hundreds of his race following in his footsteps."[85] Thus ended the career of a most remarkable musician and entrepreneur in Memphis.

Concerns about Blacks drilling and drumming at night was not confined to Memphis, but soon became a source of complaints in Nashville as well. One such band of Blacks was said to be led by a self-styled "magician":

The drilling of negroes on St. Cloud Hill and the Sulphur Spring bottoms has become an intolerable nuisance to the good citizens of those localities. Those who are drilled at the former place are led by a negro, Leander Wood, whom the respectable colored men of the city denounce as the vilest and most corrupt scoundrel in Nashville. He lives in what is known as Rocktown, a settlement of negroes over whom he has at various times essayed to exercise supreme control. He has induced the negroes who came from the country to join his bogus company by telling them that he holds a commission from Brownlow, and that an act would soon be passed by the Legislature calling out the militia. . . . They are at present drilled after dark, to the very great annoyance of the laborers and mechanics who work at the Decatur shops, who complain that they are unable to sleep on account of the noise created with their drums and voices to a late hour in the night. . . . The band of fifty negroes who drill in the Sulphur Spring bottom, are said to be under the leadership of one John Durham, a "magician," who seems to be so little known that it has been impossible to obtain a history of his antecedents. He has been circulating a petition asking for alms for negroes who he alleges have been driven into the city by the Kuklux.[86]

In Memphis, politics was still the order of the day, and the fife and drum continued apace, particularly on the Radical side of the campaign. The *Appeal* described another riverfront rally in terms that mirrored the one they had covered in July, with the usual slurs against Blacks:

Yesterday afternoon our attention was attracted by the sound of a big drum and fife, leading a Grant and Colfax procession. The display was very imposing—a big n----r with drawn sabre marching in front, while a sable companion carried a flag, two drummers and a fife played their best, and about twenty colored cotton-baggers (juvenile carpet-baggers who pick up anything lying around loose) brought up the rear. The grand procession was preliminary to a mass meeting of Republicans on the bluff at night, called by the "biggest scalawag of them all," B. Lewis. . . . Through South Memphis the dusky warrior marched, and up through town, with drums and fife, numbering about fifty by the time they reached the bluff.[87]

On September 12, 1868, the Conservative Democrats staged a massive parade of ten thousand people through the streets of Memphis, organized by the various white and Black Democratic clubs in the city, and including Black brass bands and fife and drum bands, probably reflecting the active role that Black Conservatives played in the election that year:

Next came the FIRST WARD DEMOCRATIC CLUB, in the van of which was a huge pair of long wheels, twenty feet in diameter, drawn by six horses. Mounted on them was a triangular transparency with the simple and effective motto, "Seymour and Blair." One hundred and fifty-four torches were borne in the line, and six transparencies. The most ludicrous of the latter was one representing a "carpet-bagger on November 6,"—a lean and hungry-looking individual with a carpet sack, making a "straight shirt tail" for up Salt creek. This club was headed by the West Indian colored Conservative band.[88] . . . Close following these in the line came the SECOND WARD CLUB headed by their colored band, who were doing brave service on their drums and fifes. . . . Following this band came the COLORED CENTRAL DEMOCRATIC CLUB bearing a beautiful banner, representing the white and black man shaking hands. About fifty lights were carried by them, and the body was marshaled by the veteran and portly Sam Croghan, who was gorgeously attired in grand regalia of silk and satin. Next in order, led by Tobin's 7th Ward (colored) band, came the FOURTH WARD DEMOCRATIC CLUB, which bore three transparencies and sixty torches, making a fine, though not so numerous a display as other clubs. . . . Close following the printing press came the FIFTH WARD DEMOCRATIC CLUB, numbering over two hundred torches in the line, and all of them borne by sturdy yeomen. They were accompanied by the Fifth Ward Colored Democratic Band, who were untiring in their efforts to make "music for the million." . . . Next came the TENTH WARD

CLUB, led by the Tenth Ward colored band. . . . Another mounted band of INDEPENDENT DEMOCRATS, led by Col. J. J. Dubose, came after the butchers' club, and these were followed by the NINTH WARD CLUB, bearing about one hundred and twenty-five lights. In their line was a full rigged ship, in which were about twenty persons. The motto was "Constitution and Liberty." They were led by the Ninth Ward (Chelsea) colored Democratic band.[89]

Clearly no expense was spared for the massive parade, and many of the clubs chose to hire "colored bands" for their places in it. While brass bands predominated, at least one fife and drum ensemble was present. Of course, one wonders how "Conservative" these bands actually were. Musicians being what they are, it is likely that some of them played for a Democratic rally one night and a Republican rally the next. Having only been able to vote for a year, Black musicians may not have fully understood the finer points of the Republican versus Democrat dispute, but they did see clearly how to manipulate it to make money.

As the campaign drew on through the month of September, there were mini-riots and difficulties in some places in West Tennessee, such as Mason's Depot in Tipton County. Most of the noise and fury was on the Radical side, but the Democrats held small-town rallies too. One in Bolivar, in Hardeman County, hired "Stephen Greason's band of drummers and fifers from Memphis."[90] Earlier, the *Avalanche* had mentioned this same event, and "Grayson's Band, who have been 'drumming' up so many colored volunteers for the Democratic cause."[91] The article mentioned that Grayson, in addition to providing music for the barbecue, had made an effective speech to the Blacks who attended. Stephen Grayson seems to have been a man determined to follow in the footsteps of Robert Wardlow.

Like Robert Wardlow before him, Stephen Grayson was a colorful figure who kept a hand in politics, business, and music.[92] We know little of his early life, but from his death certificate we know that he was born in Mississippi in 1826, likely a slave.[93] From Freedmen's Bureau records, we can see that he married Nancy Tillman in Memphis on January 6, 1865, and that his father was white and his mother Black. He had lived with a woman for ten years, but had been separated from her by the war.[94] He first appears in the 1867–68 *Halpin's Memphis Directory*, where he is listed as a painter, living in the rear house at the northwest corner of Linden and Main.[95] He first appears in the Memphis newspapers in 1867 as well, having been charged with two other men named John Riley and Henry Magregor with robbing an old man from Mason's Depot named Sandy Wilton. Grayson and the two others were accused of trying to sell the man a watch and, when he refused to buy it, reaching in his pocket and grabbing his money.[96]

In September, the *Appeal* mentioned the arrest of Grayson again, this time charged with assault with intent to kill.[97] The incident was more fully described by the rival *Avalanche*: "A herculean black fellow, answering to the name of Steve Grayson, was brought before 'Squire Hall, yesterday afternoon and required to give bonds to keep the peace toward an ebon hued chap of lesser muscle, who testified that he was 'done 'fraid dat n----r would do damage to his pusson.'"[98] In February 1868, the *Avalanche* reported that the habeas corpus trial of Steve Grayson that was scheduled to begin on February 6 had been postponed, so presumably Grayson was imprisoned, and his attorneys were trying to have him released, although it is unclear exactly for what he was incarcerated.[99] At any rate, by July he was out, and having been threatened with death by a man named Jack Davis, Grayson swore out a warrant against him before 'Squire Black, who placed Davis under a peace bond and bound him over for trial.[100] So far, Stephen Grayson seemed to be just a brawler with a quick temper who was frequently on the court docket. But a few days later in July, the *Avalanche* published a letter from Grayson renouncing Radicalism and endorsing the Democratic Party:

MEMPHIS, TENN, July 25, 1868 EDITORS AVALANCHE: Having been connected with the Radical party in various capacities since the dominant party have had the control of the public offices in Memphis and in West Tennessee, permit me to say to my friends and the public, through the columns of your valuable paper, that hereafter my influence and vote shall be given in favor of the nominees of the Democratic party.

Having labored long and earnestly to secure the freedom and suffrage of my own race, I, in common with all true, patriotic and honest Republicans, feel deeply the unfortunate condition in which my people are drifting, unless they take preliminary measures, and that speedily, to rid themselves of the unprincipled rascals that are deluding the colored people and swindling the public of the revenue derived by extortionate taxation of both rich and poor. I do this from none but the purest motives, and from conscientious convictions, feeling satisfied that if Tennessee is longer in Radical hands the consequences will be very injurious and destructive to the interests of the colored race. Very respectfully yours, STEPHEN GRAYSON[101]

Although Grayson stated that he was motivated by only the "purest motives," there were immediate consequences that were quite beneficial to him. Omitting any mention of his frequent fights and criminal charges, the *Avalanche* referred to him as "one of the most intelligent negroes of Memphis," noted his career as a painter, and called on Conservatives and Democrats to hire him.[102] The one Republican newspaper in Memphis, the *Post*, published a card that suggested that Grayson's legal troubles had motivated him to switch sides: "Mr. Steve Grayson has become a Democrat because, while going around the city, acting as prosecuting attorney, he took Lee Brooks before Justice Black and had himself the costs to pay. So he jumped the fence and joined the Democracy. Good-bye, sugar-coated, sweet-scented Steve. Respectfully, JOHN CHRISTIAN."[103]

Whether cynically or based on personal conviction, Grayson seems to have taken to his new political home with abandon, for in early August, his name is listed as one of the founders of the Tenth Ward Colored Democratic Club in Memphis.[104] Over the next weeks, he was involved with the formation of several other such clubs in different wards of Memphis. At an August gathering of the Tenth Ward Democratic Club, Grayson spoke tellingly about Blacks hiding their politics from white employers, and the band with which he was associated is first mentioned:

A large and enthusiastic meeting of the Tenth Ward Democratic Colored Club, Stephen Grayson in the chair, was held last night. The only white speaker was Captain Thomas Wright, who made a telling speech. He was followed by Tom Avent, Eli Glass, George Norment and Stephen Grayson. Grayson alluded to the fact that colored men employed by Southerners pretend to have no politics. He called on merchants to give preference to colored men who stood up for the Democracy and were working for its success. He also mentioned that the club would turn out in public soon, and he wanted to see all the colored clubs turn out and show their strength. During the meeting the house was surrounded by Radicals, who kept many persons away, but did not dare attempt a disturbance. This club now contains fifty names, and is daily increasing in strength. About midnight, a number of members, with a martial band, serenaded the AVALANCHE and Appeal offices. Colonel Galloway appeared at the former, and briefly acknowledged the compliment.[105]

The band that played on that occasion was probably Robert Wardlow's Conservative Band, although whether Wardlow was there is questionable, as he had apparently been ill for some time. He died two days after the rally, but his band was mentioned a week later at a rally across the river in Marion, Arkansas, now under the direction of Stephen Grayson: "Too much praise cannot be awarded the colored Democrats who, on this occasion, displayed much enthusiasm, and did everything in their power to make everything what the meeting turned out to be—a perfect success. They paraded with the Tenth ward, Fifth ward, and Central colored clubs, led by Tom Epps' band and Wardlow's old and popular musicians, under Grayson."[106]

The *Avalanche* gave a similar, if more condensed account of the barbecue, but referred to "Steve Grayson's band," suggesting that the remnants of Wardlow's band became the basis of the band to which Grayson put his name.[107] Two weeks later, the same newspaper reported that "Stephen Grayson and several other colored speakers, together with Grayson's band, will leave on the 12:40 train to-day for Bolivar, to be present at the meeting to-morrow."[108]

On the 13th of October, a large contingent of Democrats, led by General Nathan Bedford Forrest, headed for a Democratic barbecue in Jackson, Tennessee, in Madison County, and Steve Grayson's band was along for the ride: "Memphis was represented on the 12:30 train which left Tuesday, by Generals Pike and Forrest, Major Jack Hays, the chaperon—in a masculine and fluid sense—of the party; Judge Perkins and several others, besides Steve Grayson's band, which waked up the small towns and put all the big ones to sleep on the route."[109] But by November the campaign was all over, and the *Public Ledger* reported that Grayson had gotten into another difficulty: "At about half-past seven o'clock this morning, a difficulty occurred between Stephenson Grierson and Anderson Toliver, in reference to family affairs. Grierson shot Toliver in the left arm and side, the ball ranging in, and will no doubt prove fatal. Grierson afterward gave himself up to the sheriff and is now in jail."[110] That the man the *Ledger* called "Stephenson Grierson" was actually Steve Grayson was revealed by the next day's *Avalanche*, which duly reported that "Steve Grayson, colored, shot Anderson Colbert, colored, yesterday morning at their mutual residence on Butler Street, inflicting a mortal wound. Grayson capitulated on honorable terms with the police."[111] It was left to perhaps the best of Memphis's early daily papers, the *Appeal*, to give the details of the affair:

> The Steve Grayson shooting case was being examined until a late hour yesterday evening, before 'Squire Norton. The witnesses for the defense testified point blank that Grayson acted purely in self-defense, the circumstances being as follows: Grayson and Talliaferro (pronounced Toliver) occupy different ends of the same house, and on

Saturday had a quarrel, after which Talliaferro came to Grayson's end of the house, and after threatening his life picked up two half-bricks and run [*sic*] Grayson into his bedroom. Talliaferro was pursuing him thither when Grayson turned upon him and shot him with a pistol, which he had drawn in the meantime. The ball entered the left breast, below the heart, and ranged downward, inflicting a wound that stopped him in his career. He is now lying in a very critical condition, and it is thought by his attending physician that the wound may eventually prove mortal.[112]

A few days later, the *Appeal* noted that Grayson had been acquitted on the grounds of self-defense.[113] The *Avalanche* gave the same report, with the additional information that Toliver had in fact recovered from his injuries.[114] But by January 15, 1869, Grayson was again on the court docket, charged with assault with intent to kill.[115] Nothing more seems to be mentioned of those charges, but in March, a man complained that Grayson had taken twenty-five dollars to obtain workers for him, and did not produce any workers as promptly as the man thought he should have, so Grayson was arrested and taken to the Second District station house. After being brought before 'Squire Kiernan to give an answer, he reached an agreement with the man and the case was dismissed.[116] The next day, the *Avalanche* reported that he had been run down by a handcart while walking: "Stephen Grayson is a colored individual of the unfortunate species. He seems to be always in trouble, and a couple of days ago he was run down, while walking along the street, by one of the gay and festive youths who trundle the express hand-carts along the streets. Steve had the party in question before Justice Norton yesterday, but the witnesses to the transaction failed to appear, and the case was postponed till tomorrow."[117]

About a week later, Grayson was in court yet again, charged with assaulting somebody, but his appearing as his own attorney won him faint praise from the *Appeal*: "Steve Grayson was yesterday brought before 'Squire Norton on charge of assaulting somebody. The state was represented by L. E. Dyer, Esq, and another lawyer, Steve acting as his own lawyer, and so well did he plead his cause that he was triumphantly acquitted. 'Bully' for Steve, say we."[118]

By April 1869, Steve Grayson had clearly left the Democratic Party, and had joined himself to the Ed Shaw–Barbour Lewis faction of the Republican Party, as the party seemed to be breaking up into warring factions based on particular personalities. When these factions erupted in a brawl during a Republican meeting, Grayson found himself caught in the middle:

Burlesque itself was forestalled and outdone last night at Assembly Hall. Never since the memorable contest in "Pickwick Papers" has it had its equal. The hackneyed phrase of "Pandemonium turned loose" is the only expressions that would convey any idea of it. We looked for a breezy time when that meeting came off, and in the language of the good book, we were not disappointed.

It was a Hunter meeting—or rather it was to have been a Hunter meeting—quite a different thing. But it wasn't. The Fates, and Ed Shaw, and Barbour Lewis, and F. W. Louis, willed it otherwise. The way of it was this: The Barbour Lewis-Ed Shaw-F. W. Louis faction nominated a county committee. Hunter is a candidate for the Chancellorship. He knows that the committee won't nominate him for the position, and so he is determined to ignore the committee and have a new one appointed that will nominate him. That is what the meeting last night was called for. Circulars were sent to the "leading men" of the party that could read. A half dozen was all that it was necessary to print. A band consisting of four or five kettle and a big bass drum was sent around town during the early part of the evening to drum them up. By hard work they got up a crowd that half filled the Assembly Hall.

The meeting was called to order by Giles Smith, who nominated Judge Hunter for chairman. The Granny was about taking the seat, when in marched F. W. Louis and Ed Shaw, with Steve Grayson's band, drumming and fifing in the most vigorous manner, and from fifty to seventy-five followers shouting lustily. In a moment all was in an uproar. Both bands struck up "Hail Columbia," and each faction commenced to shout for its leader—Hunter or Louis. Somebody nominated F. W. Louis for Chairman, and declared him elected. Louis was about to take the seat, but the Granny already had it, and showed fight; so he moved his hand up closer, and bade them thunder away. Hunter, putting both hands to his mouth and forming an impromptu speaking trumpet, announced that Joe Lusher, Beecher and Giles Smith were the nominating committee. A roar from the Shaw faction, and a rattle of the drums drowned his words. This enraged a belligerent Hunter man, and he went for Steve Grayson, the leader of the band. The police promptly interfered, and prevented a collision, but in the melee somebody slashed a hole in Steve's bass drum. Steve was about to send him to kingdom come, when the police got his pistol away from him. Cries of "Louis" and "Hunter" meanwhile continued without ceasing, and were heard above the din and roar of the drums. And so they had it "nip and tuck," until all at once, in the middle of the din, "out went the lights—out all," and then "sich another getting down stairs you never did see." Every mode of egress was instantaneously sought. Some of the crowd sprang out on the shed, and "snaked" down the columns, but the greater part of the crowd got down the steps.

In the streets, the crowd yelled and shouted, and the drums beat just as they did in the hall. Steve Grayson just "roared" about his bass drum, and was going to do terrible things if he could "find the man that did it." He didn't find him.

After several minutes delay the lights were lit again, and all parties returned to the hall, to renew the same scenes previously enacted. The Hunter faction took the stage and the Louis-Shaw faction kept down by the door, but the drums of both parties kept up a deafening roar. Thus matters stood when we left at eleven o'clock, and thus Shaw swore they should stand until the police made them break up and go home.[119]

If Stephen Grayson becoming a Democrat had annoyed his fellow Black Memphians, his becoming a Republican again enraged the local newspapers. When he sued a Black man with the name of George Washington for having stolen four and a half dollars, the *Appeal* unloaded on him for his perfidy: "George Washington, a black moke, and Mr. Steve Grayson, the Radical-Conservative-Democratic-Hunter-Lewis-Stokes-Senter n----r, who changes his politics every day in warm weather (and twice a day in winter), had a little falling out about four dollars and a half, Mr. Grayson accusing the black father of his country of having unlawfully, fraudulently and feloniously appropriated the said money to his own use, contrary to the peace and dignity of the State of Tennessee. The 'Squire, after a patient investigation, sent George up in default of $1000 to answer to the Criminal Court."[120] But apparently, the newspapers could forgive Grayson's politics if they enjoyed his band's music, which they evidently did, for the next day, they were praising the musicians: "The APPEAL office was serenaded by Steve Grayson's band last evening about half-past ten o'clock, and very fine music they made, too. We don't know when we have heard anything more unique, and at the same time pleasanter and more inspiring than the music they made."[121]

The *Appeal*'s good mood would not last, however. On the day after the election in August of 1869, the newspaper singled out Grayson for his political waverings: "Steve Grayson informed us about six o'clock that he had voted the Senter ticket. A friend of ours who happened to see Steve vote, says that maybe he did, but if so, Stokes' name was at the head of it.[122] We will all remember Steve."[123]

In reality, it was likely that Grayson had little interest in politics, and a lot of interest in getting ahead in the best way he could. It is also possible that the Democrats offended Grayson as he was on the campaign stump with them. General Forrest had in fact made a strong speech in defense of Southern slavery at the October 14, 1868, barbecue at Jackson, Tennessee, where Grayson's band played. That occasion was the last event at which Grayson was clearly a Democrat.

In December of 1869, the *Public Ledger* mentioned Grayson as "the colored patriot who ate so much free Democratic hash in the last Presidential campaign and afterward acted as brass band for the Radical party." He was described as having recently returned from an "arduous campaign in Mississippi."[124] As the new year began in January 1870, Grayson's band was again engaged in playing for political events, but the volatility was seemingly beginning to frighten some of his musicians, as the *Appeal* recounted: "Some rich scenes took place at the mutual admiration white and black serenade last night in front of the Walker organ. Steve Grayson's band struck up the 'Yellow Gal Winked at Me.' A Johnson man called out to play 'Root Hog or Die.' The musical darky who exercises his talents on the bass drum misunderstood the request, and thought he heard the word 'fight.' He said, 'Look a heah, Steve, I didn't come head to fight for Walker; Ise a Lynn man, I is!'"[125]

Later that month, a political discussion got out of hand at a saloon on the corner of South and Main Streets, which, according to the *Edwards City Directory* for 1870, was also the location of Grayson's house at the time:

> We are informed that an affray occurred at a negro drinking saloon at the corner of South and Main streets, yesterday evening, between Steve Grason [*sic*], the notorious Radical negro politician, and some unknown negroes, in which several shots were fired. Grayson and the crowd were chuck full of whisky, having just come from a Radical caucus, and became involved in a political discussion, which Steve put a summary end to by stepping back and drawing a pistol, lamming [*sic*] loose at the crowd. No one was hit, but a speedy adjournment of that meeting was had.
>
> Nothing of the affair was on the docket at the Second District Station house, and we therefore suppose no arrests were made.[126]

In February, the *Appeal* noted that Grayson had been arrested for gambling and pointed out that he was going to jail quite frequently. He actually had always been going to jail quite frequently, but the *Appeal* never seemed to notice when he was jaunting around the state on behalf of the Democratic party.[127] In July, Grayson pressed charges against another Black man for assault, but the judge found that Grayson was in the wrong and assessed him court costs.[128] Increasingly, Grayson seemed to withdraw from politics, and his mentions in the newspaper were fewer and fewer. In 1871, he was mentioned only twice, both times in connection with Decoration Day, the commemoration of the Union dead at the National Cemetery on the Raleigh Road. There, his band performed in conjunction with the society called the Independent Order of Pole Bearers: "Two hundred negroes, armed with pikes, and styling themselves 'Pole Bearers,' paraded through the streets to-day preparatory to attending the floral decoration at the National Cemetery. The society of Pole Bearers is a branch of the Grand Army of the Republic, and is a well organized military battalion. The notorious Democratic negro Steve Grayson acted as drum-major of one of the bands."[129] The rival *Appeal* reported on the events at the cemetery itself, where Grayson's band and the Pole Bearers were again noted prominently:

The band played many of the national airs, and some mournful ones that are not national. It is odd how a dirge near becomes a national thing. There is a deep philosophical principle in this, which our learned reporter disposes of in this wise: A national dirge is the requiem of national life. It is never sung. There is no life left to sing it. Steve Grayson's excellent martial band was there, doing honor to the occasion. . . . The organization known as the "Independent Order of Pole Bearers" turned out in very creditable style. They numbered over four hundred, and presented a most respectable appearance.[130]

Stephen Grayson does not appear in the Memphis newspapers again until 1874, where he is listed as one of a number of Blacks hoping to become city policemen. The mayor of Memphis at that time, John Loague, was a member of the Radical party and supported making Blacks firemen and policemen, but his efforts in that regard failed.[131]

We last encounter Stephen Grayson at a barbecue in Bartlett during the campaign of 1878. The power of the Radical party had been broken in 1874 by an openly white-supremacist political campaign called the Bartlett Movement. However, in 1878, there were still some Black Democrats taking part in the campaign:

General Gordon next introduced George Hayden, Colored, who took the stand and made an address particularly directed to the colored people. He was down on Colonel and General Eaton, because they used to arrest the colored people for debt.

Steve Grayson—I remembers dat.

Hayden (looking into the audience and discovering Grayson)—Oh, yes, you used to help arrest us, but you were forced to do it. He then told how the work was done, disclosing how the loyal league was organized, with its adjunct, the colored league. Hayden's speech was chiefly consumed in detailing Radical sins against the colored people.[132]

One can only wonder how Steve Grayson felt as he stood there listening to a man recount how Black people had suffered under some of the policies of the Radical party that Grayson had worked for. Three months later, Stephen Grayson was dead, of dysentery, during the height of the yellow fever epidemic. One would have thought that a man so well known during his life would have warranted an obituary, but the ravages of the fever had reduced the *Appeal* to only two pages. With so much death around, Grayson's passing was noted only in a list of those who died of causes other than yellow fever. It was an ignoble and undeserved end to a man who left a such a mark on Memphis music and politics.[133]

In October of 1868, during the height of the election campaign, the white Memphis newspapers were still complaining about Black fife and drum music, which they seemed to associate not only with Radical political activities but also with Black criminality:

We have been blessed with lovely weather, and so far as it is possible to do so for the want of labor our planters are "making hay while the sun shines." To this end few of them comparatively come to town, but they send cotton in freely and order their supplies as they need them. We learn of efforts being made to induce the idle vagabond, who are found loitering about our city, to earn an honest livelihood, and as much as one dollar per hundred and board has been freely offered during the picking season, but these pests to society and armed robbers and midnight assassins prefer to stay in our midst to follow after the drum and fife nightly, uttering yells which would startle the infernal regions from their propriety. They prefer to hang around the confines of our city, robbing hen roosts, killing cattle and hogs, and occasionally an unprotected white man, rather than earn an honest livelihood.[134]

Likewise, in Nashville, the *Nashville Union* complained that the Black musicians had a habit of going armed: "The negro musicians of the Radical party who daily and nightly drum through the streets of the city, carry big pistols belted around them, in order to give a military appearance to their outfit and make other n----rs 'stand around.' M.P.'s who usually go armed in the same way will have to look out for their laurels."[135]

It is noteworthy that these accounts of the nocturnal fife and drum sessions mention exuberant yelling and defiant boasts of being free men, among other things. One of the allures of these meetings/picnics/parties was doubtless that in them Blacks seemed to be free to enjoy themselves and to assert their newly acquired rights and freedoms. These same reasons seem to have been the basis for the white objection to fife and drum music, as well as a continuing fear of what it actually portended for the future. Again, believing that fife and drum music was only used for military purposes, white Southerners assumed that Blacks were drilling and making preparations to go to war against them as a group. The occasional armed robbery or killing of a white resident of course did nothing to calm the fears.

"DRUM MET DRUM AND FIFE MET FIFE": BLACK FIFE AND DRUM MUSIC IN TENNESSEE, 1869

The beginning of a new year saw the convening of a Radical convention in Shelby County, intended to nominate a candidate for the County Commission, called together by a fife and drum band, but the enjoyment of the band was apparently the only thing the attendees could agree on. The debate on who the nominee for the position should be became increasingly contentious, and although the Black leader Ed Shaw was ultimately chosen, that decision did nothing to calm the uproar:

> A genuine Radical convention met last evening in the Criminal Court room, a most appropriate place, for the purpose of nominating a candidate for the office of County Commissioner at the ensuing election on the 6th of March: It was a regular Smith-Blewis [*sic*] crowd, and the spectacle presented by the motley crowd was dark and benighted. After a fife and drum band had surfeited everybody with all kind of airs played out of tune, the base drum being alone heard, with now and then the squeak of an ear-piercing fife . . . it was at length declared that Ed Shaw had received the nomination, all others having withdrawn, which was followed by a genuine uproar and music on the big drum.[136]

Ultimately, the strife in the convention seemed to portend a growing split in the Republican ranks, and by April, it was soon out in the open for everyone to see:

> Monday night the Shawites had a grand blowout at the Municipal Courtroom, and Shaw made a speech, in which he gave Beecher and Hunter and a few others of that clique, particular fits, making some terrible charges against them. Last night the Granny had her revenge. She called a meeting at the Criminal Courtroom, and sent around a band with trumpets and drums, harps tymbals [sic] and a hugag [sic] to bring together a multitude unto the Courtroom to hear her. But the multitude didn't come. Diligent drumming didn't bring together more than two hundred persons all told—about half of whom were white men, or friends of Shaw. . . . We learn that the tea party broke up in a general row, Shaw and Hunter denouncing each other as liars, thieves, and, in fact, everything that they could lay tongue to. Pistols were drawn and flourished, and a general wool pulling and clothes tearing ensued. About midnight Shaw and his faction withdrew from the courtroom, flourishing their pistols and swearing vengeance on the Hunter faction.[137]

A week later came another Hunterite convention, which was the incident in which Steve Grayson's bass drum was slashed.[138] It occasioned a rather mirthful editorial from the *Daily Memphis Avalanche*, which could scarcely hide its joy at the split within the Radical ranks:

> The war of the roses is still raging. History tells us of the "Battle of Spurs," the "Battle of the Books," the "Battle of the Frogs and Mice," the "Battle of the Giants," the "Battle of the Herrings," the "Battle of the Kegs," the "Battle of the Poets," the "Battle of the Nations," the "Battle of the Standard," the "Battle of the Thirty," and "The Tearless Battle," and now we have in our midst "The Battle of the Thieves and Plunderers." In Memphis the Radical party is split in twain. The members of each faction are burnishing up their old rusty sabres, and drums are beating, fifes are squeaking, banners are streaming, dung carts are rumbling, and the beligerent [sic] factions, as they snarl and growl at each other, look like a hundred-headed dog, with each head containing a separate and distinct hydrophobia.[139]

The *Public Ledger* was equally gleeful: "The sight last night at the meeting of the Radical clowns was one that would sicken and yet amuse the intelligent portion of any community. The Radicals, as it was thought, had fallen out over the division of spoils. Each greedy pap-sucker desires the lion's share of the public plunder. When the rival factions meet in battle array nothing is heard but the tooting of horns and the beating of drums, reminding one of a more martial array than is present in this motley herd of ragged blacks and dirty scalawags."[140] What was bad for the future of the Radical party politically was, on the other hand, a considerable blessing for musicians and lovers of fife and drum music, as each faction now employed musicians. The *Avalanche* gave a detailed description of both the political and the musical battle:

> Last night the Hunter faction of the Raging Rads, anxious to give back a Rowland for the Oliver dealt them the other night by Barber Lewis, sent out their light skirmishers, headed by drum and fife, to call together the adherents of the Criminal Judge, who are anxious to put him in the line of descent from the Lord Chancellors of England. The avants courreurs of the Barber faction were not to be driven from their "coin of vantage" by any such affair of outposts, and they, too, had their big drums and little drums and screeching fifes out on the rampage. . . . The Barber men, undaunted by the judicial frown of the indomitable Hunter, although he could proclaim himself in contempt, and bring the United States troops to sustain the assertion, mounted the very fortress of the Hunterites, and drum met drum and fife met fife. . . .
>
> At the east end of the room the Barber men were drawn up, music in front. . . . But the champ du mort had its focus, or rather its foci, where the opposing drums and fifes were stationed. With a glee that only the negroe's [sic] love of noise could sustain, each band tried to out-drum, out-fife, out-shriek, out-rub-a-dub and out-thunder the other. The fifers blowed until their lips were swollen to lobster size and hue; their eyes stood out with panting exertions as if rat-terriers were after them behind, and they were bound to leave their orbits or "bust." But the drummers on the big drums—there was one on each side—were ahead of the fifers. Forty-parson power hammering high doctrine into the ears of a stunned conventicle, compares with it but as the glow-worm to the sun. The small drums had the notes rattled and hailed out of them on a cataract basis. Let the reader calculate the speed with which a thirsty lamp-post committeeman swallows

a free drink in "Whisky Chute"; the rate at which atoms fly from a cotton gin: the rapidity with which a shaver's hand on Madison street clasps "a good thing," and he will have a faint idea of the flying speed at which the darkie drummer's elbows flew, as the sticks beat the punished parchment. Drum, fife, yell, cheer, groan and bellow all echoing from the walls in unmitigated dissonance, made a combination no combination negro-minstrel troupe ever equalled.[141]

Although the William Hunter and Barber Lewis factions attempted compromise, the effort failed, and soon both factions were having separate nominating conventions for Shelby County offices, with each called together with fife and drum music: "The Barbour Lewis—or Barber-poll—men met in the old cotton shed beyond the bayou on Madison street. The tom-tom band kept South Memphis with its teeth on edge all afternoon, and the consequence was a large turn-out.... The Hunter faction had their meeting on the bluff, at the foot of Union street. A drum, fife and forty tin torches had paraded the northern part of the city, but the crowd, though a tolerable fair one, was not equal to their rivals in the cotton press."[142] If Memphis residents had chafed at the fife and drum bands prior to the splintering of the Radical party, the result of the split was even more fifing and drumming than before. As the *Appeal* put it, "The rival Radical faction again made night hideous, last night, with their drums and tom-toms."[143] The Memphis newspapers' reference to "tom-toms" seems an intentional invocation of primitivism—a subtle way of invoking Africa, or perhaps suggesting that Black citizens were not entirely "civilized" and thus not worthy of exercising the franchise or being allowed to hold office. This was perhaps the first attempt, though certainly not the last, to link Black fife and drum music with ideas of exoticism and primitivism.

The next day, the *Appeal* was still complaining about the music: "Citizens in the lower part of the city, in the vicinity of South street, complain of the negroes who assemble every evening and make night hideous with drums and fifes. Cannot the chief of police, who, we are bound to say, has thus far shown himself zealous in the pursuit of his duty, devise a means to put a stop to it?"[144] The *Avalanche* agreed with the *Appeal*: "South Memphis is nightly agonized by the mean drum and fife music dealt out to them, often until between one and two o'clock in the morning."[145] Why South Memphis was the center of this fife and drum activity is unclear, but it is true that after the Civil War, Blacks had largely settled along South Street, nearest to Fort Pickering, and this was in fact the area where bandleader and bass drummer Stephen Grayson was living at the time.

Although the Democratic Party had in 1868 sought to convince Black voters to support them by appeals to reason, by 1869, there were the first glimpses of a blatant appeal to race and white supremacy in the interest of consolidating the whites against the Blacks. The *Public Ledger* invoked it in a May editorial thusly:

> The nights now in our city are wild and tumultuous, making sleep depart from all eyes and startling the innocent from their beds of rest to look out on a sea of blacks lashed into uproar by mad politicians and mean alcohol. The drum and fife are also freely used to keep alive this unnatural excitement, while the carpet-bag politicians step in to take advantage of the ignorant negro who presumes it something very great to be addressed as fellow-citizens. These negroes have their meetings, always directed and presided over by white men who have deserted race and principle that they may now, in consequence of the unfortunate times, put on and strut for a brief hour in the robes of office. But the time will come, and soon, without doubt, when these scenes will be forgotten, and every man will be assigned his proper place in the community. That the destinies of this country should be controlled by such as we see parading the streets nightly with drum and fife, who are now the recognized loyalty of the land, is quite amusing to men that have made the science of government their study for years. What do you suppose the negro knows of law, who has been working corn and cotton fields all his life long, and who is suddenly released from the chains of slavery, where he and his ancestry have been confined for years, and never permitted to look beyond? Is it at all presumable that this untutored black can think intelligibly upon a question of politics? That men, whose minds heretofore have been as blank of ideas as a spotless sheet of paper, should at the manhood of life suddenly, and all at once, be capable of appreciating the intricate workings of government, is a question too absurd for intelligence to consider for a moment. If the negro is capable of government in so short a time, we are bound to accord him superior natural powers of mind over those possessed by the white race.[146]

These arguments would eventually become the dominant ones in the Democratic Party, and would eventually lead to efforts to disenfranchise all Blacks in Tennessee.

A month later, the *Clarksville Chronicle*, under its masthead with the slogan "This is a White Man's Government—Let It Be Governed By White

Men," railed against the conduct of the Black community on Election Day,
as they had been brought into town by Radical candidates:

> It cannot be denied that the colored men were all brought to town
> by the direct manipulations of Peffer and Buck,[147] and that many of
> them came to town armed and endeavored throughout the day to
> intimidate those colored voters who wished to vote for Rice. It can-
> not be denied that the difficulty which took place in the Court House
> yard, arose from an attempt on the part of one of Mr. Peffer's colored
> friends to intimidate another colored man who had announced his
> intention to vote for Rice. It cannot be denied that when the police
> endeavored to suppress the difficulty, Mr. Peffer's colored friends
> overpowered the police and trampled the law beneath their feet. It
> cannot be denied that immediately after the police had been over-
> powered, Mr. Peffer's colored friends brought out the drum in tri-
> umph, thus adding greatly to the excitement and the danger of a
> serious difficulty.[148]

Although a May State Supreme Court ruling had restored the voting
rights of many ex-Confederates in Tennessee, the Radicals continued holding rallies in Memphis and elsewhere. The river bluff in Memphis was a
favorite place for such gatherings and was soon dubbed "Buzzard's Roost"
by the Memphis newspapers, presumably because of the large number of
Blacks who attended political rallies there. Said the *Appeal*, "Buzzard's
Roost was a howling wilderness of darkies last night, and up to a late hour
drums were rattling, fifes shrieking and B. L. and others bloviating at a
tremendous rate."[149]

At the end of July, the *Public Ledger* gave notice of a picnic to be held
at White's Station in Shelby County,[150] ostensibly for the formation of a
benevolent society, but the *Ledger* could not avoid the suspicion that the
society was a front for political activity:

> The negro population for miles and miles around are assembled to-
> day at White's Station, ostensibly to organize some kind of benevo-
> lent society, but really to be harangued by political tricksters. It is
> understood that the principal speaker will be Mr. McKenna, one
> of the Radical candidates for the Senate. As he lives a great deal at
> White's Station, in all respects, and will eviscerate his ideas from
> the summit of his own dunghill, or from a swinging limb on his own
> sour apple tree, the supposition is that he will considerably increase

his popularity and elevate the altitude of his fertile hillock several inches. The darkies call it a picnic. If they can find any nick nax they will pick the bones clean. The morning trains brought down large quantities of the man and brother and a considerable amount of his sister, while several tons unable to buy tickets were seen padding down the dirt road to the tune of "old dog Tray."[151] Mr. Sam Jones, owing to a pressing engagement elsewhere, will not be present to address the great crowd of voters.[152]

Although no fife and drum music is mentioned explicitly, this is precisely the kind of event at which it likely would have occurred. Despite the *Ledger*'s suspicions, the event was probably exactly what it stated it was: a barbecue and picnic sponsored by a benevolent society. Because membership dues were not enough to meet the costs of funerals and burials, or of maintenance of the cemeteries, the societies often sponsored large picnics to help raise funds. While these picnics were not technically political events, it was not surprising that politicians would appear at them, speak at them, and possibly even make donations to them. After all, Blacks could vote, and every vote counted. The practice of holding such picnics with fife and drum bands for the benefit of a benevolent society was basically the last purpose of Black fife and drum music in Tennessee, continuing to around 1980.

On the next day, the *Memphis Daily Appeal* noted that the Black community of Memphis celebrated the thirty-fifth anniversary of the abolition of slavery in the West Indies "with banners flying and drums beating." The article noted that the various societies were out in full regalia.[153]

The election of Conservative Republican Dewitt Clinton Senter as governor of Tennessee in August of 1869 had a chilling effect on the Black community, and an emboldening effect on white Democrats and Conservatives, although Senter himself was a moderate. The effect seemed almost immediate, as an incident involving fife and drum music in Maury County showed:

Last Saturday, the teacher of a negro school at Santa Fe, a colored man named Aleck Few, had a celebration on the occasion of the end of the session, accompanied by a drum and fife, and attempted to march through the streets of the town. When they came to the Main street of the town, however, they were stopped by several white men, who turned the column back. The negroes turned around, and as they started off, they gave three cheers for Aleck Few. They marched up to where their dinner was spread, and were enjoying themselves when the same white men who had stopped them went up and said they were ordered to have the drum stop beating. The music was squelched and the enjoyment of the negroes broken up. About night-fall one or two of the white men threw a few rocks at a small cluster of negroes, but none was hurt. The negroes behaved peaceably, and we regret that the whites did not do the same.[154]

By November, conditions for Blacks in Tennessee had evidently deterio-rated to the point that a protest meeting was called to organize a "colored convention" to meet in Nashville in December to discuss the "condition of the colored people of Tennessee": "The 'boisterous sheep-skin,' which had so long ceased to reverberate, was again heard upon our streets yesterday morning. Following in the rear of the drums was a placard, upon which was written in a black scrawl, 'Colored folks rally at the court-house at 2 P.M.' About the object of the meeting there was much speculation, not even a minority of the colored folks who make much pretension to knowledge of such matters, being aware as to what was to be accomplished."[155] The event, after failing to get the use of the courthouse, or the Second Colored Christian Church on West Gay Street, ending up gathering at the dining room of the Harding House Hotel, in greatly reduced numbers. All the same, they voted on resolutions that called for a state convention of Blacks:

> The colored are completely at the mercy of the whites; that they want the world to know they are a down-trodden race; that they bear no malice; that they only want to vote for whom they please and be paid for their labor; that they have shown a forbearance that would have done honor to the most highly educated white folks; that some people still want to make them "mere serfs and political tools," that forbear-ance has ceased to be a virtue; that security can only be secured by a combination throughout the State; and that therefore resolved that a State Convention be held here on the 13th proximo, etc.[156]

It is possible that the convention was never held, as there is no further mention of it. But as 1869 closed, the future of Black Tennesseans seemed darker and more uncertain than at any time since the end of slavery.

"WE TRUST IN GOD AND OUR OTHER FRIENDS":
BLACK FIFE AND DRUM MUSIC IN TENNESSEE, 1870

New Year's Day of 1870 marked the sixth anniversary of Abraham Lincoln's Emancipation Proclamation, and the anniversary was the occasion for a large parade and celebration of the Black benevolent societies in Nashville, as reported by the *Nashville Union*:

> About 2,000 colored people celebrated the Sixth Anniversary of the Emancipation Proclamation, issued by President Lincoln in 1863. Notwithstanding the inclemency of the weather about 600 formed in line on Broad street, consisting of members of the various colored societies of this city, Clarksville, and Antioch. They marched up Sumner street to Line, through Line to College, up College to the Public Square, around the Square to Cedar street and up Cedar to the Capitol, and then into the Hall of the House of Representatives, which had been granted them by the Representatives. In a few minutes the large hall and galleries were filled to their utmost capacity. There were three bands engaged for the occasion, one brass band and the others drums and fifes. The procession was very orderly, and the whole exercises at the Capitol were conducted in a very decorous manner.[157]

The victory of the Conservatives in the last elections seemed to reduce the number of Black political rallies, and most references to Black fife and drum or brass bands in the new year were in connection to ceremonial events rather than political ones. Such was the Memphis celebration of the ratification of the Fifteenth Amendment, which extended the franchise to Blacks, and the *Memphis Daily Appeal* covered it in amazing detail, although with that paper's usual racist terminology and consistent references to body odors. The article is nevertheless indispensable for its mention of the specific benevolent societies by name, the bands, the colorful descriptions of uniforms worn, and the slogans on the carried banners:

> Africa was jubilant yesterday, and all Ethiopia, male and female, old men and young men, matrons and maidens and mokes of all degrees, ages, kind and descriptions were on the hidady [*sic*].[158] The 15th amendment was ratified by them in a style of surpassing gorgeousness, and loudness beyond ability of ours to sing. It would require the mews of forty polecat-power to give the faintest idea of the odorous pageant—in fact, we haven't the scents, and will not therefore, try to

do so—that is in terms befitting the occasion. Suffice to say, it was grand—indeed, grand is no name for it—and after saying this we will get off from our pigasses and go into details.

The chief beauty of the fair was the secrecy with which it was gotten up, and the unexpected splendor with which it burst on the eyes of the astonished, benighted and utterly ignorant and unenthusiastic white trash who compose the lower orders of society here. For days past the telegraph had been bringing us news of how the favored race in "God's country" had been everlastingly moving things in the way of celebrations of the "Fifteenth," and how the skin of Africa, for a long time past tight with overfeeding and no work, was "bustin' out in spots," but our bosses were singularly reticent. True, we noticed that the sweeping of millinery shops, the scrapings of book-binderies, the leavings of tin shops, etc, had been searched for several days with a singular watchfulness, but it never struck us what the mokes were up to until we saw their uniforms yesterday—and then the mystery was explained. Every refuse bit of ribbon, every gaudy piece of paper, every piece of gilt tinsel, every available bit of glittering metal had been utilized, and the pageant which proudly wound its way through our streets shone in all their glittering glories.[159] To describe the costumes would require several columns of our space, and the talent of a "most extr'or'nery Jinkins," so we will not attempt it.

The gathering of the clans was effected quietly and mysteriously, the trysting place being the promenade at the Charleston depot (and here let us remark that they showed remarkable good taste and sense, for no more fitting place for the assemblage of a large body of persons is to be found in our city limits).

The column was formed as follows:

Brass band of the Sons of Ham in a wagon.

Marshals on horseback (about two dozen), gorgeous in the hues of the rainbow.

Two mokes with battle-axes (blue swallow-tail coast, brass buttons, standing collars, stripes on their pants, Epluribus unum on the seats of same).

"Pole-bearers" Band (dressed en zouave, with red breeches, etc).

Chaplain (in black, bearing a copy of the Scriptures).

Moke with flag bearing the cabalistic letters, I.P.B.[160]

Independent Order of Pole-Bearers—250 strong (numerically—rather stronger by an odorometer), bearing banners with the legend,

"Hope and Prosperity to All," "We trust in God and our other Friends," etc. The dress of this gang was black, with red trimmings.

Next game a wagon drawn by four horses on which were seated thirty-six negro girls, from six to sixteen years old, dressed in white with "low corsage."

Savalla Band United Sons of Ham—preceded by a banner with the legend, "Friendship, Love and Truth." (This crowd were dressed in dark suits, with very wide blue sashes, and enormous red, white and blue rosettes.)

Young Men's Association (dressed in dark clothing, with sashes, etc. as usual.)

United Sons of Zion, No. 1 (about two hundred and fifty strong, dark clothes with purple sashes—a good looking set of darkies, though we would hate to trust an unlocked hen-house in their neighborhood.)[161]

Banner, with the inscription, "Know thy-self, ye daughters of Zion." Band (fife, fiddle and accordeon [*sic*].)

United Forever Society (one hundred strong—the roughest looking deal in the lot. They looked like they ought to be united for life in the penitentiary.)

Young Men's Association No. 2 (about two hundred strong—a good looking set of fellows.)

Laborers' Union, (a rough lot, but honest looking.)

Daughters of Zion.

(Why, in the name of all that's appropriate, this name was taken by an unregenerate, unredeemed, rampant set of he mokes we cannot imagine.)[162]

St. John's Relief Society.

Draymen's Association.

Laborers' Union.

Mokes generally.

Eight carriages, loaded with mokesses and little mokes.

Three omnibuses, chuck full of mokes of all degrees.

Wagons, carts, etc.

"Citizens generally."

The procession, after being formed, marched down Poplar to Main streets (an accident occurring to the car with the young mokesses happening at the corner of Fourth—nobody hurt), down Main to Beale, up Beale etc., etc., out to James Park.[163]

There is much of interest in the description of this Memphis parade. First of all, several organizations are mentioned that came to play an important role in Black fife and drum band activities in later years, including the Independent Pole Bearers Society and the United Sons and Daughters of Zion. The description of the glittering costumes calls to mind the way social aid and pleasure clubs still "turn out" today in New Orleans, as well as the costumes made by the Mardi Gras Indians before their parades. The banners were inscribed with slogans that would not seem out of place at a Black event today, such as "Know thy self, ye Daughters of Zion" or "Friendship Love and Truth." But we also see that the importance of fife and drum bands seems to be waning, at least within the cities. None is mentioned in this parade, and the closest we get is an odd ensemble consisting of a fife, a fiddle, and an accordion. Otherwise, the bands in question seem to be brass bands. There are at least two possible reasons for this. It may be that African Americans in Memphis and other cities were beginning to do better financially and could now afford to buy the necessary instruments and pay the larger number of musicians required for a brass band. Certainly brass bands were customary for white processions and celebrations, and that fact was probably not lost on the upper echelon of Black society.

However, on the same day that Black societies of Memphis were celebrating the Fifteenth Amendment, the Benevolent Order No. 1 paraded the streets of Nashville to celebrate their fifth anniversary of founding with both a brass band and a fife and drum band. If annual picnics were the most important occasions for societies to have fifers and drummers, the anniversaries of their founding dates were likely the second-most important occasions for such bands: "The Benevolent Order, No. 1, and branches, celebrated its fifth anniversary yesterday by a procession, which moved through the principal thoroughfares of the city. They numbered about two hundred, and were preceded by a brass band and drums and fifes. When the marching was over, the Order assembled at Clark Chapel and was addressed by Rev. R. C. Knowles, the orator of the day, and T. J. Bell, the first ex-President of the association."[164] From this, it would seem that 1870 was sort of a transitional period in the cities, as fife and drum bands were giving way to brass bands.

Even so, the Radical Republicans were still using fife and drum music to organize Black voters in political campaigns, as the *Public Ledger* complained in an editorial. The *Ledger*, which had always had an anti-Black tinge to its stances, now became inscreasingly virulent in its hatred of Memphis's Black community and the white Republicans who attempted to organize it: "The Radicals of this county are working with great energy to elect their ticket on next Thursday. The drum and fife are heard each night in the various quarters of the city, calling together the black minions of the opposition's strength, that they may listen to the hell-deserving speeches of Lewis, Hudson and others, who are styled the leaders of the party. These men are inflaming the minds of the negroes to a considerable pitch against the whites by the most immoderate utterances and fallacious arguments."[165] Indeed, although at the state level Reconstruction was largely ending, Reconstruction in Shelby County and Memphis still had quite a way to go. Republicans had done well in the last elections at the county level and would continue to have some influence until 1874. White candidates were attempting to win over potential Black voters with participation in Black community events and music, including fife and drum:

> Our special correspondent on the spot furnishes us with a funny history of a day's pleasure by the new Radical convert, T. S. Ayres, who is moving "the spheres" to accomplish his eager wish to be Chancellor. On Saturday last there was to be a grand ratification of the Fifteenth Amendment at Collierville, and believing it good ground for pushing his popularity, Ayres found his way to the depot of the Memphis and Charleston railroad. After depositing Mrs. A. in a more genial atmosphere, the Radical candidate for judicial honors, slipped into the car set apart for the Sons of Ham who were bent on participating in the celebration. To ingratiate himself still further than mere affability, and disposed to contribute all in his power to the social feeling predominating, the dignified Ayres slipped the drum collar over his neck and "discoursed most violent music" with the sticks, while his darky compatriots enlivened the time by shrill notes on "the ear-piercing fife." It was a forcible display of peculiar fitness for the dignified office of Chancellor, and was itself convincing evidence that Treadwell S. Ayres is not above the lowest arts of the demagogue, or the most humble subserviency to besotted ignorance, to advance the interests of his ambition.[166]

Any such instance in which white people demonstrated mutuality with people of color tended to send Southern newspapers into fulminations of fury, and the *Ledger* was no exception. Although the newspapers would claim to want peace and good feeling between the races, they would always complain about incidents such as the one Ayres took part in, presumably because the social order of white supremacy and Black inferiority was being broken down by whites treating Blacks as equals.

That in the African American mindset fife and drum music did not have to be limited to things military or political was clearly shown by its employment at a large Sunday school picnic in Maury County. On the other hand, the banners that were unfurled at the picnic clearly had a political bent, and it was in fact difficult for events in the Black community to be separated from the aspirations of the race as a whole:

The Sabbath Schools of the colored Presbyterian and Missionary Baptist Churches had a grand display and picnic last Friday morning at the McGuire Grove. The colored Methodist school would have taken part in it, had it not interfered with their first day and quarterly meeting. In front came a fine carriage, in which sat the aristocratic colored ladies. Next came the inevitable drum and fife at the head of the column. A large number of mottoes were emblazoned aloft on the banners, and among them we noticed, "Let us have peace—U.S. Grant"; "Peace, be still"; "Onward and upward"; "Let there be no strife between thee and me"; "Education and enlightenment in transitu"; "Long live our Queen." Behind them was a large wagon drawn by two black dashing steeds, on which sat a number of partially colored ladies. In the centre of the group was an evergreen structure under which the "Queen of May" was to be crowned. The children were very nicely, and some of them elegantly, dressed, and looked very happy and joyous. Cyrus Webster is the teacher of the Missionary Sabbath School, and Lucius Armstrong is Superintendent of the Presbyterian School.[167]

Despite setbacks for Radicals in the 1869 elections in most counties, the party was still actively organizing for the 1870 elections, and the *Somerville Falcon* complained of the fife and drum activity in Black-majority Fayette County, at what were apparently political meetings:

The Radicals of Fayette county are organizing for active and vigorous work in the coming election. The negroes are thoroughly drilled and collected together at night to perfect their plans and preserve their organization. Stealthiness in their movements and secrecy in their counsel is strictly enjoined among them. Ask a negro what means this playing of fifes and beating of drums at night, and parrot-like, he gives the answer he has learned: "Don't mean nutin, sah, just de 'nevolent sciety." It is a sin and a shame that these poor, deluded creatures should be blinded and gulled into the belief that their former own-ers are their enemies and that their interests require them to obey the behests of Radical cabals and to assemble in midnight meetings where they will learn from the lips of their friends? The dangers which surround them and the course they must pursue in order to insure their safety. This is the only means, however, by which the carpet-bag scalawag element hope to re-rear and sustain the fallen fabric of Radicalism. We had hoped that in the coming judicial election, no political issues would be raised, but since the old dark league is again to be ushered into existence to defeat certain candidates, it is eminently the duty of the conservative element to meet the old foe with a solid front, and rally to the support of the men marked out by their leader as victims. Let it again be crushed out in the very morning of its existence by a decided blow at the ballot-box.

—Somerville Falcon.[168]

That the fife and drum meetings could really be "just the benevolent society" was beyond the realm of credibility for Fayette County's white residents. They were absolutely certain that the sounds were the harbinger of dark and evil things to come. Of course, at the same time that the *Falcon* was suggesting that Blacks were deluded by white carpetbaggers in believing that they had anything to fear from ex-Confederates, other Democratic papers were suggesting that the Fifteenth Amendment had been fraudulently ratified, that Blacks should be stripped of the right to vote, and that the Democratic Party should neither seek nor welcome Black votes or Black voters. Blacks were neither as naive nor as easily duped as the *Falcon* editor imagined.

August brought a complaint from the *Nashville Union and American* that a Black procession on Church Street with drums and "various screeches and noises" had entirely blocked the sidewalk, forcing some white ladies to cross to the other side. The paper suggested that such processions should be held in the street and not on the sidewalk.[169]

That same month, a picnic of the Pole Bearers in Memphis gave the *Appeal* another target for racist ridicule, and although a band was mentioned, no specifics about what kind it was are mentioned: "The mokes had a picnic yesterday. As usual the pole bearers . . . were out in force, with Masonic aprons and other toggery. The procession was headed by a band of n----r music, and had every mackerel in town at its heels."[170] Although the editor did not capitalize "Pole Bearers" it is clear that this organization was involved in the picnic. However, there was no specific relationship between the Pole Bearers and the Masonic Lodge, and thus it seems likely that some of the members of the Pole Bearers were also members of the

Prince Hall Masons, as the predominantly Black branch of Masonry was called. "Mackerel" was commonly used as slang for thieves or gangsters in the Memphis papers, occasionally in terms that made it seem the name of an organized gang, at other times more generically. At least one theory is that it sprang from a French word *maquerel*, which meant a pimp or procurer. However, as used in Memphis, the term seemed more often to refer to criminal gangs of thieves and pickpockets than to pimps. All the same, the activity described in the article seems to resemble what in New Orleans is called second-lining, again suggesting that these things were once found in Black communities across the South, rather than strictly in New Orleans.

By October, when a rally of two thousand Black Republicans was held in the Greenlaw Opera House in downtown Memphis, it was evident that the Radicals were hopelessly split into factions, headed by General W. J. Smith on the one hand, and David Nunn of Brownsville on the other. Despite Barbour Lewis chairing the meeting, and pushing through resolutions on behalf of Smith, the growing noise and pandemonium in the crowd led to considerable disorder. Noted the *Appeal*, "The big drum was beat every few minutes, keeping time to the terrible din and tumult." One supporter of David Nunn was stabbed onstage and had to be carried out. The end of the rally occasioned a near-riot in downtown Memphis:

> Several speakers tried to address the meeting but in vain. At last silence was obtained for a few seconds, and an adjournment carried. After the meeting adjourned, bands of negroes, headed by a drum and fife, marched up Second street, yelling at the white people on the streets. This conduct came very near creating a serious difficulty on Second street, but the difficulty was prevented by judicious parties who saw that the result would be bloody in the extreme. The time has passed when white persons can be insulted on the public street by bands of drunken and disorderly negroes with impunity; and it is to be hoped that such conduct on the part of negroes will not be repeated.[171]

Editorially, the *Ledger* warned that much was at stake—for the state had adopted a new Constitution that extended the governor's term to four years—and pointed out that the Radical party was still organizing:

> The Radicals will not die contented without another crushing defeat. They are, even now, tooting their horns and beating their old drums at night, to gather the faithful together for one more struggle. Their leaders, such as W. J. Smith, Barbour Lewis, Ed Shaw, and White

Station McKenna, tell them to keep together, wait and hope and pray, and the time will come when they will enjoy and dispense the crumbs of office. The loyal leaguers are waiting for the signal; they are fully organized and hoping their day will come. Since no more elections will occur for a long time, we must carry this one by an overwhelming majority, such as will permanently define the strength and unity of the Democratic party as opposed to Radicalism.[172]

With the election of John C. Brown of Giles County, one of the founders of the Ku Klux Klan, as governor of Tennessee in November 1870, Reconstruction, at least at the state level in Tennessee, was largely dead. Yet it had a while longer to run in Memphis, Shelby County, and some of the state's other western counties.

"THOSE EVERLASTING NUISANCES": BLACK FIFE AND DRUM MUSIC IN TENNESSEE, 1871

Early in 1871, the Independent Pole Bearers had to deal with the death of a member, and the *Public Ledger* noted especially the band playing joyful music when returning from the funeral, attracting a crowd that the newspaper referred to as "black 'macks.'"[173] This phenomenon of playing slow dirges on the way to a burial, and lively, upbeat music on the way back has been well documented in New Orleans, but it clearly went on elsewhere among Blacks in the South. Although it was at least partially attributed to celebrating the life and legacy of the deceased, this tendency was also associated with the fear that the spirit of the deceased person might attempt to follow the mourners back from the cemetery to the community.[174]

The *Ledger*, like most of the other pro-Southern papers of the day, clearly believed that the arms carried by the societies were not ceremonial but actually loaded, and that the societies themselves were neither benevolent nor religious, but actually fronts for Black political organizing. As noted before, the truth was probably somewhere in between, with Republican politicians calling on and speaking to the benevolent societies because of the great loyalty they commanded among the Black population in West Tennessee. And certainly, some Blacks were going armed; given the hostility of the majority of white citizens, they would have been foolish not to have done so. Later that same month, the *Ledger* specifically mentioned a parade of the Pole Bearers, calling them "a branch of the Grand Army of the Republic" and "a well-organized military battalion."[175] In reality, there is not one shred of evidence other than the article in question to link the Independent Pole Bearers to the Grand Army of the Republic. The latter was an organization of Army veterans, Black and white, who had served on the Union side in the Civil War, similar to the American Legion or the Veterans of Foreign Wars. While many of the Pole Bearers had been veterans of the Union army, the Pole Bearers was an all-Black organization founded by Thomas Swan, who was also a member of the Sons of Ham and who may have been a member of the Sons of Zion as well, as he was buried in Zion Cemetery, which the latter group owned. It would seem that the Pole Bearers contained members that were not veterans. With respect to their being "a well-organized military battalion," the article itself stated that the members were drilling only with sharp wooden pikes, and the best evidence is that their drilling was ceremonial in nature, intended for public occasions such as parades.

In August, the *Ledger*, with usual irritability, complained about the noise and drumming of a Black fair held in the former post office building in downtown Memphis: "The fair being held by the negroes in the old Postoffice Building was suppressed last night by the police, it being a nuisance in the neighborhood. Marching and counter-marching through the streets at night, unearthly sounds issuing from the building, and the beating on a drum by a two-hundred pound negro, was rather more than civilization could stand. They have a perfect right to hold a fair and festival, but such harmless amusements should not be turned into a scene fit for pandemonium."[176]

The same week brought a rare occasion of Black fife and drum activity to Greeneville, in East Tennessee, under the auspices of the Sons of Zion, presumably the same fraternal organization that existed in Memphis, in the western part of the state. The *Greeneville Herald and Tribune* noted that "the delegation from this place was large and dressed in all the fantastic colors and oddities required by the occasion. They were accompanied with a band—fife and drum—and before leaving treated the town to a few pieces of stirring music."[177] Although East Tennessee was certainly not free of racial prejudice, the area was a hotbed of Republican sympathies, and no political opprobrium would have been attached to Black fife and drum music there.

By September, the municipal election campaign in Memphis was in full force, and the *Public Ledger* could not resist venting its usual rage at the noise of fife and drum that accompanied Black rallies:

The barbaric age of drums and fifes is again approaching, its disciples smelling afar off an election. The war-horse has not a keener scent for a battle than has a small-beer politician for a local political contest; consequently the horrid drum and the squeaking fife can be heard nightly among the cohorts of Africa. The leaders are organizing political bands among the negroes, forming such in semi-religious associations. Almost every night you can see a lot of straggling negroes following a drum and fife, with lamentable pertinacity to some locality where noisy politicians make sensational speeches in favor of themselves or each other. The game has almost played out in Memphis; the negro political power is broken into atoms, and it would be a blessing (and that not in disguise) if the same fate was meted out to the infernal drums and ear-spitting fifes. In the name of the nine Muses—Calliope, Clio, Melpomene, Erato, Urania, Thalia, Polymnia, Terpsichore, and especially Euterpe[178]—we ask, is there no legal remedy by city ordinance or chancery injection to stop this street nuisance?[179]

The *Appeal* also noticed and described one of these parades during the campaign, probably sponsored by a benevolent society: "A squad of colored men, headed by a very heavy and sonorous drum and fife corps, marched through several of our streets last night. The managers of the parade sang out their orders in a deep base [sic] guttural tone that sounded like the rattle of empty barrels rolling down a hill. The squad carried several flags, and the paraders wore several aprons apiece."[180] Added the *Ledger* in complaint: "The colored troops who fought nobly, and who are organizing in the city for the approaching municipal contest, paraded through the streets last evening behind these everlasting nuisances, the fife and drum."[181]

In November, the *Appeal* complained that a "negro fair at the building next [to] the theater is in such full blast that the audience at the theater have their ears annoyed by the bass drums, cat-gut, fifes and cymbals every night."[182]

It was left for the *Appeal* to close out 1871 on New Year's Eve with the summary of a letter to the editor complaining about Black fife and drum music and the current municipal election campaign:

We have such a multiplicity of letters devoted to the discussions of questions of city politics that it is quite impossible to find space for them. A letter before us insists that the Honorable Jacob Thompson shall represent the Tenth ward in the city legislature as councilman. This proposition is from a gray-haired old gentleman, who, in former years served the city well in several capacities. He inveighs against drums and fifes and the hideousness of nights spent by people in the

Seventh and other southern wards. Let the people unite. They must meet and concentrate on worthy candidates. This is the only remedy.[183]

Thus the five-year experiment of Reconstruction in Tennessee largely came to an end. From a hopeful beginning in 1866, Black Tennesseans saw the gain of the franchise, the right to run for and hold office, and the organization of their people into a political force, only to see their fortunes dashed by factionalism within the Republican Party and the growing ascendancy of the Democratic Party and the ex-Confederates. What began in sunshine seemed to end in shadow and uncertainty.

Chapter 3

"THESE THINGS MUST HAVE THEIR DAY"

Fife and Drum Music, Benevolent Societies, and Black Political Organizing in Tennessee, 1872–77

Although the election of John C. Brown, a founder of the Ku Klux Klan, as governor of Tennessee in 1870 marked the beginning of the end for Reconstruction in Tennessee, things were somewhat different in the state than in other parts of the South. For one thing, although the Constitution of 1870 imposed a poll tax, it proved to not make much of a difference in Black people voting or running for office, particularly in the western part of the state. And in the eastern counties, the white population was staunchly Republican, something that was unusual in most Southern states. So the Radical Republicans continued to organize and try to get their supporters to the polls, believing that they could take back power in the state by concerted effort, and recognizing the importance of every Republican vote in a presidential election year.

"WITH ABUNDANCE OF EXTENDED SHEEP SKIN": BLACK FIFE AND DRUM MUSIC IN TENNESSEE, 1872

However, as the year 1872 dawned, the Black community in Memphis and nearby areas of Mississippi seemed focused on a different and more pressing issue: the use of convict labor to build the Selma, Marion, and Memphis Railroad, whose president was the notorious ex-Confederate General Nathan Bedford Forrest. A camp of these convict laborers led to a demonstration near Capleville, Tennessee, in southeastern Shelby County, close to the Mississippi state line:

> Sheriff Wright sent out a posse of twenty-five men yesterday to the camp where the convicts who are employed by General Forrest stop. Word had been sent to the city that a procession of negroes from

Mississippi intended to march close to the camp with drums and fifes and firearms. The posse got out there in time. A whole host of them came within three or four hundred yards of the camp with four bands and two or three hundred rifles. They marched up and down a hill some ten or fifteen times, shouting, drumming and firing off their pistols, but finally retired without making any further demonstration, seeing that about fifty armed men were prepared at the camp to give them a warm reception should any demonstration be attempted.[1]

The *Public Ledger* gave a more detailed account of the incident, which suggested that the intent was to rescue the convicts held at the camp:

Information was received by General Forrest yesterday morning that a body of armed negroes from Mississippi intended to rescue the negro convicts at work on the Selma railroad. The negroes are at work near Cabelville [*sic*], within two miles of the Mississippi line. Sheriff Wright sent out a posse of thirty men to prevent the rescue. About 12 o'clock, two hundred uniformed and armed negroes approached the camp with flying colors and drums beating. They marched and countermarched, and threatened to do as they please with the posse, guards and convicts. The posse and guards were well armed, but did not desire to bring on a fight if it could be avoided. The drunken and turbulent negroes were informed that they must make no attempt at rescue, or they would be fired upon by the guards, who were well armed and had plenty of ammunition. After taking a survey of the situation the leaders prevailed upon their followers to return to Mississippi without the convicts. As they left they made threats to return and rescue their fellow-citizens of color who pined in imprisonment. Nothing has been heard from Cabelville to-day.[2]

The use of Black convict labor to build the railroad from Memphis toward Tupelo was inevitably going to be a major provocation to Black citizens on both sides of the state line. For one thing, the use of convicts certainly resembled slavery too closely for Blacks to be comfortable with it. The laborers were kept in camps under guard. Doubtless, accounts from these camps had crept out to loved ones, and although Forrest claimed conditions were good, the death rate of these convicts was truly appalling.[3] In addition, Nathan Bedford Forrest was widely believed by Blacks to be the "Butcher of Fort Pillow" and a founder of the Ku Klux Klan. That he was the head of the railroad using these convicts as labor of course merely added fuel to the fire.

Forrest had been a slave trader before the Civil War, and in the wake of it, he seemed to look for a way to continue the system he had always known. The Thirteenth Amendment forbade slavery, except with regard to those convicted of certain crimes, and it was this exception that Forrest increasingly embraced, having first negotiated for himself the right to run a penal farm on President's Island near Memphis. Accounts of brutality led to the rescission of that contract and a takeover of the colony by the county government, but Forrest still considered himself an expert on working with convicts.[4] Forrest's behavior throughout Reconstruction was an odd combination of hatred and threats toward the so-called carpetbaggers (whites from the North who supported the Republican Party) and occasional expressions of goodwill and concern for African Americans. Toward the end of his life, Forrest would attempt to mend fences with the Black community, but in 1872, feelings were still fairly raw.

In May, Memphis Republicans met at Assembly Hall for the purposes of putting together a regular party organization and choosing delegates to the state convention in Nashville. Both a fife and drum band and a brass band were present:

Last night, from seven to nine o'clock, the vicinity of Assembly Hall, on Main street, was enlivened by the tooting of horns, beating of drums, the shrill sound of martial fifes and the discordant roar of mingled hoarse Caucasian and African voices, for the cohorts of Grant, the Nepotist, were assembled in great force to appoint delegates to the State red-hot, uncompromising, war-to-the-knife, dyed-in-the-wool convention, which is to meet shortly in Nashville, in the interest of the various army of office holders. The colored brass band made discordant sounds, both outside and in, for an hour and a half previous to the opening of business, during which time the interested were gathering principally from the various locations of Federal offices in the city and from Rotten Row and Hell's Half-acre.[5]

The "Grant ratification" meeting in Nashville was also the occasion for music by a "field band," which the *Republican Banner* described: "A field band, composed of three snare drums, one bass drum and a fife, made the music for the occasion. The engineer of the bass drum was a born genius of the race of Ham, and at every lick he made seemed to rise higher in the heaven of transport incident to musical performance."[6] The term "field band" would begin to be used interchangeably with "fife and drum band" during the next few years.

The first explicit reference to fife and drum in Fayette County appeared in an article from the community of Galloway's Switch (the present town of Gallaway) in connection with the Union League, a semisecret organization of Republicans that in most Tennessee communities was made up strictly of Blacks:

> There is but little talk of politics as yet, and we desire that there should not be for a time to come, or at least until we get our crops layed by [sic]. Some of our county candidates are pestering us a little; they get some leading negro to make an appointment and get the negroes together and manage to meet them. It seems as if it does not make any difference with the candidate which way the negro's notions lead him, whether for Grant or Greeley,[7] just so he will vote for him for Sheriff or Tax-Collector; he is anything and all things to all men for the sake of office. We think the white voters in this section of the country will vote the Greeley ticket at the November election; bitter as it is, it is the best we can do. The freedmen have their Union League, and attend weekly to their drum and fife and Grant devotion. These things must have their day and then will pass away to return no more forever.[8]

Because African Americans outnumbered whites to such an extreme degree in Fayette County, Blacks voting and running for office became extremely contentious there for many years, and Black fife and drum music became the occasion for outrage at times.

Later that same June, the *Memphis Daily Appeal* gave an account of a commemoration of the Union dead at the National Cemetery on the Raleigh Road sponsored by the Pole Bearers, which seems to have turned into something of a picnic:

> The same day the colored people had a little celebration at the national cemetery. It was intended as a solemn commemoration of the heroic dead who repose in that costly inclosure. From the surrounding country the pious people of color flocked with such banners, trappings and odds and ends of music as they could get together by long and earnest searching. Five pole-bearers with a drum, headed by a very crooked man with a hiltless sword, marched several miles to attend.

From Big Creek, Raleigh, Bartlett and from all the country round about the roaring Wolf river, these devout "men and brethren" of stanch collars and sense, with their wives and other women, gathered. They rode on mules mostly, but some were more ambitiously mounted on horses. Several trains went out from the Louisville depot, the first of which escorted twenty-five persons, the next about three hundred, including the colored band and an organization known as the "pole-bearers." This assemblage of colored persons—not a white person being seen among them—were all that attempted in their uncouth fashion to do honor to the Federal dead that rest in the Memphis National Cemetery. The occasion was one of much jollity. About twenty-five booths were improvised out of rude poles and green branches, from under which cheerful drinks were circulated; also boiled pork and strong cigars at high prices. Scattered about the cheerful grounds were all manner of catchpenny amusements to make the African heart glad and the African dime free. It was the queerest picnic, or serio-comic revel over the dead that has been witnessed since the great flood.[9]

The *Appeal*'s ridicule of the Pole Bearers for making a joyful celebration out of the commemoration was typical (and the organization eventually took steps to suppress the selling of food and drink at the Decoration Day celebrations). But the newspaper went further; by July, it was openly endorsing white supremacy:

The two drums sent down to President's Island are designed to convoke the loyal leagues on the island and from the Arkansas shore. Two hundred colored citizens of Arkansas, we are told, voted in the Curry-Wright contest,[10] and forty or more came into Chelsea from about Mound City. Instead of indulging at this late hour, local or personal jealousies, Democrats and Conservative Republicans should organize plans to defeat schemes of like character on the part of Lewis, Curry and Jerusalem Smith. They traverse the county in all directions, and gather black multitudes, who are compacted in order to place the supreme control of the city and county in the hands of Barbour Lewis' faction. All personal private causes of dissatisfaction should be subordinated to the single idea of maintaining the supremacy of the white people in the city and county, and he is the veriest of all idiots who suffers himself to be wheedled and cajoled into the embraces of Curry and his ring.[11]

That the benevolent societies in Black communities were really political was a belief that seemed to prevail in all white communities. Said the
Republican Banner in regard to Lauderdale County: "The negroes of Ripley
have organized a Union League, calling it a Benevolent Society."[12]

The Fourth of July was celebrated more vividly in Memphis in 1872, the
white community noting the restoration of their voting rights and their
recent victories at the polls. But the Black community celebrated as well,
and fife and drum played a significant role in the party:

> Too much praise cannot be given to the people of color, as they were
> termed, for the patriotism that shone forth yesterday in their every
> movement. It was evident they had pre-determined to make a great
> demonstration yesterday. They had invited people here from the
> thirty-two points of the compass, and they came from those points
> in full and imposing regalia, with abundance of extended sheep-skin
> and perforated reeds. Several cars loaded with them reached here
> from Brownsville. Several other cars loaded with them arrived by the
> Charleston road. They came on foot, on horseback, by river, by wagon
> and by stage-coach, and made an immense array. Notwithstanding
> the rain, they marched. They marched in procession nearly a mile
> long and four deep, with fifes, drums, hewgags, and wound up in
> Humboldt Park, where the great day was to be celebrated in mass.
> The festivities at this place were eminently and numerically satis-
> factory. The rush of people of color into that inclosure all day was
> simply fearful. The colored ladies were all out. It is the sad experience
> of many housekeepers that there was not a colored lady in the city
> who did not go. Those who could hack, hacked, and those cheerful
> ones, who had no alternative but walk, footed. We saw, indeed, one
> exception to this. A small brigade of miscellaneous recruits, with
> several commanders, marched out and back again, with a female
> marshal mounted on a gothic rosinate. The irregular body was the
> joy and the visible delight of the urchins. Endless variety in costume
> characterized these citizens, both female and male. The body was
> truly picturesque. It is creditable to the colored people that they had
> more than a liberal supply of cheer at the park for their guests, and
> that the ceremonies and festivities of the day were not marred by a
> single disturbance. It was the largest and most harmonious gathering
> of people that was ever witnessed in Memphis, where the object was
> fun and spreading-eagleism.[13]

The rival *Avalanche* gave a much more detailed account of the procession and the picnic, revealing that it was sponsored by the Sons of Ham:

The picnic of the Sons of Ham was the largest affair ever gotten up by the colored people of this city. It is estimated that over seven thousand persons were on the grounds—Humboldt Park—all of whom enjoyed themselves in varied ways, and only as the free American of color knows how to enjoy himself. This was the only affair at which a set oration was delivered, Judge Barbour Lewis being the orator of the day. A report of his speech will be found in another column. The procession in the morning of the different colored societies was a huge, and, in its way, magnificent affair. Societies of this city and of Nashville, Collierville and Wythe Depot participated,[14] all in full regalia with music and banners at their head. Forming on Beal and Second streets, the procession marched up Second to Auction, up Auction to Main, down Main to Beal and out Beal to Humboldt Park. The order of procession was: first, Knights Templars, mounted, followed by the colored brass band; Nashville Sons of Relief; Sons of Ham, of Memphis; Daughters of Zion No. 1; Field Band; Ornamental wagon of the Sons of Ham, occupied by thirty little girls in fancy dress; Benevolent Society No. 1, of Memphis; Field Band; Mutual Relief and Social Benevolent Society, Mount Joiners [sic] No. 4,[15] United Sons of Ham No. 5; United Sons of Ham No. 6, Wythe Depot; Sociable Relief Greenwood Farmers No. 2; Field Band; Benevolent Society No. 2; Field Band; Benevolent Society No. 3, Collierville; Daughters of Zion No. 1, in thirty carriages and five omibuses. The procession was over a mile in length, and numbered near 2000 members. All of the societies presented a neat appearance, and their quiet and orderly behavior was remarked by all.[16]

As we have seen, the field bands were fife and drum bands, probably local ensembles that belonged to the various chapters of these societies. This is also the first article that makes plain the extent to which the societies and fife and drum bands had spread into the rural areas surrounding Memphis.

While most of the various societies undoubtedly chose to participate in the parade and picnic of the Sons of Ham, a few did not. The Pole Bearers chose to march with their brass band down to the boat landing at the foot of Adams Street and embarked on an excursion across the river to Mound City, Arkansas; and some branches of the Sons of Ham and Daughters of

Zion chose to travel by boat with a string band to Bray's Island. All three kinds of bands were becoming popular in this era.[17] The *Public Ledger* claimed that the Pole Bearers marched to the boat landing with the "inevitable drum and fife" rather than a brass band. Perhaps they had both a fife and drum band and a brass band.[18]

Not two days after the "good feelings" of the Fourth, the *Appeal* was back to arousing the whites of Shelby County against the Blacks, complaining of fife and drum band activity in the rural districts:

> There is hardly a civil district exterior to this city, in which the adherents of Barbour Lewis, Curry and McLean have not a fixed, immutable majority. The "no-party" dodge, on which Mr. Curry goes bobbing up and down, in view of this fact, is most significant. While appealing to Front street for its support, he does not forget the charming condition of the country. He causes Barbour Lewis's speech to be published everywhere among the negroes, and the work of active re-organization progresses most rapidly, while he is gently pulling the wool over the eyes of innocent, unsuspecting Front street. He and McLean are sending drums and fifes into every country district. Hideous music greets the ears of every farmer, and while Curry "honeyfuggles" innocent white men and women on Front street and Big creek during the day, Barbour and Bill and Barbour's printed speech do the dirty work in black loyal leagues at night. Curry doesn't show himself very often in black assemblages. He is just now engaged in the lofty business of ingratiating himself with innocent denizens of Front street, and his achievements on Big Creek were extraordinary. In fact, half the white people in the hills had agreed that he was a very proper person until the storm of drums and of marching, howling clans led at night by Curry's and McLean's agent, dissolved the spell woven of Curry's personal appearance, so genial and smiling and bland. An innocent countryman writes us from Big Creek as follows: "Curry, the Radical-Barbour-Lewis candidate for Sheriff was up here yesterday. He is a bob-tail pacing pony, and whispered right smartly around here among the gals. It was no go however, for that very night Curry's agents came along and reorganized the Loyal League. There was drumming and fifing all over the county, and Cuffee went mad. The jig was up with the little Canadian Yankee, the Colonel, so-called. The trick was too thin. He must either be black or white, and can't ride both horses in these parts."[19]

Fife and drum music was also a feature of Black Fourth of July festivities in Clarksville, as noted by a reporter for the *Nashville Union and American*:

> Among the celebrators parading the streets was a colored gang. Martial music from a fife and snare-drum enthused them very much, causing at least eleven to join the procession, which waved red, black and yellow handkerchief-banners. One darkie thought he would be rather novel, and so he did, for he bore a demoralized umbrella, the staff of which was near nine feet in length; this umbrella was held at an angle of forty-five degrees due south, and its length reminded me that Mark Twain would call it "an eternity" umbrella. These colored people had been left by the train for Guthrie, where between twelve and fifteen hundred of their race met and celebrated the Fourth. Barbecued meat, speeches and ecstatic eloquence constituted the order of exercises, which were interspersed with mosquito choruses and bull frog solos.[20]

But it was still the campaigning for votes that was the most frequent occasion for drumming or fife and drum music, and perhaps because of the association with Black political activity, this occasioned the majority of complaints. On July 10, the *Appeal* grumbled that "Barbour, the big drum, and Curry were raising an awful din and uproar at Africa Bailey's Church, in the Tenth Ward, last night,"[21] and a day later the *Republican Banner* of Nashville mentioned that "the fife and drum were brought into requisition yesterday, to attract an audience to the market-house, where the colored candidates for Jailer had arranged to discuss their respective merits."[22]

The August 1 election for county offices occasioned a demonstration by Black would-be voters from President's Island, as well as the arrest of some who came from Mississippi and Arkansas and attempted to vote in the elections:

> About a hundred negroes came up on the rampage from President's Island, headed by a fife and drum, and marched in procession to the Fifth ward polls, with the view of depositing their votes. The Judges, however, could not see it, and politely told the leaders to go to their own precincts. After a little parleying, they concluded "they could not vote thar," and off they marched to poll number six, with a like result. Threats were made to take the town, but at last accounts, at midnight, the beleaguered negroes had subsided and the town was not "took."[23]

The election results were a disaster for the Black community, as the Conservative Democrats won nearly every county office, primarily due to heavy white voting in the wards of Memphis. The appeal to white supremacy on the part of Memphis's newspapers was working.

In September, two Black Memphis societies made a significant showing at the Tennessee Colored Fair in Nashville, with the opening being a drill parade by the Independent Pole Bearers Society. This drill was likely accompanied by a field or fife and drum band, but the Pole Bearers had also brought their brass band, as a battle of the bands was a feature of the fair: "There will also be a premium offered to the best band—the Harmonica and Benevolent bands, of Nashville, and two bands from Memphis contending, each band to play three airs."[24]

The close of the fair the next day occasioned a large procession that the Sons of Ham and the Pole Bearers dominated:

> When the colored fair was over with yesterday afternoon, a procession of about 100 colored men belonging to a society known as the Sons of Ham, favored the town with a dress parade, which, if not a large one, was certainly well behaved and disciplined. The Harmonica Band played the marching music, and intense brunette belles could be seen along each of the streets that were favored by the procession. One of these sisters of darkness, who was smiled very sweetly upon by one of the Sons of Ham, was seen to pull a pocket looking-glass out from the depths of calico, in order that she might see herself as others see her, and put it back with a complacent smile of satisfaction.
>
> Another procession of colored civilians, with red braid upon their clothes and formidable looking spears in their hands, known as the Pole-Bearers, also marched through the streets, headed by a fife and two drums, and claimed public admiration—for upwards of an hour.[25]

A few days later, the *Daily Memphis Avalanche* reported with some pride the accomplishments brought home by Black Memphians from the fair in Nashville: "Presentations were made by Vice President Nelson Walker of the Association, in a very nice speech, of two silver goblets to the United Sons of Ham, of Memphis, and another to the Young Men's Association Brass Band of Memphis. The Independent Pole Bearers Society and Brass Band of Memphis, were both presented with a silver goblet, and they deserved their honors well."[26]

The election of Thomas A. Kercheval, a Radical Republican, as mayor of Nashville in late September was a portent of things to come in the fall elections. Although the Republicans had split into Radical and Liberal factions, the latter was largely backed by only the Democrats, who decided not to run a candidate for president of the United States. Instead, they chose to support the Liberal Republican candidate, Horace Greeley. Kercheval's victory was cheered by Blacks in Nashville:

> The colored people grew very jubilant last evening, and turned out with fife and drum and took possession of the newly-elected Mayor, shortly after it became apparent that the returns from the Fourth Ward would place him ahead of Mayor Morris. In a brief speech he said he held that he was not elected by any party, but by the masses of the people, who choose him as their Mayor in preference to an aristocrat, who had had the office repeatedly. He said that, while serving through his term, he would endeavor to further the interests of the city.[27]

Throughout the month of October, with a presidential election pressing, the Radical Republicans stepped up the tempo of rallies and meetings intended to build enthusiasm for the reelection of President Ulysses S. Grant. Wherever these rallies were aimed at Black voters, fife and drum ensembles were prominently placed:

> During the afternoon yesterday, a small party of negroes—remnant of the colored troops who fought so nobly during the "late unpleasantness"—were seen meandering through the streets, armed with fifes and drums, and bearing aloft a banner on which was inscribed this legend: "Republican Rally. Speeches at the Courthouse to night. Grant & Wilson, 'Carry the news to Horace.'"[28] In this manner the information was had that there would be a gathering of Radicals at the courthouse in the evening, and soon after dark, a small, but motley and odorous party gathered about the building designated.[29]

A day later, a similar rally in Raleigh, in Shelby County, seemed to fizzle, leading the *Public Ledger* to express the hopeful theory that Blacks were turning against the Radicals, which was a wish expounded as fact by Conservative journalists every other month or so during Reconstruction:

> For some time past, General W. J. Smith and Captain S. S. Garrett have been advertising a grand Republican rally which was to come off at Raleigh last night. Drums and fifes were furnished the darkies

to blow and beat and collect the ebony patriots together for a grand demonstration. Preparations were started on a grand scale and everything was done that could be to draw together an immense assemblage of voters. But "all signs fail in dry weather," and in this county there has been a drought in Radicalism for some time. The darkies didn't enthuse worth a cent. Radical voters were conspicuous by their absence, and the multitude that came all stayed at home. Our informant says there were probably fifteen or twenty blacks in attendance and as many whites, and the colored troops fought no-body. The Raleigh darkies say they are tired of being deceived by Radical politicians, and they mean to attend to their own business in the future and let the office-seekers do the same.[30]

Certainly, incidents like the summer riots in Collierville and Osceola—in which Radical politicians withdrew, leaving Blacks to face the repercussions of the upheavals—did nothing to endear the Radical party to Black residents, at least on the local level. Yet, nothing in that was going to motivate them to vote for their open enemies in the Democratic Party either. And there was a certain tendency for Blacks to tell Conservative whites what they wanted to hear. In Clarksville, a letter writer to the *Republican Banner* in Nashville complained of the use of fife and drums in the service of Horace Maynard, of Knoxville, the Radical candidate for the House of Representatives, writing, "While I sit here writing these few lines the Maynard band is making the air hideous with doleful sounds of their cracked drums and cane fifes. The Cheatham Ring had better look out, or they will elect Maynard."[31] The writer seemed to better understand the true enthusiasm of Black voters for the Radicals. No Liberal or Conservative victory was in the offing.

The results of the November 5 elections were an overwhelming victory for Ulysses Grant and the Radical Republicans, at least in part because earlier elections in the North had been victories for the Radicals, and Southerners either failed to vote, or voted for Grant, seeing his election as a fait accompli. The *Appeal* in Memphis bitterly suggested that fraud on the part of Black voters was at the root of Grant's victory, at least in the city:

There were no restrictions imposed upon illegal voting, or upon repeaters, yesterday, in this city. The Northern elections of October dissolved partisan ties to a great extent, and no Conservative committeemen appeared at the polls to restrain or watch corrupt voters. The vote of this city was increased fifteen hundred, and these were imported colored people. There was no registration of voters, and the detection of frauds was impossible. In fact, when a circle of five hundred or eight hundred colored men began to move before the ballot-box it never stopped. It moved endlessly throughout the day. . . .

Monday night, throughout the whole night multitudes of colored men paraded the streets. Drums and fifes echoed everywhere, and the forces of Radicalism were gathered from the lowlands and from every hill and valley. They swarmed yesterday into this city, and into villages along the railways. The African vote was evoked as never before, and whence it came none can conjecture. There was not a voting place in the city (but) at which numerous black faces appeared, led by Federal office-holders. No questions were asked, no oath of qualification administered, and the same negroes might have voted a dozen times at the same place without recognition. To the masses of whites in the city, all negroes are alike and alike unknown.[32]

That the Radicals could have won in such fashion a presidential election that Southerners expected them to lose—and that Black voters played a significant role in that outcome—was especially galling, and seems to have played a role in the Democrats' decision to increasingly embrace not partisan politics per se, but the polarization of the races.

Certainly, the Black community was jubilant over the outcome, as reported in the *Avalanche*:

The grand ratification meeting and torchlight procession of the Republicans to jubilate over the result of the late elections took place last night. Though the mercury stood low, and the wind blew bitingly, before 7 o'clock the colored societies and the Grant and Wilson clubs of the various wards began to assemble around Market square, the place previously fixed upon for organizing the procession. Transparencies and Chinese lanterns had been provided in great abundance for those who desired to participate, and hundreds of colored men who belonged to no organization, carried away with the enthusiasm which everywhere abounded, took them up and joined in the demonstration.

Some of the transparencies bore very expressive mottoes, our reporter noticing the following among them: "Liberal Democrats first cousins to Republicans."[33] "Give us a Custom House." "That tidal wave has come." "A union of hearts and union of hands." "Memphis is now the Central City of Africa,—['Appeal.']" "Grant and Wilson, the people's choice." "No party lash—freedom for all." "The will of the people the law of the land." "Give us a railroad to the Pacific."

"The blue Watauga still flows." "Thieves to the rear, and honest men to the front."

Captain S. S. Garrett acting as Grand Marshal, formed with Arnold's Old Memphis Brass Band at the head. Next came the Independent Pole Bearers' Association, the club turning out in full force and J. Wiseman acting as Marshal and Harrison King as his assistant. Next came the Third Ward Grant and Wilson Club, known as the "Gewhollopers," J. H. Looney Marshal. Then the Fifth Ward Grant and Wilson Club, John Polk Marshal, and the Eighth Ward Grant and Wilson Club, Wm. Rollins Marshal. After these came three country clubs, properly officered, the White Station, Germantown and Nonconnah Benevolent Societies. The United Sons of Ham and several small clubs from wards not mentioned brought up the rear.

The body commenced to move at half-past 8 o'clock, and presented a fine appearance. Over five hundred men were in the line, which stretched a distance of three blocks. The men kept well into line and behaved very orderly, deafening and long drawn yells being the only way in which their enthusiasm manifested itself.

The following was the route of the procession: From Market Square down Main to Beal, out Beal to DeSoto, up DeSoto to Union, Union to Second, up Second to Madison, Madison to the bluff, where a stand had been erected for speaking, and where hundreds of citizens had already congregated.

At the end of the parade route, the gathered Republicans listened to speeches. But it was the words of Judge Henry G. Smith, the first speaker, which were prescient. And his cautious words would sadly be forgotten in Shelby County over the coming tragic years:

We want no white man's party. We want no colored man's party, but we want a party that shall embrace the whole of the citizens of our common country. No good can result to anybody in parties that are based upon any such distinction. It can do no good to the white man, and it can do no good to the colored man, but it is full of mischief to every man, woman and child that belongs to this country. I know you here to-night will join with me as denouncing as full of mischief to the whole country—to every man, woman and child in it—the attempt to establish a white man's party or a black man's party or any other party but one that shall embrace all—black and white—within its ranks, and which shall work for the good of the whole country.[35]

At year's end, the Pole Bearers held a procession on Main Street in downtown with their brass band, but the occasion was neither a holiday nor a political rally. Instead, the *Avalanche* noted that they marched to a picture gallery, where each member was photographed. It is sad in the extreme that these photographs are no longer extent.[36]

"A BETTER ERA IS DAWNING":
BLACK FIFE AND DRUM MUSIC IN TENNESSEE, 1873

As the new year of 1873 dawned, the Sons of Ham held the annual celebration of Emancipation in downtown Memphis, with a parade that included fife and drum music. As noted by the *Memphis Daily Appeal*, "New Year's day was also celebrated by the Sons of Ham, who paraded the streets in long lines arrayed in all the toggery of splendid regalia, with banners, drum and fife."[37] The competing *Avalanche*, as usual, gave a bit more detail with regard to the event: "Yesterday was the tenth anniversary of the emancipation of the colored people, an event which is daily remembered and celebrated by all of that nationality. In this city the various colored societies turned out in full regalia, and with brass and field bands marched through the streets, finally convening in the Exposition Hall, about 2 o'clock."[38] The parade and celebration also coincided with the annual appointment of new officers for the Independent Order of Pole Bearers, at which Thomas Swan was named president.[39]

Such processions were not always merely a matter of choice or pleasure for the members of the various Black organizations, as the *Appeal*'s River News editor complained when no workers could be found to unload boats on the Memphis levee on a Sunday that was a "society day." Failure to attend the meetings and processions would often result in a significant fine for members: "Yesterday being a 's'ciety day' with those laborers of the African persuasion and white laborers being scarce, the Elliott got but little of her freight out, and at the elevator the unloading of the Grand Tower was delayed by the same cause. It costs a darkey a five-dollar bill if he, belonging to the Sons of Ham or Pole Bearers, fails to turn out in the 'percession.'"[40] At this time, most processions seemed to be ceremonial or recreational rather than political, perhaps because 1872 had been an election year and there were but little campaigns for office in the new year. One exception was the mayoral campaign in the city of Memphis, but otherwise there was little concern with politics. It seems that Black societies in Memphis often used impromptu parades as something of a public relations exercise, and the societies' musicians often serenaded the local newspapers, perhaps for the same reason. In March of 1873, the *Appeal* mentioned such a procession of the Pole Bearers, for no apparent reason, but the newspaper noted the brass band and the fife and drum corps, "playing lively airs."[41] Such incidents, peculiarly, were both provocative and conciliatory. They were provocative in the sense that the Pole Bearers or other Black societies were by them claiming the right to the public streets and thoroughfares. The right of Black citizens to control shared social space was disputed in the South and became a major bone of contention during the later civil rights movement, occasioning some of the most shocking violence and many of the mass arrests. On the other hand, the playing of music by the bands of such societies made them seem more festive and ceremonial than menacing, which was probably an intentional public relations move. Music was a level on which whites and Blacks could agree, and some of the most positive comments in the white press of Memphis regarding the Pole Bearers were in regard to its brass band.

The Pole Bearers were apparently now the leading Black society in the city of Memphis, and about a week after their picnic, they ran advertising in the Memphis press announcing that they would be holding a ceremony for the decoration of the graves of the Union dead at the National Cemetery on the Raleigh Road.[42] The event, called Decoration Day, was apparently held in Black communities across the South and was a precursor to the Memorial Day holiday. There was also a white Decoration Day for the Confederate dead, but it was generally a week before the Union ceremony. Later, when sectional hostility between Northern and Southern whites had died down, the two Decoration Days were sometimes consolidated into one event.

Although there was little in the way of political activity during the early summer of 1873 in Memphis, the residents of South Memphis still complained of the noise of fife and drum bands in that neighborhood:

Citizens of South Memphis, living in the vicinity of the Peabody school building,[43] complain of a most intolerable nuisance in that locality yesterday afternoon, caused by a crowd of negroes with drums and fifes, who, it seems, have selected that place for a practice-ground for an amateur drum-corps. Under ordinary circumstances such noises are almost unbearable, but at the present time, when numbers of people are confined to their residences, and many to their beds, with sickness of one kind or another, it is simply intolerable. Our advice to the good people in that locality is to notify Chief Athy, who will certainly order the nuisance to be abated. Where were the policemen on that beat?[44]

On the 10th of July, the Pole Bearers' brass band made its way to the offices of all three of Memphis's daily newspapers, serenading the editors of each, and all three papers acknowledged the favor. Noted the *Appeal*: "The Poll-Bearers' [*sic*] band paid the APPEAL the compliment of a serenade last night, and, under the direction of their leader, Mr. Thomas Swan, 'discoursed most excellent music.' The band bids fair to succeed and take rank among the best."[45] Said the *Avalanche*: "The AVALANCHE acknowledges a delightful serenade last night by the fine band of the Pole Bearers, a colored organization."[46] But it was the *Public Ledger*, usually the most racially polarizing of papers, which sounded a hopeful note of reconciliation: "The Pole Bearers' band, headed by the President of the Association, serenaded the LEDGER office last night and tendered their compliments. We acknowledge the musical compliment and tender to each and every member of the band and the Pole Bearers' Association our sincere wishes for his success in life. It is gratifying to record the fact that a better era is dawning and a better understanding exists in this glorious State of ours between the white and colored people."[47] Unfortunately, the *Ledger*'s good will proved to be fickle. Within a year, the editor would be calling on all white men to unite along the color line against the Blacks.

A more patient and tolerant attitude seemed to prevail in Maury County, at least judging from the tone of the local *Columbia Herald*, which gave favorable accounts of two Black society picnics in the same August issue. From the Mt. Pleasant column came an account of a Black picnic sponsored by the Friends of Relief:

Thursday of last week was celebrated by the order of the Friends of Relief and the citizens. The society met at the church and formed a procession, marched through the town in full regalia to the Monument, to meet the brother societies from Columbia, Hampshire and Cross Bridges, then marched through the village to their church, formed the grand procession of the different societies in front, ladies second, gentlemen this, those on horseback, buggies and wagons, fourth. With thrilling and appropriate music, the vast crowd, numbering about three thousand, moved in good order to the beautiful grove of Mr. Rufus Long. After mixing and mingling as usual on such occasions, order of the day was announced by Mr. Albert Green. An address was delivered by T. A. Harris. Albert Green was then called for, who made an excuse for the non-attendance of Mr. Sims Latta, who was expected to make a speech. Albert Green then made a short and appropriate speech. A heavy rain prevented the spreading of a sumptuous dinner upon the ground, however notice was given, and all repaired to the church, where a bountiful and good dinner was spread, enough for all. Good order and peace was observed.[48]

In the same county, in the town of Ashwood, another Black picnic was described in detail by that community's columnist:

On Saturday, the 19th let., at an early hour, the denizens of this burg were aroused from their apathy by martial music of three drums and two fifes. We knew that something was going to be done. Presently a cavalcade of horsemen, with banners, sashes, and decorations, filed along the dusty road: then we were certain that something was going to be done. Then came carriages, buggies, wagons, footmen, and horsemen, but happening to observe very closely, we found that they all belonged to the Hamitic race. They were going to a sunday school celebration at Ark Valley. Well, times seemed to be so stirring and lively, we followed along, expecting to get our dinner anyhow. When we arrived on the ground, we were greeted with martial music, and the stentorian voice of command was heard above the din of the fife and drum. The children were marching and making their grand display before the speaking should begin. Felix Mayes was Grand Marshal of the day, and was mounted upon his superb charger and war horse, Bedford Forest; Joe Armstrong, 2d Marshal; Peter Fleming, Conductor of Ceremonies; Elisha Burnet, Chief Principal of sunday school; Sol Wade, Orator of the day. Mr. Elisha Burnet made a few appropriate remarks incident to the occasion, and grew very eloquent before he had finished. He is a worthy and deserving man, and much praise is due him for his interest and industry in the sunday school at Ark Valley. Mr. Sol Wade was then introduced. He opened with an outburst of oratory and eloquence, and for full fifteen minutes he held his audience entranced. After him followed a few speeches and dialogues from the children, and then singing from the school, but between each and everything that was said or done, there was martial music. They were hired by the day, and that was the way that they got their pay, and well they may, for it was soul stirring and grand. At about one o'clock the procession was again formed, and the sunday school marched to a spring hard by, and regaled and refreshed themselves under the shade of the trees, and with the cool waters of the Ark Valley spring and martial music.[49]

To the amazement of white observers, even a Sunday school picnic was an appropriate occasion for fife and drum music in the Black community.

On September 19, the Black societies of Nashville turned out by the hundreds because of the visit of Frederick Douglass, the leading Black man of his day in America, to their city for the purpose of making a speech at the Tennessee Colored Fair. The momentous occasion was described in significant detail by the *Republican Banner*:

> At 10 o'clock, crowds flocked to the Public Square, to witness the formation of the procession of societies which were to escort Frederick Douglass, the most distinguished of their race, to the fair grounds.
>
> The following are the names of the societies, with their chief officers, which formed the escort:
>
> Sons of Relief—Felix Paschal, President.
>
> People's Aid—Israel Rains, President.
>
> Young Men's Immaculate Society—A. Clarkson, President.
>
> Brothers of Love—W. C. Watson, President.
>
> Benevolent Society No. 1—Major Allen, President.
>
> Edgefield Branch Benevolent—Benjamin Williams, President.
>
> Organ Association—R. D. Campbell, President.
>
> The societies formed in the order mentioned, under the direction of Nelson Walker, Chief Marshal, and James Stephenson, his assistant. They then moved through Cedar to Cherry, and down Cherry to the Harding House, where Mr. Douglass was invited into an open carriage near the center of the line, when it moved out Cherry and on to the fair grounds, to the music of one brass and two martial bands. There were from four hundred to five hundred members in the processions. It was accompanied on either side, however, by large crowds of colored people.[50]

Memphis had had a problem with sickness since the beginning of the summer. Cholera had been reported in June, but by September, yellow fever was in Memphis. There had been complaints about fife and drum music back in June, but now, due to the epidemic, the chief of police gave an order banning the playing of all drums or other instruments on the streets:

> Owing to the great amount of sickness now prevailing in our midst, and from the nature of the disease, it is requisite to the safety of the sick that no loud, unnecessary noise should be made, all parties are

hereby requested to refrain from beating drums or playing instruments on the streets to the annoyance and discomfiture of the sick.

The police will notify all parties to cease such annoyance. A non compliance with the request will subject the offenders to arrest. P. R. ATHY, Chief Police.[51]

Perhaps not surprisingly, the Pole Bearers were the first to run afoul of the new policy, when attempting to bury a deceased member in their usual fashion: "The Pole Bearers buried one of their number yesterday, and started out to the tap of the drum. Chief Athy promptly stopped it, in accordance with the recent order on this subject."[52]

By December, the constant suspicion and agitation of the newspapers in West Tennessee succeeded in bringing about a dangerous mob-like situation, in which forty masked white men in Madison County rode through the Tenth District of that county asking for George Washington, the Black leader of the Colored Benevolent Society of that district, whom they accused of making incendiary speeches against the white people. The appearance of these masked men led to a gathering of more than three hundred armed Blacks, "amid beating drums and the discharge of fire arms."[53] From there the situation escalated and deteriorated, as the band of masked white men rode through Black communities of Madison County over and over, in an attempt to intimidate Blacks and break up the benevolent society in the Tenth District:

The citizens of the 10th district and vicinity are still intensely excited over a threatened collision between a band of disguised men and the negroes. The negroes are armed and defiant, while the masked riders are "bold and aggressive." Nearly every night during the past week, these disguised men have paraded through the country, threatening the negroes, and creating alarm and excitement. They have as yet committed no crime, and their movement it is thought, is for the purpose of breaking up a secret society among the negroes of that section. But a serious collision is imminent, as the negroes are very much exasperated, while the masked riders seem determined to break up their society at all hazards. On Wednesday night between 10 and 11 o'clock, about fifty of the maskers surrounded the negro cabins at James Exum's, 11 miles north of the city, and closely questioned the negroes, who were greatly alarmed. A young man by the name of Nat Pearson, living with Mr. Exum, took a double barrel shot gun and went out to where they were and asked them their business. The only reply they gave was, "we are here for a purpose, but will do no harm to any one." Young Pearson ordered them off. They refused to leave, whereupon Pearson jumped behind a tree and fired into them. Some fifteen or twenty shots were fired at Pearson, but he escaped to the house unharmed. The maskers did not pursue him, and it is not known whether Pearson shot any of them or not. Between 12 and 1 o'clock, on the same night, heavy firing was heard four miles south of Exum's, but its cause we have not yet learned. The country is intensely excited and preparations for a conflict are evidently going on. The authorities should take the matter promptly in hand, before serious damage is done. The negroes are exasperated and defiant, and seem to want a collision. Something should be done at once to arrest the mischief.[54]

President Grant's second term, which some had seen as a possible catalyst to better race relations, was instead becoming an occasion for strain and polarization.

"AFRICA WILL HAVE JUSTICE DONE HER": BLACK FIFE AND DRUM MUSIC IN TENNESSEE AND THE POLITICS OF RACIAL POLARIZATION, 1874

Relations between whites and Blacks in Tennessee began to deteriorate rapidly in the new year of 1874. Much of it was the result of bitterness springing from politics, as white Southern Conservatives began to realize that Black voters were never going to abandon the Republican Party in large numbers as they had hoped. On the contrary, Blacks were becoming more insistent in their demands for full and equal rights in America. Not only were they demanding the right to run for and hold office, they were also demanding an end to segregation in places of public accommodation, which eventually led to a civil rights bill, debated in Congress through much of the year. As the bill was discussed, white Southerners became more enraged, and even white Republicans in the South began to oppose it, warning that its provision for "mixed schools" would lead to the end of public education altogether. Tensions related to the civil rights bill ultimately led to a string of riots in the South, as well as a growing number of murders and terrorist attacks against Blacks.

By 1874, the Independent Pole Bearers had seemingly replaced the Sons of Ham as the primary Black organization in Memphis. Week after week, the Memphis newspapers brought reports of their balls and events, as well as their endorsement of certain candidates for office. Even Mardi Gras in Memphis was the occasion for a "grand procession and bal masque."[55]

However, the first mention of Black fife and drum music in the new year was in connection with a school tax referendum in Shelbyville, the seat of Bedford County, where the fife and drum band attracted a large crowd of second-liners:

> The public school question has been most thoroughly agitated for sometime past by the enterprising county Superintendent of Public Schools, John R. Dean, Esq., who has, by every conceivable means, sought "to keep it before the people" that there was to be an election held on Saturday, Jan. 24, for the purpose of voting an additional school tax on real estate of two mills on the dollar. This vote was only for this, the 7th civil district of the county. Grand (?) rallies and stump speeches were the order of the day, or rather of the night, and scarcely a night passed without some demonstration of this kind. The "ear-splitting fife" and "soul-stirring drum" were called into requisition, and went thundering and squealing about town, followed by 15th amendments and small boys, ad infinitum, bearing numerous painted banners and transparencies, and torch lights. It was a good time for the "hoodlums" of our town to give vent to their pent up yells and screeches, and you may rest assured they showed their appreciation of the privilege in a long and loud unearthly din. It was a good time, also, for the young lawyers of this bar to ventilate their slumbering Demosthenian talent before an appreciative public.
>
> The election came off on the 24th and resulted in the election of the two mills tax by a vote of 380 for, and 130 against. There are about 580 voters in the precinct, so it will be seen that the tax received more than two-thirds of the entire vote.[56]

The death of Senator Charles Sumner on March 11, 1874, was a major blow to Blacks, not only in Memphis and Tennessee, but throughout the country. Perhaps more than any member of Congress other than Thaddeus Stevens, Sumner had firmly and consistently demanded that Blacks have full and equal rights in the United States. He had first introduced a civil rights bill in 1872. It failed that year, but he continued to reintroduce it until his death. His consistent friendship toward Blacks, despite his break with President Ulysses Grant, led the Black societies in Memphis to plan a commemorative march and celebration: "At one o'clock to-day the different colored societies of the city, numbering fourteen or fifteen organizations, will meet at Court square, and after parading the principal streets of the city, proceed to the Pole-bearer's hall on Second street, where orations and eulogies will be delivered in honor of the memory of Charles Sumner. The demonstration will be one of the largest ever made by the colored people of Memphis."[57]

On the following day, the *Appeal* gave a detailed account of the procession and the participants in it, including three bands:

Yesterday the colored citizens of Memphis turned out in great force to honor the memory of Charles Sumner, their devoted friend. According to previous arrangement, the different societies assembled at the east side of Court square, where a very large crowd of white and black people had been attracted; some through curiosity alone, others by motives of sincere respect for the dead statesman. The streets and sidewalks for a considerable distance were densely packed with spectators, and Court square was also thronged with a great crowd.

The procession was formed in accordance with the following programme:

Grand Marshal John Wiseman, Captain Smith, Sergeants Dea and Pendergrast, all mounted and ten patrolmen on foot,

Thirty assistant marshals on horseback.

Pole-Bearers' band, of eighteen members.

First section of Independent Pole-Bearers.

Hearse, containing coffin.

Second section of Independent Pole-Bearers.

Hacks, with mayor and city officials.

Benevolent Society No. 1.

United Sons of Ham.

Sons of Zion.

Emmet Guards.

Benevolent Society No. 2.

United Sons of Canaan.

Brothers of Charitable Treasury.

Union of Zion Nos. 1 and 4.

Benevolent Society No. 4.

Young Men's Association No. 2.

Union Forever Society.

Laborers' Union Nos. 1 and 2.

Israelites' Society.

Jerusalem Society.

Union Aid Society.
Mutual Benefit Society.
Hacks, with members of female societies and citizens.

The procession formed, it moved up Second street, the sidewalks of which were thronged with spectators, while from every window and door were persons anxious to witness the demonstration. At the head of the first section of Pole Bearers was a white banner, with the inscription, "In Memory of Charles Sumner." The first section of this society, with reversed arms, preceded the hearse, following which was the second section with reversed spears. At the head of the column were three flags, two of the Union, and the others representing the society. The society's banner was furled and draped in mourning, as an emblem of the sorrow felt by the members. Four large dark-brown horses drew the hearse, which bore black plumes and contained a silver-mounted casket. On either side was an escort of honor, composed of eighteen pall-bearers, from different societies. Following the Pole Bearers' society were seven carriages, containing Mayor League and the city officials. . . .

The different societies bore banners, and in the procession were three bands. The procession was at least a mile in length, and was half an hour in passing a single point. Its appearance was very imposing, and it is stated that over eighteen hundred persons engaged in the procession. The demonstration was one of the largest ever made by the colored people of Memphis, and showed that they do not lack appreciative gratitude for the memory of one whose public life and greatest efforts had been devoted to what he deemed the improvement, liberation and elevation of the negroes of the United States. . . .

Upon arriving at the Pole Bearers' hall, on Second Street, between Adams and Washington, the societies divided ranks and formed on the side opposite the building. Mayor Loague, the members of the general council, distinguished persons and officers were then invited to seats on the plaza, where the orator's stand was located. When the societies had formed, the first section of Pole Bearers countermarched to the entrance of the hall and formed open ranks. The hearse, with its escort of honor, then drove up in front of the stand. Ten banners and flags of the Union, the Pole Bearers and Colored Agricultural society, and also the white one inscribed "In Memory of Charles Sumner," were held over the hearse. By this time the street was thronged with a very large crowd, and it was impossible for anyone to pass. From

Adams to Washington street was one dense throng of people, all eager to witness the memorial tribute to the genius and philanthropy of Charles Sumner.[58]

As was so often the case, the rival *Avalanche* gave a far more detailed account of the parade, with more specific and tantalizing information about some of the Black societies participating, particularly some of the rural ones from outlying areas of Shelby County:

Yesterday was the day selected by the colored people of Memphis to show their appreciation and respect for the memory of their greatest and foremost champion—the dead Senator Charles Sumner. According to announcement the various societies intending to participate assembled at the east gate of Court square on Second street about 2 o'clock. Thousands of people, mostly colored, were on the sidewalks, and many accompanied the procession on its long march.

The procession formed with Captain C. T. Smith and Sergeants M. Dea and M. J. Pendergast in the lead mounted, followed by a squad of ten men, who, for some reason, were not in full regulation dress, as neither were their officers.

The advance guard of the Grand Marshal, John Weisman and Assistants Coleman Thomas, Joseph Lusher, Henry Kennedy, Robert Butcher, Henry Morgan, Wesley McGree and Harrison Meyers, all mounted and with batons and sashes, were next.

A plain white banner trimmed with crepe, bearing the inscription, "In Memory of Charles Sumner," carried by the advance guard of Independent Pole Bearers was followed by a guard of honor of Pole Bearers, Nos. One and Three, 100 strong, armed with muskets, carrying their arms reversed, was next, in the center of which was the hearse, containing an elegant rosewood casket, highly mounted with silver. Four black horses drew the hearse, which was especially guarded by twelve muskets, six on either side, all the men wearing crape. The Pole Bearers proper, under command of Thomas Swan, and numbering about 300, in full regalia, with banners and flags, one of which was at full mast, were immediately after, they being preceded by a portion of the colored brass band, and accompanied by their full string band. . . .

The Brothers of Home Guards, 20 strong, from Central Point, with flag, were next. General A. Taylor was in command. The Greenwood Social, with banner, were under the command of Wilkes Anderson.[59]

The other parts of the colored brass band were next, and then came the Social Benevolent Societies Nos. 1 and 3, about 100 strong, with banners and flags all craped, and under the command of Squire Ewing and Joseph Withy.

The United Sons of Ham, 100 strong, with flags and banners, preceded by a field band, were under the command of Henry Boyd. The procession of Societies was closed by the Society of the United Sons of Zion, 250 strong, bearing banners and flags, under the immediate command of Harry S. Wilton.

Thirty or forty carriages containing colored people, mostly women, closed the procession which was fully eight squares long. All the societies were in full regalia and presented a creditable and in some instances a martial appearance. The bells of the various engine houses tolled every three minutes while the ceremonies were being conducted.[60]

A number of city officials spoke, but when Ed Shaw, the Black wharfmaster of the city of Memphis, was introduced as the next speaker, the white city officials left. His remarks, as was typical of him, were uncompromising and militant:

I say we are entitled to the same privileges as white citizens. This is the work that that great man Charles Sumner undertook, and I believe that one of the first speeches he ever made in the halls of Congress, was in '56 against slavery, when the attempt was made by the Senator from South Carolina to murder him. But it was not intended by the Almighty that we should lose his services at that time. The work assigned to him is not yet accomplished, but I believe that Charles Sumner lived long enough to see that his great work would eventually be accomplished. When the war broke out, the question was "What is to be done with the negro?" Whence did the answer come from? Our honored President, Abraham Lincoln said that the negro would have to be colonized. It was thought impossible to retain what they then called the ignorant and brutalized negro in the midst of the nation. Some declared that if the negro was set free in the Southern states that it would be impossible for civilized people to live in their midst, but the Hon. Charles Sumner came to their rescue again, and declared that the negro was a fit subject to become an American citizen, and said that he expected to live to see the day that a negro would be a companion of his in the Senate of the United States, and he did live to see it.[61]

In May, a meeting of Democrats and Conservatives at the Second District Courthouse in Bartlett, Tennessee, in northeastern Shelby County, began a movement called the Bartlett Movement, intended to unite all white voters in Shelby County against the Republican Party, which was increasingly being seen as a "Black man's party." The combination of this new political movement and the effects of white anger over the civil rights bill had a most polarizing effect on local politics. The *Public Ledger* noted it in a column in May:

> Since Ed Shaw's speech insisting on negro supremacy in Tennessee, the white men of the Republican party have weakened, and are seriously considering the abandonment of the "negro" and affiliating themselves with their white conservative brethren. . . . Candidates' cards are written, "Subject to the action of the convention when convened by the Bartlett Executive Committee." This is the popular mode at present. The "combination" or Radical negro party has bursted in Memphis, and many of its leaders during the last Mayoralty election are sliding back into Conservatism via Bartlett. They want to be "on the side of the people," you know.[62]

It was in this tense atmosphere that the Independent Pole Bearers announced their annual Decoration Day celebrations at the National Cemetery near Raleigh, a day to commemorate the Union dead. The buying and selling of food, cigars, and liquor at previous Decoration Days had been ridiculed by the white Memphis press, and this year, Thomas Swan, the president of the Pole Bearers, had endeavored to put a stop to it. The advertisement warned that "no booths or saloons will be allowed and persons are requested to have their dinners in baskets on the ground," but this provision would end up causing a considerable amount of controversy. The advertisement also noted that "the societies will march from their various halls to the corner of Beal and DeSoto streets at 9 1/2 o'clock a.m., where the line will be formed, and move up Beal to Main, and thence up Main to the Louisville depot, headed by the Pole Bearers brass and field band."[63]

The Pole Bearers' Decoration Day exercises were originally scheduled for May 28, but advertisements ran in Memphis papers rescheduling them for May 30. Nearly five thousand persons turned out at the cemetery for the events, which quickly spiraled out of control when attendees became enraged because businessmen, primarily white, had set up vending booths around the cemetery in clear violation of the advertised warning that no booths would be permitted:

Agreeable to public announcement the decoration of the Federal graves at the National cemetery, seven miles from this city, was set for yesterday. At ten o'clock in the morning the different negro societies of Memphis, headed with bands of music and bearing flags, formed processions, which paraded Second and Main streets to the Louisville depot, where, with two thousand men, women and children, they embarked for the cemetery. Train after train on the Louisville railroad left the city, each one being crammed with its freight of African Americans anxious to honor (?) the memory of the gallant soldiers who fell while fighting for their emancipation.

There are 13,902 soldiers, white and black, interred in the Mississippi valley cemetery. By two o'clock the grounds were covered with at least five thousand persons, all of whom, except half a dozen white people, were negroes. The different negro societies represented were as follows: Pole-Bearers, No. 31, of Memphis; Pole-Bearers, No. 3, of Springdale,[64] Benevolence societies, Nos. 2 and 3; Sumner Guards, Sons of Ham, and Union Star society. During the morning the societies were escorted to the Louisville depot by bands of music which played alternately, "Just Before The Battle, Mother," "Come Put Me In My Little Bed" and "Jordan Is A Hard Road to Travel." Upon arriving at the cemetery, the different societies paraded and countermarched outside of the walls of the enclosure, and attracted a great deal of attention. We noticed a small frame grocery with an arbor near by the station platform, besides a flying jenny and several refreshment and liquor stands.[65] About an hour after the crowd had assembled, the Pole-Bearers, who were armed with muskets and bayonets and battle-axes, thought no man, woman or child had a right to sell or barter anything whatever within a mile of the enclosure wherein slept the heroes whose memory they had assembled to honor.[66]

The commemoration degenerated into a riot when Thomas Swan, president of the Pole Bearers, put together a squad of his armed men and sent them against the various stands and stores that were selling food or liquor. That these had been set up against the express warnings against such in the advertising ahead of the event seemed to enrage the crowds of Blacks who had come to the event. Some of the vendors were attacked with thrown fruits and vegetables as they fled, and one liquor stand was visited by Swan and his men, who demanded payment of twenty-five dollars, at the point of bayonets, as a penalty for violating the orders of the day. The city recorder Pat Winters was also present at the cemetery and warned Swan that he had no legal authority to shut down vendors if they were not on the cemetery grounds proper, but Swan paid him no heed. That at least one white woman vendor was menaced by the crowd added to the sense of outrage in Memphis's white community over what came to be called the National Cemetery Riot.[67]

Although Swan's conduct on Decoration Day seems reckless, it needs to be pointed out that he only took the action to prohibit vendors after the Memphis press had ridiculed the Pole Bearers in previous years for turning the commemoration into a picnic, with food and drink and plenty of buying and selling. The act of setting up such booths against the express wishes of those putting on the event was of course highly disrespectful, both to the Black community and to the Union dead being commemorated, and Swan probably also felt that having a successful day was dependent on keeping the crowds from accessing liquor. Indeed, the violent behavior may have been precipitated by some in the crowd who had gotten access to liquor. Nevertheless, the actions of the Pole Bearers at the cemetery polarized the races in Memphis to a dangerous extent.

The *Appeal* of June 2 printed a letter from Thomas Swan, president of the Pole Bearers, giving his side of the National Cemetery incidents, in which he denied taking part in any robbery or extortion of vendors:

It is true that the Pole-Bearers went there on Saturday last, to strew flowers on the graves of the Federal dead. For several days previous it was announced through the papers that no booths or stands to sell liquor would be allowed. When we arrived there we found, greatly to our surprise, that the ground outside the cemetery was covered with booths. I asked the superintendent of the cemetery if they were there by his permission. He replied that they were not. He then went with me, being on horseback, and I told them it was all wrong, and asked them to close up their places of traffic, which they proceeded to do and we left. Afterward I heard that some unruly persons were snatching the vendors property, when I took six armed men and went to them, hoping to stop the pillaging and robbery. It is not true in any sense, that I, or any of my men in any way aided or abetted the conduct you so justly disapprove. My whole energy was toward discountenancing such proceedings. With regard to Mrs. Martin, I wish to say that I did not go to her place when I first went round to request the vendors to close their business, because I knew they were on their own property; but when I heard that a mob was there molesting her, I took my men there to protect her. A few days before

I had seen Mr. Martin, and he told me he would not sell liquors, as he considered it wrong, and that he had fought in the same cause, and thought it a shame for anybody to make a picnic or whiskey speculation of such an occasion. . . . Allow me in conclusion to ask how would you treat such characters, if they attended and carried on in the same manner at Confederate floral offering days? If you would take the trouble to look over your files, I think you would see that in former years you ridiculed us for allowing booths about the grounds. This year, because we tried to do away with them, you try to make political capital out of it.[68]

On June 4, the *Avalanche* reported that the grand jury had indicted Thomas Swan for extortion, and that he had been arrested and placed under a $2,000 bond.[69] The *Public Ledger* of the same day added the news that the cemetery superintendent, W. Henry Taylor, had also been indicted for extortion.[70]

In the intense atmosphere of those days in Memphis, the news that Blacks were drilling at night out beyond the city limits was the occasion for much fear and apprehension:

The chief of police was yesterday reliably informed that the negroes had been drilling in Chelsea from ten o'clock to two o'clock Thursday night. They had pickets on duty, and would not permit any white man within their lines. Yesterday Chief Athy had a conversation with Thomas Swan, president of the Pole-Bearers, and the latter stated that several members had been or would be expelled because of their insolent conduct. The object of this drilling is not known, however there are many rumors as to its purpose and some excitement among the white citizens. Should any riotous demonstration be attempted it will be met with prompt suppression by the police and sheriff.[71]

In this atmosphere, Thomas Swan called for a meeting at the Pole Bearers Hall on June 8 to discuss the recent rumors of rioting and to call for peace. The meeting was duly held, attracting a large crowd at Second and Washington Streets, including a number of white citizens. At least the drummers were present, if not the full fife and drum band:

There was a large mass meeting of negroes in front of the Pole-Bearers' hall, on Second street, near Washington, last night to hear the explanation proposed in relation to the reports concerning mobs and riots.

There was quite a sprinkling of white persons in the crowd, which seemed to increase at every thump of the drum, and the street in front of the building was a perfect jam. A stand had been erected on the plaza of the building, from which the speeches were made. On motion, the meeting was organized by electing as chairman for the occasion H. N. Rankin, colored attorney-at-law. Previous to this Thomas Swan, president of the Pole-Bearers' association stated that they had come together to ascertain if the charges laid at their doors were just and supported by facts. Various rumors had gone abroad relative to riots and uprisings among the negroes, and to show the injustice of these rumors they had invited a meeting of the citizens of Memphis.[72]

At the meeting, a number of speakers denounced the rumors of riots and secret drilling among the Black people of Memphis. The meeting's chairman, H. N. Rankin, pointed out, "Indeed, what inducement is there for the colored people to engage in or seek for a riot? A riot would cause us to suffer more than anyone else." He was followed by the Black wharfmaster Ed Shaw, who stated:

Riots, rest assured, are not for the purpose of murdering the negro, but for the purpose of plunder and robbery. It is stated that a colored barber, residing on Jefferson streets has said that the negroes in every ward of the city are organizing and preparing to fire the property of the citizens of Memphis. Now I want to know the name of this colored man, not to have him killed, but to indict him and bring him to trial. We want him to prove, if he can, that such statements are true. I know such are false, and so did the editor of the paper which published it.[73]

The final speaker of the day was Thomas Swan, president of the Pole Bearers, who gave a defense of his organization's behavior at the National Cemetery on Decoration Day:

The Pole-Bearers didn't believe in robbing and plundering; there was a clause in their constitution making such unworthy of membership. He had been president of the association for six years, and always advised good behavior, politeness, peace and order. The negroes never received credit for doing anything good, but were abused for everything tending to their disadvantage. They now began to open their eyes, and would co-operate for benefit and protection. He referred to the fact that he had been handcuffed to be carried to jail on an indictment for extorting money from Mr. Pope at the National Cemetery, but was bailed, one of his own color pawning his watch. Since then Mr. Pope wanted to compromise the matter. This we wanted to tell the white people. If I had been guilty would he had made this proposition to me? No, sir. Gentlemen, the time will come when old Africa will have justice done her, let all the pressure of the world come against us.[74]

The meeting was closed with resolutions denouncing the local newspapers and denying the rumors of riots or insurrections, followed by a public reading aloud of the Pole Bearers' constitution, with the goal of showing that it was not a military or political organization, but merely a benevolent order, providing for the health care and burial of its members.

While fife and drum music had been used but sparingly in Memphis during the 1874 campaign, it figured prominently in July at a large Republican gathering at Collierville in the eastern, more rural part of Shelby County, at which Ed Shaw spoke, and which was duly covered by the *Avalanche*:

A number of Memphis Republicans came out to this place last Saturday, and called together a large number of negroes for a general speechification. The party consisted of General Smith, Ed. Shaw, Captain Garrett, Fred R. Hunt, J. H. Smith and P. J. Mulvihill. The day was quite warm and dusty, but a large crowd followed the drums and fife to the grove selected as a speaking place. A couple of wagons were hauled up under a large oak for the accommodation of the speakers.

Mr. Ed Shaw stood flat-footed in a small spring wagon and addressed one of the blackest audiences to be found in the State. About twelve or fifteen white men approached as near the sweltering crowd as their smellers would permit, and listened attentively to all the speeches. Good order prevailed throughout, there being no disturbance except the blabbing of half a dozen drunken negroes on the outskirts. Mr. Shaw led off on the Bartlett movement, arguing that while it professed to recognize all classes and nationalities, its managers and the convention thereunder had ignored the black man, and changed the so-called Conservative movement into the most extreme Democracy. He proposed to discuss the merits of the candidates on the Republican ticket, but before he proceeded to that, he would examine the politics of the Democratic press, "or rather," said he "the expressions of the Democratic press, for they have no politics whatever except such as interests the pocket." A very appropriate scene followed this speech, and was no less a feat than that of Mr. Shaw's taking a fall through the little spring wagon in which he was standing while orating. The "bottom fell out" under the weight of his intellect, and the sudden contact with the coupling pole and his scrambling upward were the chief entertainments of the evening. It may be said truthfully that he left a good opening for the next speaker—to avoid. Shaw remarked as he arose, "You had better mind this wagon; this is the Bartlett platform anyhow; don't put me in a Bartlett wagon. It won't hold me."[75]

As Democrats in both Memphis and Nashville began to coalesce into "white man's tickets," a handful of Conservatives chose to style themselves Independents, either because they were uncomfortable with the racial polarization implicit in the Democratic schemes, or because they simply were not chosen by the committees who were organizing the tickets. Political realities of the day being what they were, these Independents had to appeal to Black voters if they were to have a chance at winning, but failure to procure a fife and drum band could be disastrous to a Nashville rally:

Bearing in mind the appointment of the Independent candidates to address the voters of the 10th ward at the Exposition building last night, a representative of this paper repaired to that place for the purpose of noting what might be said and done. Owing to a mysterious neglect on the part of the people in that neighborhood, the candidates were not honored with a crowd. After waiting sometime in vain, and holding a consultation, they resolved upon a little matter of form, and with a dejected mean submitted to the fates.

Maj. J. R. McCann mounted a lumber pile, and to the few who were present, said: "Gentlemen! We have all been in the country to-day, and have labored very hard. We intended to have a fife and drum here to-night, but by some misunderstanding they have failed to make their appearance. We will speak at the schoolhouse in the Thirteenth district to-morrow night to a large crowd, and hope you will all be there to hear us. We will also address you at this point some time during the canvass. Thank you, gentlemen."

With this the candidates withdrew. The UNION AND AMERI-CAN man walked leisurely away musing upon the evident fact that the candidates meant to explain the absence of the sovereigns by the lack of a fife and drum. Our reporter mused upon this matter with the greater interest because there was a drum at hand, and because he had heard it thumped lustily in an endeavor to draw a crowd. There was no fife and in this fact probably consisted the fatal mistake.[76]

If so, it was a mistake that they would not repeat, for the next day's *Union* carried the brief notice that the "Independents found that fife and put it on duty yesterday. They had out a drum and fife and a placard advertising the oratorial feast which was to come off in the Thirteenth district last night."[77] A few days later, the same Independent candidates held a rally at McKee's School in the Tenth Ward, where the earlier rally had failed to come off, and the fife and drum were again employed.[78] The Independent candidates' use of fife and drum music for their campaign was seemingly the first instance of a pattern that would soon become evident throughout the South. Politics in the region was generally divided into a predominantly Black Republican Party and a predominantly white or all-white Democratic Party. The Republicans generally were the party that employed Black fife and drum musicians. But, from 1874 on, whenever a third party appeared, fife and drum music would emerge from the shadows with it. While there may have been many reasons for this, at least in part it reflected known political realities. Most third parties in the South were predominantly white affairs whose motive in opposing the Democratic Party was due to its being dominated by wealthy landowners. The third parties, often based around poor yeoman farmers demanding economic or land reforms, knew that their only hope for defeating the Democrats was by "fusing" with the Black-and-Tan Republicans, hence the use of Black fife and drum music, an aural clue to reassure Blacks that this new party was a potential ally for them rather than an enemy. Such fusion worked on occasion, and the opposition combination could win at least local offices.

But if the fife and drum music could work wonders at getting crowds to rallies or the polls, it was much less enjoyed by others in Nashville, including the editors of the *Republican Banner*, who seemed to portray it as a provincial and backward thing in a city wanting to be viewed as metropolitan:

We believe Nashville is the only city of metropolitan pretensions in the world where local politicians and office-seekers advertise as persistently with "the spirit-stirring drum and ear-piercing fife." In this respect it can claim the palm, for enlightened provincialism, over all other over-grown villages. It is a cheerful thing to contemplate, that from now until next November, the same inevitable mulatto fifer will continue to swell out his cheeks, and the same irrepressible unbleached American will continue for the next hundred days to belabor the sheepskin, to the infinite delight of the bare-footed small boy and the imminent demoralization of hack hordes and sidewalk pedestrians. Will the nuisance ever abate?[79]

Nashville did indeed seem to have an abundance of fife and drum bands in comparison to other cities in the state. In addition to their usual use for political organizing, they were also frequently used to advertise businesses and products, a phenomenon not found elsewhere to any great extent.

In Nashville, as the Democratic candidates began to hold rallies, they boldly invoked white supremacy and attacked the Independent candidates, whom they linked to the Republicans. At a large Democratic rally at the corner of Market and Broad streets in Nashville, General J. M. Quarles stated that "the fight is now between the negro and the white man," and "I would roll logs at 40 cents per hundred before one of my children would go to a negro school." He furthermore stated, "The independents say they are not Radicals. If they are not, by whom do they expect to be supported, and who is it beating their drums for them every day?"[80] Yet another Independent rally broke up in a stampede after what the *Republican Banner* called a "trivial accident," but before it did, that paper gave a description of the drums used to convene it: "The twinkling stars looked down smilingly last night upon a crowd of Independents, congregated at the Chattanooga depot to hear their leaders. When the rattle of the little drum, with goose quills on the other end of it,[81] had ceased to 'snare,'and the 'bum, bum, bum, bum' of the bass had departed on the breeze, the candidates came forward to address the audiences."[82]

The elections of August 6 brought an overwhelming victory for the Bartlett Movement in Shelby County and led to flourishes of triumph from the *Ledger*, mingled with the paper's usual threats and taunts against the Black community.

The impact of white supremacist rhetoric used to secure an electoral victory extended far beyond politics. Shortly after the elections of August 6, newspapers started reporting murders and assassinations of Blacks by whites. Typical was the murder of a Black musician, Robert Banks of Nashville, by a white man, William Kellam, at the resort town of Kingston Springs, west of Nashville:

Robert Banks, a colored musician, was shot and killed yesterday afternoon by William Kellam, a white man, at Kingston Springs. Banks was standing in front of the saloon, and was approached by Kellam on horseback, who asked him if he did not want to shoot with him.

The negro replied, "No sir." Kellam replied, "Then I will shoot with you," and immediately drew a revolver and fired one shot, which took effect in Banks' abdomen, producing a wound from which he died soon after. Kellam was under the influence of liquor. He subsequently fled to the woods.[83]

The incident elicited considerable outrage in the resort town, with the citizens asking Governor Brown to offer a reward for Kellam's apprehension. Governor Brown, receiving the request of the residents of the town, agreed, and duly offered a $500 reward for the arrest of William Kellam. Despite the reward, Kellam was apparently never captured or tried for the murder of Banks. He is in fact never mentioned again in the newspapers.

After the riotous events of the summer, white Tennesseans were notably jumpy, even in Middle Tennessee, and when Blacks gathered, particularly with drumming, there was significant concern, as in this incident from Fayetteville, in Lincoln County: "Some excitement has prevailed above town near the river, because some negroes were holding meetings at a cave, calling the members together with a drum. A gentleman who has investigated the matter says the organization is a benevolent society or something of that sort, and no harm is intended. The colored folks, he says, manifest no dissatisfaction, but, on the contrary, are orderly, as industrious as usual, and are now preparing their fall and winter supplies. There is, our informant says, no cause for uneasiness."[84]

The occurrence of fife and drum meetings south of the city of Memphis was complained of by a contributor to the *Appeal* styling himself "Suburb," who seemed to link the music and drilling to the stealing of chickens and robbery of stores:

Do we live amid civilization or barbarity? Are our lives safe, or unsafe? Will lazy scoundrels, who make a living by sounding forth ignorant and incendiary speeches in order to obtain office or create riot and butchery, be permitted to pursue their hellish avocation until evil untold shall be showered down upon us? If you but lived one week in the suburbs of this city you would come to the conclusion that you dwelt amid the rattle and booming of the battlefield. From early eve till dewy morn you might hear the dulcet sound of the rifle, the shot gun, the musket, the pistol and the blunderbuss, accompanied frequently by the soft and soothing strains of the drum and fife, performed upon by African troubadours in search of hen-roosts and grocery stores. Let us invite immigration to our peaceful homes.

When a man with gun in hand is compelled to watch the dear ones of his household every night go the year, I think it high time that some sapient brain should find, amid these volumes which form mountains of law, some protection for him who desires to live in the suburbs of a city said to be situated in a civilized community.[85]

The *Appeal*, after publishing Suburb's letter, responded to it by way of an editorial:

We commend this communication to the attention of our city and county officials. Whatever assumes the shape and form of nuisance can and ought to be abated. In the prevention of the armed assemblages alluded to by "Suburb," and the indiscriminate shooting indulged in by idle, lazy and vagrant negroes, lies, we think, the solution of the difficulties now complained of, and which fill the public mind with apprehension for the future. It does not do to lock the stable door after the horse has escaped; and so, if we would avoid the consequences of such affairs as that of Gibson county,[86] we should suppress these unlawful assemblages, prohibit the beating of drums and enforce the laws against indiscriminate shooting: and this, we submit, should be attended to at once. As we have said before, there is no time to lose. An ounce of prevention is worth a pound of cure.[87]

The *Appeal*'s suggested ban on the beating of drums in the county did not stop E. A. Benson's music store in Memphis from proudly advertising that they would sell a set of drums and fife for twenty-five dollars, "consisting of one bass, one tenor and one fife, all calf heads, and sticks complete."[88] As long as there was a Republican Party to engage in elections, business was likely quite good.

Throughout August and September, almost nothing had been heard from Thomas Swan, the president of the Pole Bearers, but suddenly, on November 1st, the *Appeal* gave a funeral announcement for Swan, which had to have come as a shock to Memphis's Black community, as he was a relatively young man: "On the evening of October 30th, THOS. SWAN, late President of Pole Bearers Association. Funeral will take place from his late residence, corner Main and Auction streets, this (SUNDAY) afternoon at one o'clock. His friends are invited to attend."[89] The *Avalanche* reported it as well: "Thomas Swan, President of the Pole Bearers, and a man of considerable prominence among the colored people, died yesterday, and will be buried today."[90]

Of Thomas Swan, little can be determined prior to his ascension to the presidency of the Pole Bearers. He first appears in the Memphis press in 1866 as the co-owner of a Black dance hall in the Pinch District that was shut down by the police, on which occasion he was arrested.[91] He does not appear in the pages of Memphis papers again until after he became president of the Pole Bearers. From the 1870 census, we learn that he was a mulatto male and twenty-eight years of age, and that he had been born in Tennessee, so he was likely born a slave. His wife, Salina, was also a mulatto woman, twenty-eight years of age, and from Louisiana. Swan was described as a "laborer." In the 1868–69 *Edwards City Directory*, Swan is listed as a driver for McKinney, Bryson and Company, a furniture store. In the 1871 *Edwards City Directory*, Swan's residence is said to be at the "head of Main," presumably the same house in which he died. By 1874, the *Boyle-Chapman Directory of Memphis* lists Thomas Swan as an undertaker, with an office at 232 Third Street in downtown Memphis. The Memphis city death records for 1874 show that Thomas Swan was thirty-one years old at the time of his death, lived at Main and Auction, and died of "typho malaria."

The *Public Ledger* gave the first account of the funeral of Thomas Swan, as it involved a large parade of Pole Bearers and other Black societies of Memphis and Shelby County:

Five hundred negro Pole-Bearers, in full regalia and headed by bands and banners, turned out yesterday to bury their President, or Colonel Tom Swan. The procession was very imposing and was surrounded by hundreds of negroes who followed it along the streets. The barbaric display and pageant passed down Main street amid the roll of muffled drums. The hearse was drawn by four white horses, and was escorted by a guard of honor. In rear of the plumed hearse two negroes led Tom Swan's trotting horse, which was harnessed up and decorated with black streamers. The Pole Bearers carried their pikes reversed, and they presented a military appearance. The society is both benevo-lent and military, the majority of its members having served in the Federal army during the last war. Swan was a most influential leader of the societies, and as President of the Pole Bearers occupied no insignificant position. It will be remember that last spring he led his armed Pole Bearers to the National Cemetery and participated in the ceremonies of plundering booths and robbing white people and then collection an illegal tax from them of twenty-five dollars, for which he was indicted by the Grand Jury of the Criminal Court, but grim Death stepped in and has brought about a no. pros. of the case. Swan was not a bad man when compared with other negro leaders in our midst, but he was manipulated by the white Radicals who controlled him and his Society for selfish and political purposes.[92]

The *Daily Memphis Avalanche* gave a much more extensive account of the funeral, and estimated the crowd at much higher numbers than the five hundred referred to by the *Ledger*:

The funeral procession of Thomas Swan (colored), Sunday, was one of the largest ever seen in Memphis. It was over one mile in length, and contained at least 2500 persons, in carriages and on foot. Swan was the President of the Pole Bearers, the largest organization of blacks in the city, and a member of the Sons of Ham and Sons of Zion, all three of which turned out in force. A colored brass band preceded the procession, after which came the Sons of Ham, then another brass band and the Pole Bearers, nearly 1000 strong. The hearse, drawn by four iron gray horses, came next. The casket was a fine metallic one. A guard of honor of the Pole Bearers walked by the side of the hearse, which was followed by the horse that Swan drove whilst living, the harness and trappings of which were entwined with black. Two of the Pole Bearers led the horse. Two carriages containing Swan's family followed and then came footmen in citizen's dress, about 500 in number. They were followed by a line of hacks and carriages fully half a mile in length, which closed the procession. The only white Radical that had the nerve or respect to attend the funeral of this prominent and influential Republican, was Commissioner S. S. Garrett, who was in his buggy solitary and alone, near the tail end of the procession.[93]

But far more controversial were the alleged dying words of Thomas Swan, as supposedly told to his attending physician Thomas H. Clark, which were published in the *Avalanche* and from there were reprinted in numerous newspapers around the country:

I have something to say to you for the benefit of my race, to whom I have been devoted. I feel at peace with God, whom I thank and give praise for His great mercy to me. I feel at peace with all mankind, and oh! that I could speak personally in tones of persuasion to my color to make peace with their white friends, cease all this galling strife that now renders life and happiness so uncertain. Say to my people, for I believe you to be our true friend, to cut loose from all those politicians, white or black, that continue to sow discord among the races. We know it is hard to overcome the prejudice of any class and particularly the fears of our simple, uneducated people. Say to them to shake off those fears, for they are unfounded in fact. Let them become free and untrammeled in the exercise of their political rights. Let them struggle to be free like all other nationalities that compose this community and sustain only those men who have living interest in the soil. I could speak forever on this subject, but your admonition to quietude cannot be disregarded. I will say, however, one farewell word to my people—the last, too, that I will ever say on earth: My people, endeavor to cultivate more attachment for the worthy people of the South; be true to them and worthy of their confidence; and remember a dying friend says to you that peace will surely follow.[94]

Although an earlier letter of Swan's printed in the *Appeal* shows him to be a decent writer, and possibly capable of speaking the last words attributed to him, this statement was diametrically opposed to the positions he advocated during his life, and it was met with a certain skepticism. At some point, it became generally known that Thomas Swan did not in fact utter the words attributed to him shortly before his death, although how that fact was established for certain is not known. What is known is that Swan's attending physician, Dr. T. H. Clarke, eventually went insane, and the fact that he and not Swan wrote the words in question was attributed to his insanity:

A gentleman gave information at the station-house last night that Dr. T. H. Clarke, who resides on the Raleigh road, had become insane. Dr. Clarke, it will be remembered, wrote Tom Swan's confession (the President of the Pole-Bearers). It is now well established that Swan never uttered such statements, and that the whole affair developed in the romantic mind of the learned doctor. Since that time, as well as before, the doctor has been taking great interest in negro politics, and was most active in getting up those love-feasts or social mixtures of which the fair ground and other picnics were examples. This of itself was a vast undertaking, well calculated to drive distracted any sensible citizen, but we understand the doctor had been reading works on spiritualism and broke down beneath the praying test, consequently lost his reason.[95]

Thomas Swan was buried in the Zion Cemetery south of the city of Memphis, which today is located in South Memphis along South Parkway. Presumably there was not a marker placed at the original burial site, but in 1880 the Pole Bearers raised the money for a monument to be placed at the grave: "A meeting of the Pole-bearers and the friends of the late Thomas Swan was called by S. Farris, president, and F. B. Davis, secretary of the society, to meet at the Exposition building, last Sunday afternoon (June 6th) at three o'clock, when the monument, selected by the committee, was exhibited. Elders Patterson and Morris officiated at its dedication. The monument was erected with appropriate and imposing ceremonies over his grave, in the cemetery of the United Sons of Zion, No. 1, on the following morning (June 7th) at eleven o' clock."[96] Despite playing a significant role in the history of Memphis, both politically and musically, today, Thomas Swan is almost entirely forgotten. The indexes of books about the history of Memphis do not show even a single mention of the man. Thomas Swan deserved better.

"A NEW AND WELL-GROUNDED HOPE": BLACK FIFE AND DRUM MUSIC IN TENNESSEE AND THE POLITICS OF CONCILIATION, 1875

The year 1874 was perhaps the high-water mark of Black political power in Tennessee, but the results of the elections that year mostly broke that power. With the Democrats firmly in control, there were noticeably fewer mentions of Black fife and drum bands or Black public events in the pages of Tennessee papers in the years that followed. Of course, it does not follow that there was necessarily less fife and drum music, just perhaps that it was not at public events or other places where the white press was likely to encounter it. Also, the press had been referring to Black fife and drum music as "inevitable" for many years by 1875, and as it ceased to be "novel" they may have simply quit mentioning it. A number of articles describing Black events in 1875 do not mention any music at all. At the same time, several other trends may have been conspiring to make fife and drum music rarer as well, including the tendency to switch to brass bands in the larger cities, and perhaps the association of fife and drum bands with Black secret organizations and drilling, which the Black community may have sought to curtail to some extent in the interest of peace. Even so, it seems likely that fife and drum bands persisted in rural areas, and they would continue there for nearly a hundred years to come.

The awareness of Democratic rule cast a pall over Black Emancipation Day celebrations in Memphis on New Year's Day 1875, which was noted by the *Avalanche*, but misunderstood:

> There may not have been many people thinking about it, but yesterday was Emancipation Day. Twelve years ago their martyr President—he wasn't a martyr then, but, according to certain writers, he became one afterwards—promulgated that proclamation which made those who were slaves free. In years gone by the negroes have generally celebrated the day with great pomp and parade, turning out men and women by the thousands. It is beginning to get too much like an old thing, however, to enthuse the emancipated any more. They want civil rights now. About 150 Sons of Zion, Sons of Ham and Pole-Bearers combined turned out yesterday afternoon, and, with the colored band, marched down Main street and around Beal, DeSoto, Union and Second to their hall, where they disbanded. No crowd followed them, as is usual with negro processions and, as they marched along in the cold, drizzly rain, none of them looked as if they were excited over the turnout. At the hall the proclamation was read and speeches made by some of their leaders.[97]

While the *Avalanche* noted the reduced numbers and subdued nature of the 1875 Emancipation Day event, it failed to recognize the true reason for the change, attributing it falsely to ingratitude or a demand for more in the way of civil rights. Rather, it seems likely that African Americans in Tennessee saw little to celebrate as the new year dawned, with their political power broken and both the local and state governments under the control of their former masters, with a governor who had in fact been a founder of the Ku Klux Klan. For the first time since Emancipation, Black Tennesseans could not look at the future with hope, but only with apprehension. True, the newly elected Democrats promised to defend the political rights of the freedmen, but the rhetoric of white supremacy and the color line during the last year's campaign made those promises seem empty and hollow. Furthermore, the weather matched the mood of the celebrants: the *Public Ledger* noted rain and even a few desultory snowflakes in downtown Memphis on that day.[98]

Decoration Day, the commemoration of the Union dead, had always been an important day of celebration for Memphis's Black community, but in the wake of the riots the previous year, the white ex-Federal soldiers of Memphis took control of the event in 1875 and invited the ex-Confederate soldiers to attend, leaving the Black community out of the picture alto-gether.[99] To make sure that the Black community made no commemora-tion of their own, the arrangement committee voted a resolution to ban all parading or ceremonies other than those at the cemetery itself: "Resolved, That it is the sense of this meeting that there shall be no street parade and no ceremonies, except at the cemetery, to which all who desire to do so are cordially invited to attend and assist in decorating the graves."[100] Thus were Black Memphians excluded from an event they had largely created.

There were still occasionally Black picnics and public processions, but they hardly elicited more than a line in the Memphis press by 1875. A mention by the *Appeal* of a June parade by the Black Odd Fellows and the Sons of Ham was typical: "The colored Odd Fellows and Sons of Ham had a public parade yesterday."[101] What kind of music the parade featured was not mentioned at all.

The first really interesting news of the year was picked up by the *Public Ledger* in late June: "President Henley, of the negro society known as the Pole Bearers, has invited Gen. Forrest, Gen. Pillow, Congressman H. Casey Young and Alderman Henry G. Dent to attend a negro barbecue to be held at the Fair Grounds on the Fourth of July."[102] "President Henley" was Hezekiah Henley, a blacksmith, who became president of the Pole Bearers when Thomas Swan died. He seemed to be a Democrat by temperament, and far more inclined to seek a rapprochement with ex-Confederates than his predecessor Thomas Swan had been. Whether this was Hezekiah Hen-ley's true political belief, or simply a pragmatic course given the disastrous events of 1874, is of course unclear. But what also has to be noted is that Dr. T. H. Clarke, the physician who attended Thomas Swan in his last days and wrote the false confession published in the newspapers, was said to be greatly involved in getting up "love feasts" between the white and Black communities, so it has to be considered that Clarke may have suggested this course of action to Henley. At any rate, an invitation from a Black society to ex-Confederates in general would be unusual news, and in par-ticular an invitation to General Nathan Bedford Forrest—a former slave trader, general at Fort Pillow during the massacre of Black troops there, and founder of the Ku Klux Klan—would be provocative indeed. That being said, there were signs that Forrest was changing as well. He had decried "bushwhacking" and "whitecapping" of Blacks in Madison County by men that he described as "deserters from the armies during the Civil War," and had taken a prominent leadership role in the outrage meeting held against the Gibson County lynchers. The stage was being set for one of the most unusual incidents in the history of Memphis.

The *Appeal* of July 1 brought the publication of a letter of response from those invited to speak by the Pole Bearers at their Fourth of July barbecue:

MEMPHIS, TENN. June 29, 1875. To H. Henley, President of Pole-Bearers:

Your courteous invitation in Sunday's APPEAL to the undersigned to be present at the celebration on the Fourth of July, by the colored citizens of this city and county, calls for a respectful reply. In this invitation, you request us "to address you such suggestions and advice for our mutual action as your well-cultivated experience may indicate as necessary to lead us in pursuit of industry and reciprocal blessings," etc. Feeling that the prosperity and happiness of both the white and colored races in the southern States, in a great degree, depends upon kindly relations and a good understanding and mutual friendly offices, we will probably all accept your invitation to be present, and some one of our number will address you upon matters affecting your interest and future welfare; but we will, as far as possible, avoid all discussions of existing political questions or issues. We are, respectfully yours,

GID J. POWELL
N. B. FORREST
M. C. GALLOWAY
H. G. DENT
CASEY YOUNG[103]

The Pole Bearers' bold stroke in inviting ex-Confederate Democrats to speak on the Fourth of July seemingly motivated the Sons of Ham to do the same, for the *Avalanche* of July 1st brought the following letter from Reuben Carr, the president of the Sons of Ham:

EDITOR AVALANCHE—Hearing of no effort on the part of our people to celebrate the coming anniversary, July 4th, we as a people, embracing near a dozen societies, will meet in a general body on July the 5th at Alexander Park, head of Vance street, and would desire through your columns to invite Governor Isham G. Harris, Colonel A. J. Kellar, Judge T. W. Brown, Hon. Joseph Gronauer, Colonel Gilbert Moyes and Dr. A. T. Shaw to be present, and address us upon subjects connected with the history of our Government, and anniversary of the day we celebrate, being authorized to do so by our committee.

REUBEN CARR,
President Sons of Ham.
By J. H. SAILOR, Secretary.
MEMPHIS, TENN., June 30, 1875.[104]

Evidently, a certain degree of bitterness and hostility had developed between the Pole Bearers and the Sons of Ham. The latter organization was older, having been founded before the Civil War, but in the last couple of years it had been eclipsed by the younger Pole Bearers society. The claim that they had heard of "no effort on the part of our people to celebrate the coming anniversary" was of course utter nonsense, because the decision of President Henley of the Pole Bearers to invite General Forrest to speak at their barbecue was the talk of the Memphis press, if not the average citizen on the streets, and it seems unlikely that the Sons of Ham would have extended invitations to other ex-Confederates had they not seen the Pole Bearers do so. At any rate, they seemed determined to avoid the Pole Bearers' large event at the Fairgrounds and staged their own event at Alexander Park instead.

Soon there was even more confusion, as one of the Sons of Ham branches, the United Sons of Ham No. 1, announced their own picnic at Humboldt Park on July 5, featuring the Rev. T. J. Manson, the Hon. Ed. Shaw, Rev. Elder Martin, and other speakers. Notably, and possibly significantly, the speakers for this event were entirely Black, and perhaps the event was organized as an alternative for those Black Memphians who didn't care to hear white Southerners speak at their barbecues and picnics. This announcement now meant that three competing Black events would be held on the same day.[105]

The day was one of the most momentous in Memphis history, involving gestures of racial reconciliation, but also Black control of numerous social spaces, such as parks and fairgrounds, and marching in the streets with fife and drum and brass bands. In some ways it would be the last glimmer of Reconstruction-era Black confidence and pride:

> Yesterday was intensely hot. It was a scorcher. Yet the streets were, all day, filled with people, and the whole population surrendered itself to the spirit of "the day we celebrate." Picnics were in order and every park and available place in the neighborhood of the city was filled with holiday-class crowds who seemed bent on making the most of the occasion. The old fair ground was the principal point of attraction on account of the white speakers who had consented to assist their

colored fellow-citizens in celebrating the day, and the largest number of persons were there congregated.[106] The colored people had other picnics, but this was by long odds their best display. The white people enjoyed themselves in many ways, the Germans at the Mannerchor picnic and the Irish at the picnic of St. Peter's orphan asylum. Court square at night was a great point of attraction with all classes and the speeches of the several orators were well received. Firing and the popping of crackers was continuous for forty-eight hours. There were quite a number of bonfires, a few places were illuminated, many flags were displayed, and only one or two accidents marred the general joy. We may, therefore, vote the Fourth a success.

The Fourth of July was yesterday celebrated by the different colored societies of this city, the turnout being large and evidencing much interest. As early as eight o'clock in the morning the sound of the drum and fife indicated that the colored organizations were assembling at different points for the purpose of marching in procession to their respective picnic grounds. In and around Court square the negroes congregated in great number, for the central location of this beautiful park renders it a kind of rendezvous upon any public occasion when a demonstration like that of yesterday is to be made. Thither the negroes congregated, and among the crowd we noticed quite a number from the country. While no demonstration was made among the white citizens, inasmuch as the Fourth was the day previous, yet many were solicitous and not a few were anxious to know what would become of the proposed peace-gathering of the whites and blacks at the Fair grounds, to which place the Independent Order of Pole-bearers had invited a number of prominent southern gentlemen, whose previously announced acceptance (published last week in the APPEAL) had become generally known. There was no little anxiety as to the probable result of this meeting and conference, and it was quite natural that its approach had aroused some degree of interest, especially among the thoughtful of our community. From the number of societies and the display made by them, it was evident that the negroes intended making at least a great jollity yesterday, for men, women and children were flocking about the streets in anticipation of the procession of the organizations. By eleven o'clock the different processions had formed, and, headed by bands of music, paraded along Second, Adams, Main, Madison, Beale, and other streets through the city. From the following may be seen what organizations were in the procession:

Band of Music.

Different Societies of the Independent Order of Pole-Bearers with Flags and Banners.

Memphis Baptist Sunday-School Union.

Guards, in Uniform, and bearing Wooden Guns.

Band of Music.

Carriage containing Officers of the Society.

United Sons of Ham (three societies).

Carriage containing Queen of the Day and Maids of honor.

Twelve Carriages containing Female Members of the Societies.

Band of Music.

Benevolent Society No. 2.

St. John's Relief Society.

United Sons of Zion No. 2.

Carriages containing Officers of the Organizations.

The different picnics were largely attended and very much enjoyed. Over two thousand colored persons were present at Humboldt park, where the Sons of Ham gave their entertainment. At Alexander park the Sons of Ham No. 2 gave their picnic, which also attracted a very large crowd, the principal feature being dancing. The exposition building was thronged with colored visitors, the attraction being an entertainment given by Avery Chapel benevolent organization managed by Anderson Montgomery and George Rash. At all of the above places, the colored people did justice to the festivities and pleasures incident to the Fourth of July. The greatest occasion, however, was the entertainment given at the Fair grounds, five miles from the city, by the Independent Order of Pole-Bearers.

Excursion trains on the Charleston railroad went out several times during the day, every car being packed. By two o'clock there was a crowd of colored people present estimated at three or four thousand. The different societies of the Pole-Bearers, with three bands of music, were there under charge of President Hezekiah Henley, Grand-Marshal John Wiseman and Assistant Grand-Marshal Sam Farrish. Headed by the Pole-Bearers' brass band, of which Mat Stephens is leader, and Steve Brown assistant-leader, the societies formed outside of the gate and marched into the inclosure. The crowd increased with the arrival of every train, and by three o'clock at least five thousand persons were on the grounds, which presented a real gala appearance. In one of the long halls were spread fifteen or more tables laden with refreshments and edibles too varied to mention. The north hall of the building was devoted to Terpsichore, whose votaries seemed never wearied of the pleasure afforded them.

The invited guests were General N. B. Forrest, General Gideon J. Pillow, Colonel M. C. Galloway, of the APPEAL, Captain J. Harvey Mathes, of the Ledger, Alderman Henry G. Dent, Major Minor Merriwether and Dr. Clark. These gentlemen procured a hack, in which they proceeded from the city to the Fair grounds, where they were received with much enthusiasm by President Henley of the Pole-Bearers; Grand-Marshal John Wiseman, Assistant-Marshal Sam Farrish, and other officers of the organization. The gentlemen were escorted to the main stand, where, in accordance with the programme and invitations, General Forrest, General Pillow and Hon. Casey Young were expected to address the colored people.

The exercises were opened by President Henley, who said: Gentlemen, as representatives of the Union, of which we are members, we come out to join you as the representative of the people. We are glad to see you here, for we are come not to discuss or to take part in politics, but to pull down the political and to bring about peace, joy and union. When that is done there will be a mighty shout. I hope all who are here to-day will be pleased, and can say when they return to their homes, God bless the Pole-bearers! I will now introduce to you Brother G. W. Lewis, of the Pole-Bearers, who will read my address of welcome.

G. W. Lewis then read the welcome address, as follows: Gentlemen, white friends of the city of Memphis and Shelby county, it affords us great pleasure on this auspicious day to greet you one and all with heartfelt respect, and bid each of you gentlemen, an affectionate welcome. We sincerely thank you, honored sires, for your presence on this momentous and memorable occasion. Let me assure you gentlemen (I speak for my people), that we feel cause for renewed encouragement, and entertain a new and well-grounded hope for our future success. When we remember that this sacred day we have assembled to commemorate is sanctified and made dear to the heart of every true citizen of this great commonwealth by the baptism of American liberty, sealed by the blood of their fathers in 1776, we earnestly pray that our future generations may proudly recall this auspicious period as the moment in which fraternal discord has taken its leave forever from the manly and intelligent hearts of united American brotherhood, resolved that peace and forbearance that stays the angry passions of men, shall prevail henceforward from one end of this great land of ours to the other, in which, through God's providence, our colored race may be permitted to enjoy a becoming and permanent part. In our heart of hearts, gentlemen, we again reiterate our grateful thanks for the kind consideration you manifest, in your presence, with our people to-day, which we will endeavor to appreciate in the future, and for which we thank each of you, gentlemen, at this time.

The reading of the above address was frequently applauded, and at its conclusion the band played a quick air.

President Henley then said: "General Forrest, allow me to introduce to you Miss Lou Lewis, who, as the representative of the colored ladies, will present you with a bouquet to assure you of the sincerity they entertain for the objects of the occasion and as an offering of peace."

Lou Lewis then advanced to where General Forrest was standing and presented the bouquet with the following remarks: "Mr. Forrest, allow me to present you this bouquet as a token of reconciliation and an offering of peace and good will."

General Forrest received the bouquet, and in response said: Ladies and gentlemen, I accept the flowers as a memento of reconciliation between the white and colored races of the southern States. I accept it more particularly as it comes from a colored lady, for if there is any one on God's earth who loves the ladies I believe it is myself. This day is a day that is proud to me, having occupied the position that I did for the past twelve years, and been misunderstood by your race. This is the first opportunity I have had during that time to say that I am your friend. I am here as a representative of the southern people, one more slandered and maligned than any many in the nation. I will say to you and to the colored race that the men who bore arms and followed the flag of the Confederacy are, with very few exceptions, your friends. I have an opportunity of saying what I have always felt—that I am your friend, for my interests are your interests, and your interests are my interests. We were born on the same soil, breathe the same air, and live in the same land. Why, then, can we not live as brothers? I will say that when the war broke out, I felt it my duty to stand by my people. When the time came I did the best I could, and I don't believe I flickered. I came here with the jeers of some white people who think I am doing wrong. I believe that I can exert some influence, and do much to assist the people in strengthening fraternal relations, and shall do all in my power to bring about peace. It has always been my motto to elevate every man—to depress none. I want to elevate you to take positions in law offices, in stores, on farms, and wherever you are capable of going. I have not said anything about politics to-day. I don't propose to say anything about politics. You have a right to elect whom you please; vote for the man you think best, and I think, when that is done, that you and I are freemen. Do as you consider right and honest in electing men for office. I did not come here to make you a long speech, although invited to do so by you. I am not much of a speaker, and my business prevented me from preparing myself. I came to meet you as friends, and welcome you to the white people. I want you to come nearer to us. When I can serve you I will do so. We have but one flag, one country; let us stand together. We may differ in color, but not in sentiment. Use your best judgment in selecting men for office and vote as you think right. Many things have been said about me which are wrong, and which white and black persons here, who stood by me through the war, can contradict. I have been in the heat of battle when colored men asked me to protect them. I have placed myself between them and the bullets of my men, and told them they should be kept unharmed. Go to work, be industrious, live honestly and act truly, and when you are oppressed I'll come to your relief. I thank you, ladies and gentlemen, for this opportunity you have afforded me to be with you, and to assure you that I am with you in heart and in hand.[107]

The *Avalanche* gave their description of the event from a bit of a different perspective, although their account of the speeches differed only little from those given above:

Yesterday, the 5th of July, was by general consent, observed in this city as the anniversary of American independence. The colored people turned out en masse, either individually or as members of societies, and spent the day in festivities at one of the parks, or at the Fair Grounds.

Early in the morning the clatter of fire crackers and discharge of fire arms were heard in all parts of the city; bands of music were playing at society headquarters, and members were assembling, clothed in regalia of variously colored sashes, aprons, rosettes, cockades; while marshals and assistant marshals moved about carrying swords and batons, and employing themselves in assembling their societies. The jubilee of the Pole Bearers at the Fair Grounds was largely attended, where, agreeable to an invitation, addresses were made by General G. J. Pillow, General N. B. Forrest and others. Hourly trains were run on the Memphis and Charleston railroad, commencing at 8 o'clock in the morning, and at noon a large assemblage of colored people had gathered there. The distinguished invited guests arrived about half past 12 o'clock, and, upon reaching the gate, received an evidence of their perfect equality with their hosts by being required to pay 25 cents admission. The different lodges of Independent Pole Bearers had not yet arrived, and the party spent a few minutes in walking though the spacious halls, which were arranged with tables all loaded down with meats, pies, cakes etc., upon which a few of the earliest comers were vigorously employed. At 1 o'clock several heavily loaded trains had arrived, and the scene inside the enclosure was a very animated one. The busy preparations for dinner and the hum of a thousand voices were now and then relieved by the sharp cries of the man peddling lemonade at a nickel a dipper dull and the loud calls of the men who were raking in the quarters on the game of chuck-a-luck. Owing to the intense heat of the sun, the vast crowd was confined to the two halls, and to the grand stands which overlook the race-course. Owing to the fact that Generals Forrest and Pillow rode to the grounds in a hack, the programme arranged for their reception by the Pole Bearers was not carried out.

At 2 o'clock the Pole Bearers arrived and marched from the railroad to the grounds in excellent order, with beating of drums and flying colors, the rays of a summer sun being reflected from hundreds of tin spear heads. Having reached the grand stand, Hezekiah Henley, President of the Society; John Wiseman, Grand Marshal; and Sam Farris, Assistant Grand Marshal, were introduced to the guests by Dr. Clark and after some further delay the crowd gathered on the stand and the exercises of the afternoon were commenced. During a part of the time there was considerable confusion on the stand, and at times it was difficult to hear the speakers. A disturbance occurred while General Pillow was making his address, in which blows were exchanged between two colored men, but quiet was soon restored.[108]

Indeed, it was a grand occasion for both white and Black Memphis, but despite the hopefulness it produced, it did not lead to any lasting improvement for Blacks in Memphis or elsewhere in Tennessee. General Forrest, assuming he meant the magnanimous words he spoke to the Pole Bearers that day, would be dead within two years, and was thus in no position to keep his promises. Blacks would not leave the Republican Party in any large numbers, and slowly their political rights were obliterated by poll taxes, the Australian ballot law (which effectively barred illiterates from voting), white primaries (when the Democratic Party primary was basically the only election which mattered), and a simple refusal of county registrars to register Black voters at all. Laws requiring segregation on public transport and in public places began to appear by the 1890s. The speech of General Forrest to the Pole Bearers would be forgotten altogether, until it resurfaced in the 1990s, resurrected by neo-Confederates who were hoping to rehabilitate Nathan Bedford Forrest's image. In their view, Forrest was transformed from the founder of the Ku Klux Klan to "America's first white civil rights advocate" and the Pole Bearers to which he spoke were called a "predecessor to the NAACP." All of this of course was nonsense. Forrest may have made an enlightened speech to Black folks for his day and time, but he was certainly no advocate of the Civil Rights Act of 1875, which required integration in public places. And the Pole Bearers, regardless of its occasional involvement in political matters, was in fact a benevolent society, no different than the Sons of Ham or the Sons of Zion. The group never expanded beyond the Mid-South, and in no sense could it be considered a civil rights organization. All the same, July 5, 1875, at the Fairgrounds was an example of what perhaps could have been in Memphis.

On July 9, the ghost of Thomas Swan was briefly revived, of a sort, when county undertaker Jack Walsh was arrested on charges of perjury in connection with swearing under oath that he had purchased an oval glass hearse from Swan during the latter's final illness. The county attorney apparently determined that Walsh had never purchased the hearse from Swan, and the grand jury indicted him. He was released on a $2,000 bond to await trial.[109]

Black picnics and barbecues could be advantageous to politicians, even after the power of the Republican Party had been largely broken. One such event held at White Station in eastern Shelby County allegedly attracted several white Democratic candidates for office.[110] But in the wake of 1874, white politicians attending Black events and asking for the votes of Black citizens could backfire. When the *Ledger* claimed that one of the men who attended the White Station barbecue was Congressman H. C. Young, he made a point of visiting the paper's offices the next day to inform the editor that he did not attend the barbecue at White Station, as he had been out of town. With typical political legerdemain, however, Young stated that had he been in town, he would have attended it.[111]

August 6 brought yet another street parade and picnic, this one by the Sons of Ham and the Daughters of Zion, with the picnic held inside the

Exposition Building in downtown Memphis.[112] No longer did the newspapers think it important to mention the music at such events.

The same held true for a description of a society and Sunday school picnic at Bond's Station (Ellendale), mentioned in the *Appeal* of August 13 by a Bartlett columnist, who by his initials was likely Nicholas P. Blackwell, an early resident for whom the current high school in Bartlett is named. The event he described was sponsored by the Social Benevolent Society No. 4, an organization that is known to have sponsored fife and drum picnics in the Ellendale area, and which still exists today in that community:

To-day I attended the turn-out of the Social Benevolent society, No. 4, and Sunday-school celebration of Full View Sunday-school—both colored organizations. Lewis Atkins, a well-to-do, energetic and enterprising farmer, is president of the society, and Thos. Cheatham vice-president. They are both representative men of the colored population hereabouts. Albert Thornton is superintendent of the Sunday-school—the right man in the right place. The meeting today was in a grove on the farm of Mrs. N. J. Bond, near Bond's station. The exercises were principally such as is common at Sunday-school picnics—singing, recitations and music. The members of the Sunday-school, in these exercises, showed that they had been well-instructed, and their performances would have done credit to those who had better chances. The society is, as its name imports, a benevolent association. The motto is "Friendship, Love and Truth." The design is to render aid to the indigent, helpless and sick of the colored race, more especially to the members of the order; and I can say from personal knowledge that it is doing much good in securing aid to the sick members—medicines and medical attendance. And another thing, it is doing a noble work in the cause of temperance. The effects are seen in the neighborhood. These are good things. The social feature was clearly exhibited to-day. By invitation I attended. I found a large crowd on the grounds. Several of my neighbors (whites) came to witness the exercises, and they all will testify that better order was never had on such an occasion. The dinner (a barbecue) was excellent, served up in nice style. The notable feature of the day's doing was the freedom from restraint so often seen and felt when the whites intrude or are present at such gatherings of the colored people. This was a breaking down of the "color-line"—a cordial interchange of thought and word between the two races that a year or two ago would have been impossible. And I am confident from the treatment we (the whites) received, the hospitable welcome they gave us, that the "better day" of good feelings and confidence is near at hand. This was finally impressed upon my mind by the spirit manifested and the manner in which the remarks made by your correspondent in the speech he delivered to them was received. Speed the day when mutual good feeling and confidence shall exist between the two races here in the south. N. P. B.[113]

As the summer was ending, the Wilson County columnist for the *Nashville American* mentioned a number of Black events, at least one of which involved fife and drum music:

The negroes of Mt. Juliet and vicinity had a grand barbecue and picnic Saturday. A great many were present, and strong to say, the day passed off without a fight. . . . The Lebanon negroes picnicked and had orations delivered at the Cave Spring last Saturday. The various benevolent organizations turned out in full force and paraded the streets. . . . Some martially inclined negroes of Lebanon make night hideous and life a burden with a cracked bass drum and squealing fife, with which they nightly parade the streets until a late hour. A dozen tom cats in a back yard are a positive luxury when compared to the diabolical din raised by these noisy musicians.[114]

In early September, a procession to the French picnic in Memphis (probably of white musicians) led to a racial brawl after a Black man was bumped by a white man on the Main Street sidewalk:

While the procession to the French picnic was passing down Main street yesterday afternoon, John Brown, colored, being very much interested by the music of the snare-drum, was jostled somewhat unexpectedly by a white. Brown used violent language, and with a stick, aimed a blow at the white man, who, with another man, rushed upon Brown and chased him into Goodbar & Gilliland's store. They struck him with a chair, and as the negro, who ran to the back door, was trying to get out of the building, one of his pursuers stabbed him twice in the arm and once in the back, inflicting slight wounds. Brown and one of his assailants, Michael Leary were arrested.[115]

Although there was not much mention of politics in 1875, the previous year having been an election year at the federal, state, and county levels, a campaign for municipal officers in Nashville led to the year's last mention of fife and drum activity: "Another meeting was held on the corner of College and Whiteside streets. Nearly one hundred dusky citizens were present, and were delighted with the musical strains of three drums."[116] Despite a few publicized mentions, Black fife and drum music seemed to be retreating from the public eye.

"TOO MUCH MUSIC BECOMES A NUISANCE": BLACK FIFE AND DRUM MUSIC IN TENNESSEE, 1876

America's centennial year was also an election year, but even that fact did not bring an increase in fife and drum band activity in the state of Tennessee. The trend toward brass bands continued and accelerated, while accounts of fife and drum bands declined. And many annual traditions of the Black community, such as Emancipation Day and Decoration Day, seemed to fall by the wayside as well.

Instead, the first mention of a fife and drum band came in connection with the campaign of John Flippin, Democrat, for mayor of Memphis, but it is not entirely clear whether the band in question was made up of whites or Blacks, as Flippin was a Conservative candidate: "The municipal canvas, which has been thus far devoid of interest, apparently opened last night in earnest. Early in the evening the Flippin band—drums and fifes, followed by a number of men and boys, some bearing transparencies, paraded the streets in the northern part of the city, and rallied the citizens to the Ward meetings, announced in yesterday's papers."[117]

On January 13, the voters of Memphis rejected John Loague and the Radical Republicans and elected John Flippin as mayor. The Black community seemed to turn on Barbour Lewis, the Republican boss in Shelby County, as well as Ed Shaw, the ranking Black Republican in the county:

When Barbour Lewis reached the tenth ward polls he was surrounded by a crowd (mostly colored people) who hooted at him, and plied all manner of questions by way of expressing their contempt for a man who had so deliberately endeavored to mislead the ignorant of their race by arousing malicious passions. At one time it seemed as if some of the colored men would mob this champion defamer, but the efforts of Mr. Clapp, secretary of the Democratic executive committee, prevented such an act, if any of this nature were intended, and Barbour Lewis, sneaking into his hack, was driven away mid

the jeers of the crowd, many of the negroes shouting and yelling. . . .
Barbour next visited the seventh ward polls, on Beale street, being
accompanied by three or four sniveling colored voters with a fife and
snare drum. As the ex-congressman stood by, doubtless charmed into
gentle feeling by the national airs, a well-known negro roustabout,
Bill Greene, approached the hero of deception, and with the strength
of a bear, embraced Barbour Lewis to his heart's content, at the same
time saying, "Farewell, Barbour; we must part forever; may the Lord
take a liking to you, for we n----rs can't." This elicited some merri-
ment, and the veteran trickster was so astounded that he crept into
his carriage and was driven away. In a few minutes thereafter John
Loague's first-lieutenant and Barbour Lewis' henchman, the illustri-
ous political scavenger, Ed Shaw, drove up in his buggy, and met with
such a hooting by the negroes that he deemed it advisable to seek a
more congenial locality.[118]

The Democratic sweep also removed all the sitting Black members of
the Common Council from city government, and all the Black candidates
for school visitor were defeated as well. Yet the Black community seemed
to join in the celebrations of Flippin's victory.

In March, a Pole Bearers ball at the Pole Bearers Hall in downtown Memphis was the occasion for complaints from residents in the vicinity, although
the kind of music offered at the event was not mentioned.[119] A couple of
days later, the *Home Journal* in Winchester, Tennessee, mentioned a fife
and drum band with a large transparency marching through the streets at
11:30 p.m., presumably some sort of Republican political activity. It was of
course an election year.[120]

Late in July, the *Ledger* was reporting on a drill of the "black military
company" on Second Street downtown involving a fife and drum band. The
company was not further identified, but was likely the McClellan Guards:
"The black military company indulged in a drill on Second street last night.
The men marched well, and went through the different evolutions to the
sound of the fife and drum."[121]

By August, Nashville was having the usual election campaign activities,
and as always, fife and drum were a big part of it:

Yesterday afternoon some negroes, with drum and fife, might have
been seen going through the streets bearing aloft a piece of canvas,
on which was imprinted, "Speaking by the candidates to-night on the
corner of Vine and Crawford streets." Shortly after dusk the musicians

with their drums and fifes met on the designated corner and began blowing and drumming away at a terrible rate. The music soon collected a large crowd, composed of all colors, and who entertained a wide diversity of opinion as to politics. When the band stopped playing a negro mounted a large box placed by a lamp post, and proceeded to give the crowd some advice as to how they should act while the speakers who were to follow after him were addressing them. A score or more of candidates then spoke. The crowd was not particularly attentive, and indulged in all kinds of jests and badinage.[122]

It may not have been connected to politics, but a similar noisy situation developed night after night in downtown Memphis at the corner of Second and Washington Streets, where both a brass band and a fife and drum band held practices, which annoyed the *Public Ledger* to no end: "Those residing around the intersection of Second and Washington streets now wince nightly under the horrid braying of brass instruments at the hand of a colored band now practicing. The beating of drums and the squealing of fifes also add no little each evening to the entertainment of the residents. Too much music becomes a nuisance in any neighborhood."[123] Perhaps not coincidentally, this was the corner where the Pole Bearers Hall was located.

In September, a Democratic rally in South Nashville occasioned another fife and drum demonstration, and the speeches on that occasion seemed particularly aimed at Black voters, attempting to recruit them to the Tilden and Hendricks ticket: "Yesterday afternoon a drum and fife with the usual accompaniment of boys, paraded the streets of South Nashville and by their strains called the attention of the dwellers there to a banner borne by one of the party, on which was announced the fact that a grand rally would be held at the Democratic pole on the corner of Ash and Summer street. Between three and four hundred assembled, and were addressed by various gentlemen."[124] Fife and drum music was certainly not as common in the Democratic Party, but they often employed it if the goal was to recruit or attract Black voters. After all, it worked in attracting a crowd.

In November, at some occasion (otherwise undisclosed) that attracted a large number of Black people into the city of Knoxville, the *Knoxville Daily Tribune* complained of an incident where rural fiddlers were drowned out intentionally by the members of the "colored drum corps." The motive might have been jealousy between the city-dwelling drummers and the country fiddlers: "The rural fiddlers were very indecorously treated, last night, by the colored drum corps, which seemed to take malicious delight in drowning out all the finer touches of "Rake her down, Sal," and "Sugar in the Gourd," by their infernal uproar. The best part of the performance was thus hopelessly lost. There should have been more respect paid to the musical performers from the country."[125]

November 6 was the final day of campaigning before the election and became an important day for Republican rallies in East Tennessee, some of which involved Black drummers, as reported by the *Knoxville Daily Tribune*:

> The Republicans had a demonstration at Loudon, and also one at Maryville. At half past four o'clock, the black boys in blue, under their veteran commander, Abe Cline, marched down to the depot, preceded by a drum corps, and were followed at a wide interval by a white squad carrying transparencies, for it is a noticeable fact that they will not affiliate with the 'man and brother' in daylight. Arriving at the depot they all got aboard the train, which was chartered for the occasion, and if "loyal Blount" isn't enthused, it will not be the fault of Knox county Republicans.[126]

The *Tribune's* reference to Republican hypocrisy when it came to racial matters was telling, in the light of what was coming. While the elections were a sweep for Democrats at the local and state levels, the national result was indecisive. As the year came to a close, America still did not know whether the Republican Rutherford B. Hayes or the Democrat Samuel J. Tilden would be the next president, and the resolution of that confusion would come at the expense of African Americans in Tennessee and across the nation.

"A PERFECT REIGN OF TERROR": COMPROMISE, BETRAYAL, AND BLACK FIFE AND DRUM MUSIC IN TENNESSEE, 1877

The centennial year of 1876 should have been a time of great rejoicing in the United States, but the aftermath of a disputed presidential election left bitterness and acrimony that led some to threaten a new civil war. The results were not announced for some time, and when the Electoral Commission that Congress had created declared Republican Rutherford B. Hayes the winner, Democrats everywhere—and particularly in the South—cried that there had been fraud and threatened to refuse to accept the results. The resulting crisis led the Republican Party to decide that remaining in power was more important than the fate of African Americans in the South. They made an informal agreement, called the Compromise of 1877, in which Rutherford B. Hayes agreed to remove the last federal troops from the South and to appoint at least one Southern Democrat to his cabinet. By some accounts, he also agreed to stay out of the South's internal affairs with regards to race relations. As the federal troops were the only protection that Blacks had in the Southern states, without them they were at the mercy of the ex-Confederates. They were soon restricted by segregation laws, then denied the right to vote and hold office, and eventually terrorized and murdered with impunity.

In June, the citizens of Memphis were treated to a full dress parade by one of the city's Black volunteer militias, the McClellan Guards, under its captain, James Glass:

> The company numbers 27, and were armed with the improved needle gun. Despite the short time they have been drilling, the company made a good appearance yesterday, and showed they had the right stuff in them. Their uniform is blues, with white trimming and white cross belt. The command, headed by a band, marched through the principal streets having in the procession a hack also, the young colored woman who in the evening presented to the Guards a handsome banner. This presentation took place in the Exposition Building, where the Guards were holding a picnic last night at ten o'clock.[127]

The Fourth of July occasioned more appearances of the various Black societies of Memphis and their bands, as the *Memphis Evening Herald* reported the following day:

> In the city, business was generally suspended, and the holiday observed by nearly all classes of our citizens. The band of the Christian Brothers College paraded the streets and serenaded all of the newspaper offices and reminded the people that the picnic of the St. Peters orphan asylum was in progress at James' Park. The Pole Bearers and Sons of Zion, two colored societies, also were out with bands and flags. The Peabody Hotel was the centre of attraction and the fine dinner served up at this hostelry was in keeping with the reputation of the proprietor and did honor to General Peter Tracy, who had spread himself in getting up an elegantly printed bill of fare, such a one as only Tracy can print. . . . The colored people also celebrated the day. The Pole Bearers at Alexander's Park and the Sons

of Zion at the Exposition building. The order of Chief of Police Athy, prohibiting the discharge of fireworks within the city limits, was generally observed, and the day passed without a single accident or fire. Hurrah for the Fourth of July.[128]

The *Appeal* gave its account of the Fourth a day later, but also gave a bit more detail about the Black community's celebration:

The colored population did honor to the Fourth of July by indulging in parades and a number of entertainments. At Alexander park the Pole-Bearers gave a mammoth picnic, which was largely attended. All night the grounds were illuminated, as was also the great terpsichorean canopy, on the floor of which two hundred or more darkies could be seen enjoying the dance. At the Exposition building the Sons and Daughters of Zion gave a grand ball and festival, to the delight of about five thousand colored persons who were present. At both places good order prevailed. The above entertainments constituted the Memphis Fourth of July, which was unusually quiet, the chief-of-police having wisely interdicted the firing of guns, torpedoes, crackers, etc.[129]

Of note though is that none of these events involved fife and drum bands. All of them were accompanied by brass bands instead. The trend away from fife and drum bands, particularly in the cities, was noticeable.

An exception was the Fourth of July celebration of the Black community of Bristol, in the far northeast corner of Tennessee. This event was unusual, both for the use of fife and drum, and for being a rare instance of the music in the eastern portion of the state: "The colored people had a dinner and supper at Conway Hall, and the schools had a gay procession through the town to the music of fife and drum, with banners appropriately inscribed."[130]

In Nashville, fife and drum music always accompanied political rallies, and the announcement of Major W. Hooper Harris as a candidate for mayor of that city was no exception, as duly reported by the *Nashville American*:

Maj. W. Hooper Harris announced himself a candidate for the Mayority [*sic*], in a speech of an hour and a half, last night on the Public Square, to a crowd of between 200 and 300 people. As usual on such occasions, the drum and fife were brought into requisition that those who had ears might, by the sound of both, be directed to the spot. Maj. Harris began his speech by referring to the tune last played, saying that though he would not be able to talk like a "mocking bird," he would still talk plainly on those subjects which bore upon the canvass.[131]

Late August saw the emergence of a disturbing feud between white and Black farmers in the Sixth Civil District of Shelby County, about seven miles northeast of the city of Memphis, which led to the death of a Black man named Henry Davis. Events soon escalated, and it became apparent that a gang of white men was intent on intimidating Black residents, and perhaps whites as well.[132] The gang was led by Mack Williams, and the whole Sixth District was soon under a reign of terror from him and his associates. Memphians would soon read in their morning papers that Williams was holed up in a house in Bartlett, surrounded by sheriff's deputies and refusing to surrender.[133]

All of the various cases arising from the Big Creek affair came before Esquire Galloway on the afternoon of August 29 at the criminal courtroom in Memphis, and were summarily disposed of. Mack Williams was ruled guilty of murder and assault, and was ordered to be held for trial in the Shelby County Criminal Court. John Harrell, who had also been charged with murder in the killing of Henry Davis, was dismissed. However, a white man named W. D. Allen had filed complaints against Arch Humphreys and Taylor Jones, two Black men whom Allen claimed had shot at Mack Williams and H. L. Pugh with intent to kill. Neither Humphreys nor Jones could post bond, and they were jailed.[134] Galloway's rulings put an end to the disorder in Big Creek, at least for a time.

However, in October, the troubles in the Big Creek area resumed, with two Black men shot as they were on their way to a benevolent society meeting in the area. As in August, members of the Mack Williams gang were involved.[135] Although Williams had been held for trial in September, the newspapers from that month contain no mention of a trial, and the *Avalanche* of October 4 supplied the information that Esquire Galloway had set a bond of $2,500, which Williams evidently supplied; he was consequently released. Williams's friends made the claim that Blacks were trying to break into his father-in law's house when the shooting occurred.[136]

The *Ledger* on the afternoon of October 4 gave an account of the surrender of Mack Williams and his gang, which differed very little from his earlier surrender in August, and which did nothing to end the terrorism:

On Wednesday morning last, about 6 o'clock, a negro called at the house of T. T. Taylor, the deputy sheriff and informed him a that a negro boy had been shot by seven or eight white men on the night previous at or near the place where Henry Davis was killed a few weeks since, and wanted him to go and arrest the parties, whom he supposed were led by Mack Williams. Mr. Taylor immediately summoned a posse of men and went to the house of Pugh and Williams, some four miles northwest from Raleigh on the Point road. On reaching Williams' house they found it locked, and one of the posse discovered a number of men armed with guns about a hundred yards west of Williams's house, on the Point road. Taylor immediately proceeded to the point where they were standing, on the side of the road, but as soon as they discovered the deputy sheriff and his posse coming toward them they retired into a dense thicket. Mr. Taylor called for Williams, and that notorious worthy came out with his crowd, all armed with double barreled shot-guns. Mr. Taylor informed them that a negro had been shot by Mack Williams and John Harrell, and he was there to arrest them. Mack Williams and Harrell denied that they had anything to do with the shooting, and that they could prove an alibi. Mr. Taylor demanded their surrender, which they agreed to, but objected to giving up their guns. Mr. Taylor arrested them and disarmed them. The gang consisted of Mack Williams, John Harrell, B. L. Beloote, N. W. Warmick, J. T. Warmick, R. T. Hindman and C. N. Heathcock. The guns and pistols were surrendered, and Mr. Taylor and posse carried the prisoners to Raleigh and brought them before Esquire M. B. Pryor for trial. No black or white man could be found bold enough to swear out a warrant against the desperadoes, and Esquire Pryor discharged them from custody. The desperadoes left Raleigh in triumph, having browbeat and overawed the community. After they had left a negro swore out warrants for their arrest, saying that he was afraid to do so while they were present.

One of the witnesses to the shooting of Sidney Meriwether made the following statement: "About eight o'clock on last Tuesday evening Sidney Meriwether and Henderson Lanier, (negroes) were returning from Memphis going home, and when near Williams' house, probably two hundred yards, they were halted by Frank Mannus, who was armed with a gun, and he asked them "what in the hell" they were singing for and disturbing his family. Lanier apologized, and said that he was not aware he was disturbing any one, and if so, he would not do so any more; they proceeded up the road on their way home, and Frank Mannus still followed them, cursing and abusing them, and when they were near Williams' house, say thirty yards, Mannus halted them and commenced punching Lanier in the side with his gun, and at the same time two or three other men rose up out of the corner of the fence, armed with guns, and attacked Sidney Meriwether and run him up in the corner of the fence and shot him. As soon as the gun fired Lanier broke and ran off and was shot at twice but not hit.

All of which has excited the negroes very much, and a great many have refused to go into the field to work and pick cotton, and are actually afraid to leave their houses after dark; it is a perfect terror to them throughout the whole neighborhood. This is not confined entirely to the blacks but extends to the good and quiet white population of that particular neighborhood.[137]

The *Appeal*, as was typical, gave a different account of the incidents, placing the blame more on the Black community:

Growing out of the Mack Williams affair, a bad state of feeling has sprung up in the minds of the negroes living on what is known as "The Point," a locality in the sixth civil district, lying between Wolf and Hatchie rivers, some five or six miles from Memphis. Some two or three weeks ago, while Mr. John Harrell was sitting on his front porch, engaged in playing the violin, a wagon passed the house on which were two negroes, George Washington and Tilman Boggs. After passing the house, a gun was discharged from the wagon, and seven bucs shot lodged in the door over Harrell's head. Boggs claims the discharge to have been accidental, and no action was taken by Harrell until now, when he has taken out a warrant and placed it in the hands of Constable Pope for Boggs arrest, subsequent information and developments inducing the belief that the shot was directed purposely at him. Tuesday night Sidney Meriwether and Henderson Lanier, colored, were passing on the public road, singing. Lanier says that Frank Manus, a white man, called to them to know why they were making such a noise, and ordered that it be stopped, alleging that it alarmed his wife and children. Manus then, as Lanier states, followed them forty or fifty steps, and halted them, punching Lanier with a gun. At the same time two men came from the roadside and attacked Meriwether. Lanier heard the shot that Meriwether received, at which he ran off, without identifying the men who attacked his comrade. Manus voluntarily appeared at Raleigh, on hearing that

Lanier had sworn out a warrant, and delivered himself to Esquire Pryor, who, after waiting a reasonable time for the prosecutor to appear, and having such testimony as Manus produced, discharged him. The shooting of Meriwether took place within a few steps of where Mack Williams killed a negro some weeks ago, both Williams and Manus prove that they were not near when Meriwether was shot; and beyond the statement of Lanier as to Manus there is no proof as to who did shoot him. All the suspected parties have appeared at Raleigh in expectation of arrest, or under arrest, and no prosecution has resulted. There is a very bad statement of feeling between the blacks and whites, which is liable to result in an outbreak.

The white people in that neighborhood complain of the turbulence of the negroes in arming and assembling, besides picketing the road, beating the drum, and acting in other ways indicative of hostility. On the other hand the negroes complain that they are in fear of attacks at night, or being waylaid and killed by the white people. There is a feeling of distrust, and the immediate result of the uneasiness on the part of the colored laborers is damaging to the planters in the neighborhood. The wives and children of some of the whites have been afraid to stay in their houses at night, but have taken refuge in the woods. While this is not an exaggerated statement of the condition of affairs, it is believed that, like in all such excitements, the fear of the parties involved may magnify the danger. It is to be hoped and expected that a few sensible men of both sides will meet and adjust the difficulty without further trouble. There is no trouble in making arrests, but it is almost impossible to make a case. Sheriff Anderson is a determined officer, who with his deputies seldom if every fail to apprehend those he is in search of. A good deal of excitement still prevails among both whites and blacks, but there is no probability that any additional injury will result.[138]

It would seem that the Black societies beat drums at their assemblies in the Point area to call their members to meetings. As was the case throughout Reconstruction, the beating of drums, and even singing, was enough to outrage white residents.

Mention has been made already of the McClellan Guards, but by November, the Memphis papers began to mention another Black volunteer militia, the Zouave Guards. They first appear in connection with a festival they intended to have on November 7, but due to inclement weather, the event was postponed and rescheduled: "Owing to the unfavorable weather, the Zouave Guards have concluded to postpone their festival, which was to have come off at Zion's Hall last night, until next Wednesday and Thursday, the 14th and 15th insist., on which occasions they expect to parade the principal streets at 4 o'clock p.m."[139]

November brought more turbulence to the Point community in the Sixth Civil District of Shelby County, as members of the Mack Williams gang fired into the cabin of a Black man named Scott Smith, as reported by the *Public Ledger*, which, despite its anti-Black tendencies, showed a degree of exasperation with the terrorism committed by the gang:

> For months there has been trouble between Mr. MacWilliams and his friends and the negroes who live at what is known as the Point, in the Sixth civil district, some four miles from Raleigh, in this county. The roads have been picketed and negroes returning from Memphis have been shot on divers occasions by the gang. Arrests have been made, but so far no punishment has been meted out to the guilty parties. The leading farmers and best citizens of the locality have nothing to do with these bloody affairs. They condemn all such affairs and threaten to organize and rid the district of both the white and black violators of law.
>
> Last Saturday night Scott Smith, a peaceable negro, residing on the Taylor place, in the neighborhood, heard an alarm outside his cabin. He went to the window and discovered ten or twenty white men outside who clamored for admission. Smith opened the door partially, when a volley of firearms was heard. Smith was wounded in the head and arm. Two negro women who occupied the cabin with Smith made narrow escapes. At least twenty shots were fired into the cabin by the banditti. The gang left without doing any further violence, they believing they had killed every person who was in the cabin. The wounded negro, Smith, recognized Mack Williams as one of the party who fired into his cabin. Smith came to Memphis to-day to seek legal address and protection, both of which he is entitled to under the laws of the State.
>
> A perfect reign of terror exists in the Sixth civil district. Magistrates, good citizens and witnesses are overawed, and prosecutors had better leave that section of the country if they attempt to give information on the murderous gang of midnight raiders. About a week ago a negro man on his way home from Memphis was badly shot by some assassin in this neighborhood; and on last Thursday night Frank Means, a white man and a friend of McWilliams, was

shot at and badly wounded as he was returning home from Memphis. The good citizens and large planters complain that these murderous rows are injuring them, their colored hands being driven from their plantations by midnight marauders. It is time that the citizens of the Sixth civil district should organize a vigilance committee, arrest all violators of law, turn them over to the sheriff, and prosecute such violators to the bitter end.[140]

Accounts of fife and drum activity in Chattanooga were fairly rare indeed, for reasons that are not at clear. Perhaps it did not happen there often, or perhaps the newspapers did not often report it. One of the few accounts of the phenomenon in that city dates from November of 1877, and it is actually not made clear that the "men and boys" performing were Black, but it seems likely that they were: "A bass-drum, fife and a number of noisy and disorderly men and boys made the "wee sma' hours" of morning hideous by unearthly sounds. The men and boys should have been hushed up and decent people allowed to sleep."[141]

In December, the Memphis mayoral race heated up, and the incumbent mayor, John Flippin, who had been elected as a Conservative, had evidently fallen out of favor with the white Democrats, who decided to run John Johnson as their candidate. Flippin therefore held an integrated rally of white and Black voters, hoping to build on the old Radical coalition of Blacks and poor whites, and toward that end hired a "colored brass band" to play for his rally.[142] The same brass band made a visit to the *Appeal* office on the afternoon before the rally: "The thanks of the APPEAL are tendered to the members of the colored band for a serenade yesterday. The band was in one of the wagons employed to drum up an audience in the streets for the Flippin ratification meeting at the Greenlaw Operahouse last night. The APPEAL has been the best friend of the colored man, and advises them as to their true and substantial interests, which are identical with the interests of the white people of the south, who belong to the Democratic and Conservative party."[143] All of this activity would have once been accompanied by fife and drum, but the brass bands were largely supplanting the fife and drum bands. One reason might have been new city ordinances, such as one in New Orleans that was reported by the *Memphis Evening Herald*: "When any one attempts to march through the streets of New Orleans with fife or drum, he is taken to the lock-up."[144] Although there were likely ordinary reasons for such ordinances, such as the prevention of horse runaways, it is interesting that they only began to be enacted in the wake of the so-called Redemption, the capture of local, county, and state governments by white

Democrats called Redeemers, which was made possible by the Compromise of 1877. With the close of Reconstruction, fife and drum activity seemed to be retreating from the public eye, and perhaps going underground.

Chapter 4

"SO IMPORTANT A PART OF THE MACHINERY"

Black Fife and Drum Music in Tennessee
During Redemption, 1878–92

From 1878 on, the number of mentions of Black fife and drum activity declines year by year in Tennessee newspapers until, in the early years of the twentieth century, it disappears altogether. It might be tempting to discern from this that the music itself began to disappear as well, but that may not be an accurate conclusion. For one thing, most Tennessee newspapers throughout the period were white-owned and aimed at a white audience. Because of that, they generally only mentioned Black fife and drum in connection with highly visible events, such as parades or political rallies. With the end of Reconstruction, there were fewer Black parades in public places and fewer Black political rallies. What events there were (picnics, for example) were more private and less likely to be covered by the press. The rise of segregation also limited white exposure and contact with Black fife and drum music, at least outside of rural areas. The few Black-owned newspapers in Tennessee were no different, as they were aimed at a decidedly middle-class Black audience that generally was uninterested in something they probably regarded as "primitive" and "rural" in nature. Articles from the *Nashville Globe*, a Black newspaper, routinely mentioned brass bands and jazz bands, as well as organizations such as the Grand United Order of Odd Fellows or the Prince Hall Masons, and they mentioned the older benevolent societies only rarely, generally in the columns from small towns. Despite the fact that the paper existed for over ten years, fife and drum music is almost never mentioned in it.

Regardless of the lack of public visibility, there is reason to believe that Black fife and drum music continued throughout this period—primarily from the fact that it was still going on in rural areas of Shelby, Fayette, Tipton, and Haywood Counties in the early 1970s, and it is unlikely that it would have died out and then reappeared. Instead, it seems that researchers and musicologists began to stumble onto something that had been going on all along.

"THE RENEWED INFLICTION OF AN INTOLERABLE NUISANCE": BLACK FIFE AND DRUM MUSIC IN TENNESSEE, 1878

As New Year's Day 1878 dawned in Memphis, the city was in the throes of a vigorous municipal election campaign. John Flippin, the incumbent mayor, had run and won as a Democrat, but that party had refused to endorse his reelection and instead nominated John Johnson to oppose him. This led Flippin to campaign to the Republican Party and the Black community, though nominally still a Democrat. Further complicating matters was the emergence of a new, multiracial party, the Workingmen's Party, which was determined to organize at the ward level in Memphis and run candidates for all local offices. The campaign led to the usual rallies with brass band performances:

> Yesterday afternoon a colored band, in a spring wagon, blew their horns and pounded drums through the streets, in order to drum up a Flippin rally in the fifth and tenth wards last night. On the corner of Main and Madison the horses hitched to the wagon refused to pull—they reared up and sat down in the mud several times, nor would they move until a Johnson darky caught hold of them and said, "Come on, Flippin won't be elected mayor." This seemed to inspire the Democratic horses, and they moved on slowly. Even the horses kick against the bon ton child of fortune who is running down the aristocratic and independent fusion racetrack as a candidate for mayor.[1]

The next day, New Year's Day, brought a parade of the Independent Order of Pole Bearers, which the *Appeal* referred to as a "semi-military organization," in honor of the Emancipation Proclamation, with their brass band.[2]

Flippin's campaign, now vying for the Black Republican vote, began making use of fife and drum music at rallies, as duly reported by the *Public Ledger*:

> By means of considerable advertising and the spasmodic use of a wheezy little drum and a squeaking fife it became known last night that a Flippin meeting was to be held at a colored church in the Ninth ward. The Flippin orators were there, but not the crowd. Only seventy-five or eighty persons attended, and they were mostly Johnson and Anderson men.[3] Colonel Eaton seemed to be the general manager of the affair so far as the Flippin side was concerned. He urged the colored men to support the Republican party by voting for

Flippin, the opponent of the Democratic nominee. . . . Ed Shaw . . . is still on the Flippin side. Shaw is the big gun, who goes to all the meetings and usually has an escort preceded by such a band as the one which enlivened this occasion.[4]

That Ed Shaw carried with him a bodyguard comes as no surprise, as 1878 Memphis was probably not a collegial place for a Black politician, and threats were undoubtedly a regular occurrence. On the other hand, the presence of a fife and drum band with his bodyguard seems quite remarkable, to say the least. It is probable that both the guards and the band were provided to him by a benevolent society, possibly the Pole Bearers.

The importance of music, especially drums, in elections was not lost on the *Daily Memphis Avalanche*, which commented on it in an editorial: "Live and learn. The drum has, in this election, become so important a part of the machinery in ward politics that future candidates for the Mayoralty will do well to buy up all the old drums in town and keep their sweet music from drawing the voters to his opponent's 'whooping up' meetings."[5]

In June, a letter to the editor of the *Nashville American* complained about the preponderance of fife and drum music in Nashville during the political campaign, arguing that it was not only a nuisance, but incompatible with the ambitions of a big city:

"The ear-piercing fife and the spirit-stirring drum" is with us again, probably to remain until the fate of an alarming legion of candidates for county offices is decided away yonder in August, unless public indignation at the renewed infliction of an intolerable nuisance should consign it to the limbo of other ancient provincial absurdities long ago retired before the march of civilization and enlightenment. The municipal authorities should prohibit this abominable mode of advertising the street corner oration of candidates. Certainly some other method can be devised to give notice of such meetings than filling the streets with the deafening din of tortured sheepskin and the shrill shriek of a fife—blocking the sidewalks with the inevitable processions of juvenile Africans, frightening horses and endangering the lives and property of the citizens. The city has a further right and reason to protest against a custom which presents it to the visiting stranger in the light of a frontier village of the beginning of the century, instead of a city of some pretension to metropolitan dignity. The candidates' meetings may be advertised by sending around the usual banner, but the drum and fife should not be permitted to call attention to it. Those condemned to spend the summer months in the city should be exempted from this daily annoyance.[6]

By July, the Workingmen's Party had morphed into something called the National or Nationalist Party. This was probably the formal name for what historians have generally called the Greenback Party or the Greenback Labor Party, but it is worth noting that the Memphis press referred to it exclusively as the National Party, and its members as Nationalists. Being a working-class party inspired by organized labor and the European theories of socialism, it was of course a biracial organization, as almost all third parties in the South would be from then on. And perhaps for that reason, the National Party employed Black musicians extensively for their rallies and conventions. One such band paid the *Appeal* office a visit, and received a compliment in return: "The colored band employed by the National party to drum up the crowd for their ratification meeting at the Greenlaw opera house last night, serenaded the APPEAL office yesterday afternoon, and rendered excellent music."[7]

Given the political realities of the day, the Democrats also employed both a Black brass band and a Black fife and drum band when they held their large ratification meeting on the bluff in downtown Memphis. Blacks had voted heavily in the Democratic primary in June, and a number of Blacks were said to be supporting the party. The *Appeal* gave a description of the occasion:

The big Democratic rally was held on the Bluff last night. At seven o'clock the gun-squads began firing salutes, which were kept up till eight o'clock. At that time, the stand, which was erected on the south side of the Chickasaw Guards drill-ground, was filled, as were also the seats in front of the stand. A big bonfire out on the edge of the bluff lighted up the entire grounds, while the lamps of the stand shed a brilliant light far over the large crowd of citizens. Seats were provided for twelve hundred persons; these seats were filled, and far beyond and all around the speaker's stand, crowds of people, both white and colored, stood up for three hours and a half and listened to the speakers. At least two thousand people were present.

The Bluff City band (colored) made music for the occasion, and enlivened it considerably. A colored drum and fife corps also discoursed good music for the rally.[8]

The *Memphis Evening Herald* noted with amusement that the Democrats had likely hired Black Nationalist voters to carry their transparencies and play the fife and drum:

> It came off last night, that big Democratic "rally" which had been postponed from the previous evening. A brass band paraded the streets during the afternoon. At night, a bonfire on the bluffs and the firing of cannons announced to the public that the "unterrified" were to have a grand ratification meeting. A transparency with the words "Democratic and Conservative Rally, to-night, on the Bluffs" handled by a National voter, with the usual accompaniment of two drums and a fife was carried through the business portions of the city. A large stand had been erected within the enclosure of the Chickasaw's parade grounds on Front street, between Monroe and Union. This was brilliantly illuminated and the Bluff City brass band, colored, discoursed some very pretty pieces of music previous to the commencement of the speaking.[9]

Somewhat amazingly, the *Avalanche* became a fervent supporter of the Nationalists, the party of socialism and organized labor, and missed no opportunity to ridicule the Democrats during the campaign. As they noted, fife and drum music did not always work to draw a crowd, particularly when the Democrats employed it:

> From the grand stand of the grand rally it had been announced. The drummer at sundown slung his instrument from his sable neck, and perspired as he fought it unmercifully. The fifer puffed out his sweat-oozing cheeks, and blew his blow on his shrill instrument. The boss drum man hammered like one mad, and the commingled martial sound pierced the sultry air and summoned the unterrified to a "Grand Rally of the Democrats of the Third Ward at Ball's Hotel!!!!!!!!!!" Away they beat and blew and blew and beat. The wagon drivers on the corner listened attentively, and the small urchins gathered around and admired the pluck of those sweating musicians. On they labored, harder they worked, more frenzied became their wondrous stretch of energy. For two hours they kept up the din spurred on by the management who, each moment looked for the assembling of a vast horde of voters mad with eagerness to drink in the Bourbon eloquence. Still the fifer cracked his jaws and the drummer strained his

brachial muscles to their utmost extent. Finally there came a halt. The vexed atmosphere was relived from such excessive vibrations, the fifer sought relief by twitching his lips nervously, the drummer by gently rubbing his elbow. They lifted their voices unanimously and swore the jig was up, their contract completed and more. Then Mr. Moss, the orator of the evening looked around for his audience of the unterrified who were to meet him in the grand rally of the Third Ward. Tin pans, old tubs and dry goods boxes were overturned in the search, but the audience could be found nowhere concealed. Mr. Ball, the hotel proprietor, said his bar-keeper and barber could be gotten as a nucleus if Mr. Moss and the trio band would do their part in the contribution. The band rebelled, and Mr. Moss suggested an adjournment till to-night had better be taken. The debate ensuing on this motion was long and loud. Several divisions were called for, and it was only after tellers had been appointed and the ayes and noes taken that the motion was found to prevail. Then, the hotel keeper went back to his work and the other hand of the crowd strolled out. The enthusiasm of the Bourbon ticket then had its pleasing illustration.

A reconsideration was taken later on the arrival of about a dozen persons. The scruples of the musicians were overcome and again began the noise. The dozen was increased to twenty, and of these the grand rally of the Third Ward consisted.[10]

A day later, the *Avalanche* gave its rationale for its support of the National Party, reported National activities, and poked fun at another Democratic rally:

The white men and the colored men in the country are uniting on the National ticket in behalf of good officers and unity of feeling. . . . Tuesday the colored people have a "grand excursion, barbecue and campaign rally" at Raleigh, going by trains on the Louisville R. R. . . . Attend a Democratic meeting and then attend a National meeting, and see the difference in the enthusiasm. The laboring men are in earnest this time. . . . The Democratic fife and drum made a loud noise in the Ninth Ward last night, and drew to the sound of eloquence one hundred men! Analyze the glorious 100 however. Twenty were from the Second Ward, that hopping-up crowd that always moves out from the Courthouse; thirty were Nationals. The remainder hearkened to the Bourbon pibroch. Try it again, boys.[11]

A few days later, the same paper again noted the prevalence of fife and drum bands in connection with the election campaign, giving details of several rallies and barbecues:

> At Raleigh the colored people had a large excursion, though the attendance of candidates was not so large as at Kerrville. Brother Eldridge went out for the Nationals and talked to the crowd in his straight forward, earnest, honest way. In the city, the sunset marked the beginning of the noise of drum and fife summoning the voter to his ward meeting. In the Eighth Ward the Democrats tried to get up a meeting near the Poplar street market. When the AVALANCHE's seven-league-boot-man came by at nine o'clock about a dozen and a half of men were loafing around like the shadows of lost souls in purgatory. Orville Yerger was there, but failed to find a subject for his blood-warming eloquence.[12]

The *Appeal* was of course as partisan for the Democratic Party as the *Avalanche* was for the Nationalists, but it noted the delight that the city's Black residents took in the campaign, notably because of the fife and drum music involved with it:

> Hundreds of colored folks, the male sex especially and ranging up from youth to old age, enjoy the present political campaign hugely. They love to hear public speakers, especially when they go for each other in a lively personal manner, and they adore the noisy drums and the vile squeaking of the wry-necked fife. Whenever a squad of four, armed with a base [sic] drum, a snare drum, a fife and a transparency, parade the streets a hundred or more colored boys and men are sure to follow. They enjoy the music, believing it to be delicious. People do not agree about schools of music, however, and those who love the music of Verdi, Beethoven, Donizetti, etc. have no use for the clamorous and startling music of Richard Wagner, now called the music of the future.[13]

What did drummers get paid for playing in campaign rallies and events? An article in the *Avalanche* listed the going rate for drummers in Democratic rallies, and it was likely the same for the other parties as well: "As it costs $1 each to get men to walk behind the Democratic drum in a Ward meeting to 'add on the 'rousement,' how long will the bar'l last 'em?"[14]

In the *Appeal*, National rallies were inevitably described as failures, just as Democratic ones were described in the *Avalanche*, but the *Appeal* at least noted the prevalence of fife and drum bands at Nationalist functions:

> The third ward National rally, advertised to take place at the corner of Adams and Second streets, proved an entire failure. The fife and drum supporters paraded the streets, but to no effect, and "not a sheep stirred" as the disappointed dozen wended their steps elsewhere. The Nationals of the fourth and sixth wards, gathered to the strength of some three hundred, met at the corner of Beale and Main streets, opposite the old Galt house, to hear their advertised speakers. Mr. Marcus Jones presided, and introduced the candidates as they appeared on the platform. The third ward fife and drum were used at intervals of addresses.[15]

A day later, the *Appeal* gloated that "that fife and drum did not draw from the first ward as the Nationals of the third expected. And that transparent coffin was an insult offered our country trustee that others than gentlemen can only engage in."[16] But further down the same local column came a brief notice that would seem minor but proved to be ominous: "Yesterday, upon the request of Dr. Erskine of the board of health, Wharfmaster Kallaher ordered the use of a tug to convey the sanitary officer down the river, in order to meet the John Porter, said to have on board cases of yellow-fever, and instruct such steamer to pass on without landing."[17]

In the event, the Democrats won the elections of August, but soon the whole city of Memphis proved to be losers. New Orleans and Mobile had epidemics of yellow fever in July, and by August, cases were being reported in Memphis, despite numerous precautions taken by health officials. Thousands of white residents fled, but not all communities welcomed people from Memphis, as it was believed that yellow fever was transmissible from person to person (the role of mosquitoes in spreading yellow fever not being known at that time). Because Black residents seemed more resilient and resistant to the fever, possibly through acquired immunity, they served many essential functions in the city of Memphis during the epidemic. Blacks served as policemen and firemen, and the McClellan Guards and Zouave Guards patrolled the city and kept those in the quarantine camps from escaping and entering the city. When the first killing frost came in October, Memphis was a shell of its former self, its population reduced by half, the city basically bankrupt. It would soon surrender its charter to the state and legally cease to exist. November brought an advertisement in the *Appeal*, a statement from Samuel Farris, the president of the Pole Bearers, regarding what his order did to help the victims of yellow fever:

> As a society we, with the help of God, have been able to care for about seventy-seven sick members, buried ten, and extended a helping hand to thirty-eight different destitute families outside of our own order, at a cost of eight hundred and fifty-seven dollars and sixty cents, without receiving a dollar from any source except our own treasury. In conclusion we unite in thanking the good people of all sections of our country who came to the rescue of the poor people of our city at a time when death and starvation stared, especially the colored people, in the face. We pray that God may smile upon those who stood by the people without regard to race or class, and with a devotion to do more for our race than we even could do for ourselves. May God bless them all, we pray.[18]

Memphis was now smaller and sadder, but toward the end of November, some social events and festivities began to reappear. The *Public Ledger* noted a barbecue sponsored by the Pole Bearers: "The colored people held a barbecue last night at the Poll Bearer's hall [*sic*], corner of Second and Washington. Judging from the samples sent the LEDGER office, of the various eatables that graced the tables, it must have been a tempting feast. It is in charge of Miss R. Dickson, Miss A. Blair, Mr. J. Wiseman, R. Washington, William Stephens and other respectable colored people. It was such a success that it will be repeated Saturday night, when there will no doubt be a large crowd."[19] Despite the devastation, there were signs that Memphis's spirit and culture were continuing unbowed.

"THEY ARE ENTITLED TO THE THANKS OF THE COMMUNITY":
YELLOW FEVER AND BLACK FIFE AND DRUM MUSIC
IN TENNESSEE, 1879

The new year found Memphis economically depressed and demoralized. There was no mention of any kind of Black parade or musical event until May, when there was an announcement of a proposed brass band battle at Alexander's Park on May 21, between the Pole Bearers' band and the Young Men's Association Band. Ultimately, the event did not occur, due to "objections raised by the leader and manager (the bass drummer) of the

Y.M.A. Band."[20] The two bands in question were arguably the most popular Black bands in the city.

As was usually the case in Memphis, the Fourth of July occasioned street parading and picnicking in the city's Black community, with brass band music:

The fire brigade paraded early in the morning, and the Light Guards (white), M'Clellan Guards (colored) and the Zouave Cadets (colored), and Sons of Ham paraded in the evening . . . the colored folk had a ball at the Exposition building, and there were a number of private gatherings. . . . Our colored citizens entered heartily into the celebrations of the day. They appeared on the streets in holiday attire, and patronized the fireworks display in large numbers. During the day the colored military companies turned out and paraded the streets, headed by a brass band. They presented a fine soldierly appearance. The Sons of Ham on foot, and the Daughters of Ham in carriages, also engaged in a street parade, headed by a band. They carried flags and banners, and attracted no little attention as they passed through our principal streets. The colored people enjoyed and celebrated the fourth in their own way, and were the recipients of many flattering compliments from their white friends. At night they attended entertainments at the Exposition building and other places.

At James Park, the Sons of Ham, colored, gave a picnic for the purpose of raising funds to replenish their treasury, the amount so received to be dispensed among their sick and to provide burial for destitute members. Over five hundred persons were present.

At Alexander Park, four colored churches, composed of Avery chapel, Beale street church, Collins chapel and the Middle (Chelsea) Baptist church, held a church union picnic to raise means for church purposes. This was the elite picnic among the colored people, over one thousand persons being present.

The Memphis Zouaves, a colored company, assisted the two colored picnics by parading in their behalf, and contributed otherwise toward making both a success. They merit praise from their colored brethren.[21]

Unfortunately, within a few weeks, Memphis would again be in the throes of a yellow fever epidemic. Although the fever was not as severe in 1879, its recurrence heightened racial tensions, as the city sanitary authorities felt that the Black residents should be relocated to camps outside the city rather than being allowed to remain at home. The Black community, many of whom owned their homes, naturally resisted this initiative. As in the 1878 epidemic, the McClellan and Zouave Guards helped to maintain order, and when the fever was over, Memphis had been even further depopulated, to around 40,000 people, half Black and half white. The mustering out of the Black militias at the end of the epidemic was noted by the *Appeal*:

> The colored troops having been paid off by the city government broke camp yesterday, and no longer are the white tents seen on the bluffs. The paragraph is written with a view to introduce the well-known lines—And they folded their tents like the Arabs, And as silently stole away. But the sentiment is not in keeping with the truth. The M'Clellan Guards and the Zouave Guards struck their tents openly and not silently, and they marched away with parade, colors flying, drums beating, etc., to their homes. The colored troops, while on duty for the city, performed their task in a commendable manner, for which they are entitled to the thanks of the community. They are troops to be relied upon in yellow-fever times.[22]

Nashville also apparently had such a Black militia, known as the Spence Cadets, and they apparently had at least a drum corps, if not fifers. They are mentioned in connection with the annual Jubilee Day of Fisk University, a institutional holiday intended to commemorate the Jubilee Singers, who first began touring the world on October 1, 1871:

> At 10 A. M., the teachers, students and many friends of the Jubilee Singers spent the rest of the day at Clifton, about two and a half miles from Jubilee Hall. The good cheer of the party, the surrounding hills and river scenery and last, but not least, the ample repast made the day one long to be remembered for the pleasure it afforded all present. The Spence Cadets paraded and made the river and surrounding hills re-echo with the sound of the drum and cheers of the company. They were addressed by Prof. H. K. Spence and Mr. J. D. Burrus.[23]

December brought complaints from Memphis residents in connection with disorderly gatherings of street musicians downtown at the corner of Fourth and Washington Streets. It is unclear exactly what occasioned these gatherings, which were described as being interracial, but as it was the Christmas season, perhaps they were inspired by the holidays:

Citizens in the vicinity of the corner of Fourth and Washington streets complain of the intolerable nuisance created by the gathering of boys of all colors, grades and conditions, from morning until night, and even long after everybody ought to be in bed seeking rest from the labors of the day. These crowds indulge in rude behavior, vulgar, profane and obscene language, sometimes changing the monotony of the bedlamic pastime by fighting, etc. A hand-organ, a drum and a squeaking fife orchestrates occasionally for the amusement of the crowd. The details of what occurs there as related to us by a sufferer, call loudly for police interference.[24]

The addition of a hand-organ to the usual fife and drum was unique, to say the least, and quite original. But Black fife and drum music was clearly becoming less and less visible to the public eye.

"THANKS TO THE WORLD—MEMPHIS REDEEMED": BLACK FIFE AND DRUM MUSIC IN TENNESSEE, 1880

The new year of 1880 saw more mentions of fife and drum in Tennessee newspapers than the previous year, as it was an election year, and election campaigns always led to fife and drum activity. There was also a third party in the campaign, and third parties in the South seemed to have generated more fife and drum activity as well, since any third party effort knew they would be unsuccessful without some sort of fusion with the predominantly Black Republican Party in the Southern states.

However, the first article of interest in the new year appeared in February, when the *Daily Memphis Avalanche* reported the establishment of a lodge of the Independent Pole Bearers No. 2 "near Bartlett." This chapter was established at Oak Grove and was associated with the Oak Grove Missionary Baptist Church. Both the society chapter and the church still exist: "The News says the Poll Bearers No. 2 [*sic*] organized a lodge near Bartlett last week under a charter from the State of Tennessee, Henry Becton, Robert Bartlett, Wm. Bowles and Archie Redditt being the charter members.[25] The lodge is for charitable and benevolent purposes only, and is composed of many members who are of the best class of the colored people."[26]

The already-noted trend toward brass bands rather than fife and drum bands was seemingly accelerating, as the Republican mass meeting to ratify the nomination of Garfield and Arthur on the bluff in Memphis featured the Pole Bearers' band, which "occupied a space on the stand and played a number of airs to draw the masses to the spot."[27] Perhaps the highlight of the speaking was the speech made by the Black political leader Edward Shaw, who so often provoked white Memphians: "The speaker then went into a discussion of the 'fraud' question, alluding, among other things, to the cannon taken from Memphis to Helena, Ark. to carry an election. Since the war, he said, 36,000 colored men had been killed. Yet they speak of raising the 'bloody shirt.' Who wouldn't raise the 'bloody shirt' under the circumstances. Give us our rights as fellow-citizens. That is all we want."[28]

While the Republicans thus rallied with a brass band, the National Party, or Greenbackers, held a rally at the Greenlaw Opera House that involved fife and drum musicians, although it was evident that their numbers had been greatly reduced since 1878:

> The greenbacks held counsel at the Greenlaw opera house last night, but they failed to arouse much enthusiasm, despite the fact that two of their biggest southern guns were on hand to eloquently illustrate their principles, and the good to be derived by the general adoption of the policy they hope to advance. Judging from last night's effort, the greenback party is hardly the coming power, for instead of increasing as their ball rolls, it is apparently melting to smaller proportions. . . . Something near the hour of 9 o'clock the Chelsea greenback club, twenty or thirty strong boys and rag tags included, preceded by a fife and drum with a few banners, marched noisily down Main street, and entered the opera house. The boys failed to rally in anything like a respectable force, and the movement indicates a rather slender following.[29]

At least part of the problem was that the 1878 alliance between the Black Republicans and the Nationalists was breaking up, as evidenced by a confrontation between Ed Shaw and a white Nationalist at a rally near the intersection of Pigeon Roost Road and Hollyford Road southeast of the city:

> A free-for-all political hurrah was had at Nabors' Grove, Pigeon Roost road, last Saturday. The conspicuous figures in the entertainment were Harry Hill, National candidate for criminal court judge, and Ed Shaw, Republican candidate for sheriff. The eminent statesman who is willing to serve the county as criminal court judge made a speech which we have heard commented on in severe terms. His appeals are said to have been directed to the worst passions of the colored

mob, who seemed to predominate. Ed Shaw delivered a characteristic harangue. Mr. Irwin, a Nationalist, made a statement which the colored candidate for sheriff politely designated as a a lie. Mr. Irwin struck Shaw, and there was a little fight, in which neither got hurt, as they were promptly separated. Rev. James Lott was on the ground, as Shaw's friend, it is supposed, and some of the spectators say he went to his buggy for a pistol when the hostilities commenced; but as no weapon was displayed, it is not absolutely certain that the great divine desired to shed anybody's blood. A spectator reports that the colored people did not seem to fancy Shaw, and that the colored drummers endeavored to drown his voice by everlastingly banging their drums. As Shaw aspires to the position of leading peace-officer of the county, he ought to have been smarter than to provoke a fight in his first campaign speech.[30]

However, the same column of the same paper gave a briefer account that offers different and contradictory information, putting the incident on Sunday instead of Saturday, and on the Hollyford Road instead of Pigeon Roost Road. Since Hollyford Road (modern Airways) and Pigeon Roost Road (modern Lamar) cross each other, it is possible that Nabors' Grove was located where they meet, but as that location was at that time beyond the taxing district limits, the city directories of that era offer no information in that regard.[31] The county political scene soon became a frantic effort on the part of Democrats to find a way to prevent Ed Shaw from being elected sheriff. While the newspapers claimed that their opposition was due to Shaw's corruption and not his color, many Democrats made statements to the effect that his candidacy was a threat to "our people." By the end of July, the *Appeal* was whipping up sentiment by blatant appeals to racial conflict, complaining that the "Radical drums and fife stampeded a horse attached to a delivery wagon, and also a saddled horse, last evening."[32] But that was mild, compared to the rest of the column:

People from the county complain of Mississippi negroes crossing the line into Tennessee for electioneering and voting purposes at the August election. . . . "If intelligence is worth anything, and is superior to ignorance, then the white people of Memphis and Shelby county who are Democrats will elect their ticket over the negroized ticket headed by Ed Shaw." Such was the remark uttered to an APPEAL commissioner by a prominent Memphian yesterday. . . . It is well known that on election day the negro Republicans will attempt to capture the polls or voting precincts in several wards. This should not be permitted by the white men of the Democratic faith. The vile abuse heaped on such men as Major Murphy on election day by such violent negroes as Ed Shaw will not pass unrebuked if repeated on the fifth of August.... If every Democrat goes to the polls and works for the success of the ticket during election day, the ticket will leave Memphis with from twenty-five hundred to three thousand majority. It is too late at this day to drop back into negro Radical rule. The white race of people predominate in this county, and such is far better for the black race than if a Radical gang, headed by a negro, should take possession of the important county offices.[33]

The *Public Ledger* of the same day noted the fife and drum band at a Republican rally on the bluff, probably the same band that had frightened the horses: "The republicans held a 'rally' last night on the bluffs. There were the usual accompaniments, such as a big bass drum, little kettle drum, fife and a small cannon. It was near nine o'clock before the speakers appeared upon the platform. The crowd was a mixture of white democrats, black republicans and slightly tinctured nationals."[34]

The enthusiasm of Blacks for political campaigns was a constant annoyance to the editors of the Memphis newspapers, who felt that they should ignore such things and attend to their labors instead. Wherever they could, the editors called attention to the lack of available labor, blaming it on Black citizens: "On account of the political campaign this fall negro labor is going to be scarce. Many will prefer to run around the country behind a drum and fife and listen to stump speaking, rather than picking cotton or working upon steamboats. Some enterprising individual could do well by securing about one hundred of the emigrants now coming south and employ them in unloading boats as they arrive. All masters of steamboats would prefer to employ them if they could be made reliable. The negro will not do to depend on."[35]

In August, a Nationalist rally on the Collierville square was accompanied by a bass drum, attracting a crowd of over a hundred, mostly Blacks, to hear the Shelby County attorney general G. P. M. Turner speak on behalf of the National Party:

A grand rally of nationals came off here on Saturday, the last day of July. At any rate that is what it was called in the printed notices posted up around town for several days before. A colored man with a big drum called together a crowd of about 30 white men and 100 negroes at the usual speaking place, near the corner of the public square. Attorney-General G. P. M. Turner mounted the stand, and without introduction began his oration. His mellow voice floated smoothly over the rough piles of brick, lumber, sand, and other material collected for new buildings at "the usual speaking place," and was wafted by the passing breeze all up and down the lateral streets and about the public square, in cadences mellifluous as "the breathing flute's soft notes." The streets and stores were full of people, trading, talking and walking about, persons of different colors and political opinions who did not care a dime whether Gen. Turner led or followed the national party. One colored gentleman was explaining to a group of his Senegambian brethren the nature and consequences of Adam's fall, which "brought death into the world and all our woe." But Gen. T. soon broke up these side shows, for when, after speaking a short time, he became enthused with his subject and gave utterance to his sentiments in tones as loud and deafening as the fog horns upon the Atlantic cost, his audience became gradually larger until every man in hearing who could possibly do so rallied to the spot regardless of political preferences or "previous condition of servitude."[36]

On the same page, the *Avalanche* also gave an account of a Nationalist rally at the Beale Street Market that featured a fife and drum band:

The crowd was not large, and the dark night was made blacker by the color that predominated. The colored brother was in a decided majority; in fact, it was only here and there that a light speck indicated a person of the Caucasian race. Being a party of the people, the national greenback managers showed their contempt for the luxury of the bloated bondholder by failing to provide any stand for the speakers or reporters. A table that had up to that time borne only chickens, beets and geese, was set out as a rostrum for the speakers and the reporters were fain to get a place wherever they could. The Avalanchian, being especially favored by providence, secured a seat at one end, and deposited the broadest part of his person on a meat bench, between the scaly feet of several young nationals of decided color. In front, one of the faithful engineered a transparency with characteristic mottoes thereon, and two others lured the passer by to the spot with the inspiring racket of a drum and fife. When the crowd had finally assembled, it was composed of about equal numbers of nationals and republicans. They were counted, to see if there was enough to get up a respectable cheer, and the orators fell into line back of the vegetable and poultry table.[37]

The *Avalanche* had been an enthusiastic supporter of the Nationalists in the election of 1878, proclaiming that it was the party of the working people and of racial reconciliation. Two years later, the paper had come around to full endorsement of the Democrats and white supremacy. Apparently the emergency of a Black man, Ed Shaw, running for Shelby County sheriff was enough to bring them back into the Democratic fold. In the end, the Democrats largely swept the elections of August 5. White Republicans voted against Ed Shaw for sheriff, although he was their own party's nominee, and many Blacks voted for Phil Athy, the Democratic candidate for sheriff, either because they had personal dislike for Shaw or because they feared a wholesale repercussion upon their community should he be elected.

A month later, in September, Memphis held a huge festival and parade to announce that the city was now recovered from the effects of the late epidemics and was now ready and "open for business." The parade involved both Black and white citizens and was said to "eclipse all other processions of like character ever gotten up in Memphis."[38] The *Appeal* gave a detailed description of the divisions in the parade that included Black musicians:

The second division, under the command of Captain S. T. Carnes, moved in the following order: The division was preceded by the Young Men's association brass band, a colored organization. The Bluff City Grays followed the Chicks with a turnout of twenty men. The Light Guards came next, with sixteen men. The Zouaves were next in line with twelve men. The Hannibal Guards closed the military division with a turnout of sixteen men.[39] The military companies were followed by the Plumbers, Gas and Steam Fitters association, who made quite a respectable turnout.

The third division, commanded by Marshal Robert Galloway, was as follows: Music was furnished by the Pole-Bearers band, colored. The Danbury fire-engine, surmounted by the horns, came first. The Vollintine engine, with its eagle perches aloft, followed. Then came the Desoto engine, bearing its swan with her young. The Washington engine came next, with its bust of Washington, and the motto "In God We Trust." The Hook and Ladder company concluded the display of the department, having an elegant canopy, under which a lad was seated.[40]

The long day of parading and speeches was ended with a fireworks display on the bluffs overlooking the Mississippi River, for which there was actually a published program, one of the entries of which was "Thanks to the World—Memphis Redeemed." One wonders if the words were celebrating the end of Reconstruction as much as the recovery from the fever.[41]

October brought items in the Memphis papers that some Black citizens were organizing to support Hancock and English, the Democratic nominees for president and vice-president, and this met with considerable approval from the *Appeal*: "The colored people who will support Hancock and English in November will hold a mass-meeting to-night at the Greenlaw Operahouse. There should be a colored Hancock and English club in every city ward and country district. The Pole-bearers band will head the colored Democratic procession on the streets at 3 o'clock this afternoon. To-night the colored Democrats who will vote for Hancock and English will hold a mass-meeting at the Greenlaw Operahouse."[42] However, the next day's *Avalanche* account of the resulting gathering gave far more coverage to the drum corps than the brass band:

A call was printed in Sunday's newspapers, signed by a large number of colored men. Its object was to form a colored Hancock and English club at the Greenlaw opera house Monday might. The call read, "Broom's operahouse," but this was a mistake.

Between 7 and 8 o'clock last night a colored band played several lively airs on the balcony in front of the opera house, and the crowd began to assemble. By 8 1/2 o'clock probably 60 colored men were present, nearly all seated in the parquette. The white men were much more numerous, and the assemblage, white and black, aggregated about 200.

Then a small colored man with a big drum, followed by a large colored man with a little drum, the latter by a herculean colored man bearing aloft a transparency with the legend: "Seventh Ward Colored Democratic Club," and in their wake a half dozen more colored men of assorted sizes marched up stairs. They filed into the side door leading to the dress circle, and once inside, the men ceased to beat the drums and looked around for seats. But upon another colored man saying in a slightly elevated tone: "beat de drums, I tole ye," four brawny arms began swinging like sledge hammers, four drum-sticks began vigorously pounding due inoffensive drum-heads, a great cheer leaped from a hundred throats, and the time for action had arrived.[43]

The year was almost devoid of fife and drum references in Nashville, where they were usually numerous, but there was at least one mention, in connection with a political rally in October: "After a laborious performance by a drum corps, a small mixed crowd of two hundred gathered last night on Broad street, in front of a saloon, between Market and College, to hear Cols. R. E. Thompson of Lebanon, and John H. Savage, of McMinnville."[44] Locating a rally in front of a saloon was probably a good, if novel, idea for collecting a crowd, although whether the "drum corps" included a fife is left unclear by the article. Clearly, at least in the cities, the trend was toward brass bands for most Black social and formal functions, with fife and drum music relegated to political rallies and events in the rural areas.

"THE BOYS OUGHT TO BE IN BETTER BUSINESS": BLACK FIFE AND DRUM MUSIC IN TENNESSEE, 1881

By the new year of 1881, fife and drum music or drum corps music was largely relegated to informal squads of boys in the Black community of Memphis who emulated the Black militia companies that they admired during processions up the streets of the city. Almost all formal events in the Black community involved the larger brass bands, but the young boys still chose the fife and drum: "A squad of boys, several dozen strong and in variegated summer garb, marched to the melody of a snare drum down Main street near 10 o'clock last night. Their commander appeared familiar with Upton, and gave orders after that military author's directions, and he didn't seem to think there was any burlesque about his share of the business. A motley throng followed, and sleepy street car mules showed signs of alarm at the youthful warriors."[45] The boys were doubtless inspired by the kinds of events that were described in connection with the Fourth of July by the *Memphis Daily Appeal*:

Alexander Park. At the above-named place, yesterday, the Independent Pole-Bearers, a colored organization, and their friends, indulged in a grand picnic. The Pole-Bearers, headed by their officers, paraded on the streets in the fore-noon. At the park a promenade concert and dancing were the attractions of the day and night.

The colored people of the city and surrounding country enjoyed the Fourth yesterday at Estival Park, where a review and dress parade of the colored military companies, who, in the forenoon had a procession on the street was given. Several civic or benevolent societies participated. During the day and last night scores of entertainments were presented on the grounds, and dancing was indulged in up to an early hour this morning.[46]

The boys continued at their drilling and drumming practice throughout the summer, much to the annoyance of nearby residents and the *Public Ledger*: "Idle darkies of youthful years delight in pounding the base [*sic*] and rattling the snare drum in spots where they think nobody will complain at the nuisance. It becomes awfully monotonous and disagreeable to the neighbors after three or four night's performance, lasting from three to five hours a night. The boys ought to be in better business."[47]

Perhaps because of similar complaints, in August, the *Nashville American* reported that Councilman Parker of the General Council of Nashville had put forward a proposed ordinance to prohibit the beating of drums or other noisy means of advertising political meetings. It passed on first reading.[48] Whether the ordinance passed the other two readings and became a law is something the Nashville papers remained silent about.

"TO THE GREAT ANNOYANCE OF DECENT PEOPLE": BLACK FIFE AND DRUM MUSIC IN TENNESSEE, 1882

In the new year of 1882, fife and drum activity started early, as Memphis was having a campaign for school visitors, which we would today call school board members: "The shrill fife and the rattling drum sent forth their discordant tones upon nature's caloric last night. It was only an effort to marshal the darkies and their friends and arouse a little interest in nominations for School Visitors."[49] But the political scene in Tennessee soon became extremely confused, to say the least. Since 1878, there had been three parties: the Republicans, the Democrats, and the Workingmen's/National/Greenback Party. The latter was now back to calling themselves the Workingmen's Party. But during 1882, both the Democrats and the Republicans split into factions that ran separate slates of candidates. The nature of the dispute was over Tennessee's high bonded debt, much of it having to do with railroads. Both parties split into factions that wanted to adjust the debt, called "Readjustors," and those that wanted to raise taxes to pay off the bondholders, called "high-tax" on the Republican side, and the Blue Sky Party on the Democratic side. So in effect, there were now five parties running for local and state offices in Tennessee, and the result was more than the usual amount of rallies and mass meetings, with a resulting increase in Black fife and drum music.

The *Public Ledger* of Memphis noted the use of fife and drum music in connection with a high-tax Republican rally in the Chelsea neighborhood of Memphis in July:

> The high taxers, or railroad debt paying Republicans held a grand ratification meeting in Chelsea, Thursday night. General Williamson, W. M. Porter, Trobridge, and other leaders of the faction thought it to be a favorable time to pierce the low tax lion in his den. They invaded the peaceful suburb headed by a fife and drum, followed by a juvenile company of senegambians,[50] armed with wooden guns, who executed the manual a la Chickasaw Guards. As they passed Tom Graham's corner they were at a reverse arms, as if going to a funeral; and it proved to be a funeral for the high taxes. When they came to a halt on Fourth street there were only about ten men and as many women and boys present. General Williamson opened the ball, telling the little crowd that they must beware of the bolting wing of the Republican party. A voice: "You're a high tax, ain't you." "Yes, we are a high State credit party." "Den you is a bolter and had better go home." Thereupon General Williamson subsided and was followed by Porter and Trobridge. Porter designated all the leaders on the other side as General and Colonel So and So. A voice, "Dey must be all big men and I reckon bigger dan you." "Oh! go home" and other like observations. This chilled the ardor of the speakers, and they finally determined to go home, and they had done well to remain there before they spent money on such a cold trail. The Democrats have nothing to fight in Chelsea except the Shea and McMahon ticket.[51]

The next day, the *Avalanche* printed a reference to fife and drum music in their daily "They Say" column, which was given to popular conversations and rumors on the streets of Memphis: "(They say) that with the campaign comes the drum and fife, the blatherskite orators, the noisy yelling mob, the street corner and pot house politicians, the night meetings in wards and on the bluff, and many other ills that the free American ballot slinger is heir to every few years, or oftener if desired."[52]

In September, a report from a Chattanooga correspondent of the *Nashville American* mentioned the use of fife and drum music in connection with a campaign rally for Judge Joseph H. Fussell, the gubernatorial candidate of the Blue Sky Party. The high degree of fragmentation in Tennessee politics in 1882 made the Black vote crucial to candidates' election hopes, and the use of fife and drum bands was viewed as a way to attract Black voters to rallies:

> Gen. Bate and ex Gov. Marks addressed a large and enthusiastic crowd at the Court House Saturday morning and night. The telling remarks of both were lustily cheered by the true Democrats, and it is unsafe to wager on their opponents on the result of the Hamilton county vote. As I write a drum and fife are parading the streets calling the Fussell-Hawkins-Beasley crowd together to listen to their honied words at James Hall to-night. It is a mighty poor crowd of supporters that have to be called together with fife and drum.[53]

The highly fractious campaign led to increased tensions between the factions, and a degree of harassment against various candidates. The use of city authority to threaten or harass candidates and musicians was noted by the *Daily Memphis Avalanche* in early October: "Attorney-General Turner was so much engrossed by the minstrels last night that he forgot to have Gov. Hawkins arrested for incendiary utterances at the Greenlaw opera-house, as he had threatened. . . . The drum corps who furnished music for the workingmen's meeting last night were arrested on their return to the city, for playing in the streets. The workingmen were very indignant at the action of the police, claiming that it was unfriendly and unwarranted."[54]

As plenty of other articles indicate, the Memphis police usually took a decidedly hands-off approach to public fife and drum activity, even late at night, so the arrest of this drum corps seems suspicious, to say the least. It would seem that they were probably targeted because they had been hired by the Workingmen's Party. Further details were given about the drum corps, procession, and rally in an article elsewhere on the same page of the *Avalanche*:

> There was a meeting of the labor unions of South Memphis at Charley Barrell's Garden, Ft. Pickering, last night, which was largely attended. The meeting was augmented by a delegation from Chelsea Union No. 6, which marched the entire distance to the sound of martial music, led by Mr. R. A. Clark, vice-president of the Trades Assembly. It would naturally be supposed that workingmen would be rather verdant in the mysteries of conducting a campaign, but the vim which they are inaugurating the present one augurs well for them. There

were delegations from several ladies' unions present, who seem to take great interest in the success of the labor ticket.[55]

The use of fife and drum musicians and the integrated nature of the meeting were undoubtedly related, and as the Black delegates spoke of their realities and hopes, the meeting was constantly harassed by hecklers:

Mr. Epps was then called on. He is a colored man of probably 70 years of life, and gave a characteristic speech, resembling very much in appearance old Milt Barlow, of minstrel fame. He said: I want to be a free man; God made me free and equal with everybody, and if we wish to remain so, we, the men that make fortunes for the rich, must try and do something for ourselves. We must find out the cause of meat being 18c and 20c per lb, which places it beyond our reach, and try and remedy the great evil. We can only do that by joining ourselves together in a band of brothers, a band so strong that monopoly can-not break it.

Mr. Epps gave some applicable anecdotes of slavery time, which would equal Billy Emerson in pith and point. He advised all to stand together, for united we could stand, divided we would fall. We have seven hardworking men that we want to send to the legislature, and we can do it. They know the needs of the laboring masses from bitter experience, and they will do their best for us. At this point a gang of roughs attempted to disturb the meeting by calling out, "Hook!" "Hook!" but they were summarily checked.[56]

Mr. Waite then took the stand, but on attempting to speak was again interrupted, when quite a commotion ensued, which resulted in the mob being put out of the garden. . . . Mr. Martin, of Kerrville, was called to the stand. Mr. Martin expressed his thanks for the honor of addressing a band of workingmen, and gave a series of the wrongs endured by the small farmers of the country. He said we of the coun-try send you greetings. We are with you in the attempt to break the shackles of the old parties, and will be with you in November. If the young man who attempted to break up this meeting had made the same attempt in the second civil district, he would never have known which end went out first. It was a disgrace to the community. In the time of slavery we were respected by our masters, but to-day the rich look down on anyone who is poor. To-day he was offered 10c a pound for cotton that he had labored twelve long months to raise, and had to pay 19c a pound for meat. A few weeks ago they gave us

50c a hundred for picking cotton, and the landlords swore they could pay no more. We organized a union and every laboring man in that district joined it, and to-day are getting $1 a hundred. You here in the city have twice the chances we have to band together, but rest assured if you can stand together here, we of the country, will stand like a rock on the labor platform.[57]

The *Public Ledger* of the same day gave a differing account of the police interference with the Workingmen's drummers: "A number of political pow wowers, who played the bass drum and fife along Main street after midnight, were warned to give other people a chance to sleep hereafter, and allowed to go."[58] A day later, the *Ledger* stated, "Memphis is a musical community, so far as the fife and bass drum can make it so."[59] Even the usually good-natured *Avalanche* was evidently tiring of fife and drum bands by October, or the people of Memphis were, for the "They Say" column was fairly nasty toward drummers: "(They Say) That the Memphis drum corps should never be permitted to accept an encore. . . . That a drum and fife corps has no legal right to march through the streets of the city at one o'clock in the morning and disturb the slumbers of quiet citizens with infernal noise—not music. Other people outside of the drum corps have legal rights that are bound to be respected and all midnight nuisances should be abated by the police even if they appear under the guise of music."[60]

Although there was not as much mention of Black fife and drum music in Nashville, it certainly went on, as this description of a Fussell rally indicated:

Yesterday afternoon a huge white banner was borne along the streets by some colored boys with drums. The many people whom it passed read upon it an announcement that the "Citizens Democratic legislative candidates" would speak at the Decatur depot at night. Thither a reporter took his way on a street car at 8:30. Upon arriving there he found no one, and upon inquiring at a neighboring house, learned that only one man was present when the candidates arrived. They were greatly disappointed, and as their audience was already unanimously for them, it was decided to adjourn the meeting sine die. The audience wended its way to a saloon not four miles off for consolation, and there the reporter found it, and was told that the candidates were previous in leaving, as fully five hundred men came up after they left. Whether it considered itself equal to five hundred, or was given to capricious freaks of the imagination, could not be discovered. But further inquiry failed to corroborate the statement.[61]

A couple of days later, people were complaining about another fife and drum band in Memphis, as reported by the *Appeal*: "The attention of the police is called to an incendiary band, composed of two bass drums and a hysterical fife, which every now and then perambulates the city to the great annoyance of decent people."[62] A week later, the same paper noted that "the ear-piercing fife and the loud-sounding drum are in order for a week to come."[63] The elections in early November brought an end to much of the fife and drum activity, at least that which was in the public eye.

"THIS IS A FRIGHTFUL NUISANCE": BLACK FIFE AND DRUM MUSIC IN TENNESSEE, 1883

As the years progressed, the newspapers started giving less attention to Black parades and picnics altogether. When they were mentioned, it was generally in the briefest of terms, unless there was some sort of fight or trouble at them. Music was often not discussed at all, and when it was, it was generally a brass band rather than a fife and drum band. The *Appeal's* account of a Black Fourth of July picnic in Covington, Tipton County, was typical: "The colored people were also patriotic enough to go in for a big picnic near town, which they kept up nearly all night."[64]

Although the newspapers did not mention any specific fife and drum music incidents in Tennessee during 1883, a bitter editorial in Nashville's *Daily American* suggests that there was a considerable amount of fife and drum music in that city, at least enough to make an editor angry:

There is one reform which we hope to see instituted by the new municipal government, and that is the abolition of the abominable custom of advertising political meeting with drum and fife. This is a frightful nuisance and unworthy the dignity of a cross-roads village. Every election we have in the city is dreaded more for this infliction than any other. Strangers from other cities who witness this antiquated method of attracting public attention smile at our verdancy, and often ask the meaning of the grotesque parade of the drum corps followed by gangs of yelling street gamins. The deafening noise disturbs business men in their counting-rooms, school children at their books and frightens horses in the street, and licenses the roustabout to yell and jostle people on the sidewalks, and in every other way make the sidewalks hideous.

Nashville ought to have outgrown this provincial and clumsy method of advertisement. The banner announcing meetings or public speakings could be carried around quite as well without the monotonous and deafening rattle of drums. There is too much of it. There ought to be an ordinance against it. It is one great comfort of the close of the municipal election just past, and we fervently pray that we shall be delivered from it during the election next year. Nobody desires it. Everybody feels relieved that it will cease at least until another election, and that—"Silence, like a poultice comes, To heal the blows of sound."[65]

"THE DRUMMER AND FIFER ARE WELL-DEFINED ENEMIES OF SOCIETY": BLACK FIFE AND DRUM MUSIC IN TENNESSEE, 1884

In March of 1884, the *Daily American* in Nashville gave a lengthy obituary for a most remarkable Black man, a fiddler and drummer named Fleming Higgins. His accomplishments, as listed in the article, show him to have been a most important figure in the early years of Black fife and drum music in Tennessee:

Fleming Higgins, the old colored man who died in North Nashville recently, was born in Rockingham county, Va., in 1795, eighty-nine years ago. He came to Nashville in 1810, seventy-four years ago, and enjoyed good health all his life, dying of old age. He was a remarkable old man. He was a stone mason by trade. For many years he was the leading violinist of the town. He furnished music at the old Nashville Inn, at the ball given by the citizens to Lafayette in 1825, and also at the Hermitage on the occasions of Lafayette's visit there. He was the musician at the reception to President Monroe in 1819, and played the violin at nearly all of the public and private entertainments given in the early days of Nashville. He beat the drum at all parades and musters of the old State militia. He beat for the Harrison Guards and Nashville Blues, and beat drum for the volunteers when they were being raised for both the Florida and Mexican wars. He was called in those days "Flem, the fiddler and drummer." He helped to build the foundation of the Hermitage Mansion. He worked on the rubble stone work of the State Capitol from its commencement to its completion. He could remember men, days and dates, better than many men who could read and write. He could not be beaten in prompting and giving orders in the ball room, never making mistakes. Old Hickory thought well of Flem and often had him at the Hermitage to make music.[66]

By May, the *Avalanche* was reporting the coming of election meetings, with the usual attendant drum and fife music: "(They say) That ward meetings, conventions, stump speaking and elections are coming around again with the squeaky fife and noisy drum in torchlight processions; the office-seeking and hungered candidate will break out from his lair in the jungle of obscurity and will tear around town for a few weeks."[67]

While some residents and newspapers complained about the annual noise or music of elections, music stores were of course thrilled, as the need for drums and fifes was a windfall for them. One such store, Hollenberg's in Memphis, ran an ad in the *West Tennessee Whig* in Jackson, Tennessee, in July, proclaiming "Drums and Fifes for Campaign Cheap."[68] A week later, the *Avalanche* in Memphis was continuing to remind people that the election campaign and fife and drum music were about to rev up in earnest: "(They say) That the rolling drum and the squeaking fife are heralding the approach of the office-seeking contest. The drummer and the fifer are well-defined enemies of society and should be suppressed as nuisances and destroyers of the public rest at and after midnight."[69]

The majority-Black Haywood County was a hotbed of Republican politics, but accounts of fife and drum music there were rare. One exception was in connection with a speech held by Judge Frank T. Reid in Brownsville in July, where a bass drum was beaten to try to ramp up enthusiasm at an otherwise tepid meeting:

BROWNSVILLE, TENN., July 25—Judge Frank T. Reid spoke here to-day to an audience consisting of 250 negroes, 50 Democrats and 25 white Republicans. His speech was a duplicate of what has been reported from other points. His appeal to the old Whigs fell stillborn, as there was [sic] not more than six, if that many present. It was the coldest political meeting ever seen in Brownsville. One negro did most of the applauding on the base [sic] drum. A glowing tribute to the magnetism of Blaine did not wake one cheer. Reid says duty and not ambition is what forced him from the bosom of his family into this work.[70]

For some reason, the election of 1884 proved to be a difficult one for Republicans, and the Memphis papers reported that, even with the device of fife and drum music to try to build up enthusiasm, there was sparse attendance at Republican rallies compared to Democratic ones: "Their meetings, in spite of the darkies' fancy for the drum and fife, have not been anything like so largely attended during the campaign as those of the Democracy. The crowds at the ward meetings of the latter are always large—larger than they have been in several years, and the greatest interest seems to be taken in the contest by all classes of people. The success of the ticket depends upon this being kept up until the polls close."[71]

The fife and drum phenomenon seemed less pronounced in Chattanooga and Hamilton County, despite the fairly large Black community there, and was rarely mentioned, but in August of 1884, a highly competitive sheriff's campaign brought drum corps into the streets: "The Sheriff's contest is waxing warm. It promises to be one of the most exciting contests ever held in the county. The chances to-day are strongly in favor of Conner, the Independent. The strong fight is being made against the so-called court-house ring, but it is manipulated by very shrewd, influential men, who thoroughly understand how to conduct elections and have a strong hold on the negro vote. To-night, mass meetings were held in all parts of the city, and the drum corps are parading the streets followed by the howling mobs."[72]

Despite the frequent calls for an ordinance against fife and drum bands, Nashville rallies were still convoked by them, including a large Republican gathering at the Public Square in August: "The Republican rally, that has been the subject of much anticipation for many days past, was held last night on the Square. By the inviting notes of fifes and drums, a large crowd of 1,500 to 2,000 persons, mostly negroes, had gathered to hear, discussed from a party standpoint, the political issues of the hour."[73]

While campaigns were usually vigorous in Tennessee, the 1884 one, particularly in Memphis, was lukewarm and lackluster according to the *Avalanche*, whose editor was hoping a gubernatorial debate might stir things up:

> The debate between Gov. Bate and Judge Reid Saturday night will act as a reviver of political interest in Memphis. There seems to be now actually no sort of concern about politics. There is no beating of drums, no torchlight procession, no betting of consequence, no speech making and no inspiring racket. A lively debate between the gubernatorial candidates can scarcely fail to arouse the enthusiasm

of both parties. The average citizen too is anxious to see how the two orators can chaw each other up and yet manage to survive.[74]

All the same, the Nashville papers received the usual complaints against fife and drum bands, such as one sent to the editor by a man who signed himself "Inquirer" under the heading "A Sufferer's Complaint":

> Is there no law to protect people who drive good horses? In the day time they are liable to run into one of the abominable fife and drum processions which are allowed to beat through the streets at will. They are generally headed by an ignorant fifer who has no judgment, and had rather see a horse run away than stop his delightful music. In the evening here comes a bicycle with a headlight that will scare any horse, particularly when the ride runs right into the horse without warning, as was done last night in front of the Nicholson House and a very fine animal injured for a $10 bicycle. Ladies who drive are in constant danger.[75]

The government of the Memphis Taxing District proposed an ordinance that seemed aimed at Black churches in particular, banning any assembly of people in any church for any purpose after midnight, and specifically mentioning the beating of drums:

> An ordinance was presented by T. J. Graham declaring it a misde-meanor for any number of persons to assemble or remain assembled in any church building or place within the Taxing District after 12 o'clock at night, to the disturbance or disquiet of any person or per-sons in the District, whether such assembly be religious, political or otherwise, or whether the disturbance be by loud speaking, preach-ing, singing, shouting, beating drums or otherwise, and any person being at and a party of any such assembly creating such disturbance shall be guilty of a misdemeanor and upon conviction therefor before the president of the Board of Fire and Police Commissioners shall be fined not less than $1 nor more than $50. Passed on first reading.[76]

The end of the election on November 4 brought defeat for the Democrats by and large, but the *Appeal* could not avoid a celebration anyway: "No more will the drummer drum nor the fifer fife, and there will be rest for the weary until the next political contest."[77] A week later, the anti–fife and drum ordinance in Memphis was up again before the Taxing District Board, but this time it was referred to the district attorney for revisions.[78] On the same day, committees were meeting in Nashville to plan for a large torchlit procession of Democrats on November 13, to which had been invited two "colored drum corps."[79] The next day's account of the parade made it clear that at least one of the participating bands was a "colored field band" (that is, a fife and drum band).[80] It is probably noteworthy that, without exception, all of the year's mentions of Black fife and drum bands were in connection with political activity.

"HEADED BY A FIFE AND DRUM": BLACK FIFE AND DRUM MUSIC IN TENNESSEE, 1885

By 1885, fife and drum music was not nearly as visible in the state of Tennessee as it had once been, yet in March, the genre of music figured in a debate in the General Assembly over a proposed voter registration law, which was intended to combat alleged voter fraud. A legislator asked if there had been any proven instances of voter fraud: "Mr. Binns stated that a man named Keegan, from Washington City, had marched a column of negroes up to the polls in the Thirteenth District, headed by a fife and drum, and taken possession. Mr. Ruhm said there had been a rumor of that kind, but the Democratic grand jury, after examining a large number of witnesses sent before it by the Democrats, failed to find an indictment. He had heard of no ballot box being taken possession of except in the contested election case just decided in the Senate."[81]

The lone Nashville account of what was likely fife and drum music was from October, at a political rally for Thomas Kercheval, who had been mayor before and was running again:

A Kercheval meeting at the corner of College and Whiteside streets was largely composed of the women peculiar to that neighborhood and the irrepressible bootblack element. Young Mr. Ashcraft was the first speaker, and his fervidly eloquent attacks against the "pontoon ring," as he designated the present administration, received the unctuous approval of several stout and greasy looking colored ladies, who interpolated such expressions as "Dat's so, honey!" "You's right, honey!" between his oratorical flights. A drunken Kerchevalite then took the platform, and hanging his hat on the cross-piece of a lamp post near the stand, held forth in earnest, but unintelligible denunciation of all who voted for "bills," as he called Mr. Kercheval's opponent, despite the frantic attempts of the drum corps to silence him. He was followed by Ed. Gregory, who announced that he was a candidate for the City Council and that he had rather suffer defeat with Kercheval than to be elected on any other ticket. A young man named Clemens attacked the present administration and the reform ticket in a vein of scathing satire, which was highly delectable to his enlightened auditors. He was followed by Messrs. Slowey and Dick Bryant, the latter confining himself principally to criticizing the conduct of his namesake, Dr. Bryant, in supporting the Reform ticket. After a short recess Mr. Kercheval arrived, and closed the meeting by reminding the colored voters present that they owed most of their civil liberties and material comforts to his exertions in their behalf.[82]

"FOR SHOW AND STREET PARADES": BLACK FIFE AND DRUM MUSIC IN TENNESSEE, 1886

The new year of 1886 in Memphis brought an announcement of a New Year's Day parade of the Pole Bearers to be followed by a festival in the evening.[83] The Pole Bearers and other Black societies had often marched on New Year's Day in previous years, but it was generally referred to as a celebration of the Emancipation Proclamation. By 1886, there was no mention of that, perhaps because Black people in Tennessee typically celebrated Emancipation in August rather than January. In older years, the newspaper would likely have mentioned the music involved, but no music at all is mentioned in this particular notice.

June brought a few political rallies, including one with a fife and drum by the "Independent Republicans" in Nashville, occasioning a bit of gentle ribbing from the *Daily American*:

As we write, a banner with a strange device, a wheezy, asthmatic fife, a discordant drum which a muscular individual is thumping with furious heat, files sadly by. Four grief-stricken individuals, and a cur of low degree with a brief but interesting tail, are the adjuncts to the instruments of torture. The banner is a drooping, careworn rag but like the dog, it too has its brief and interesting tale. It proclaims that Judge Frank T. Reid and other Independent Republican nominees will assail the popular ear to-night from the proud eminence of an inverted goodsbox. Ere this is in print these patriots will already have given specific instructions as to the necessary ways and means to save the country. Their idea of what is necessary is so simple that a child can understand it.[84]

In July, the mention of Black drummers in connection with a female baseball game in Chattanooga was the first instance of a phenomenon that would become far better known in Nashville than Chattanooga: the use of Black drummers or fife and drum bands to advertise baseball games. The *Chattanooga Commercial* gave a fair amount of detail: "Three hundred spectators, two negroes with bass and snare drum, two policemen and some sober and semi-sober members of the defunct Chattanooga base ball club were in attendance yesterday afternoon at the Ball Park, when the Harts of this city, with a female battery, succeeded in defeating the Independents by a score of 16 to 15 runs and a million, or less, errors."[85] Although the editor did not give any specific reason for the drummers being there, it seems likely they were hired to advertise the game, which is the same purpose for which such drum corps and bands were later employed in Nashville. Fife and drum music would become a distinct feature of Nashville baseball for many years.

However, in August, it was politics and not baseball that brought fife and drum to the streets and parks of Nashville. A rally sponsored by the Independent Republicans was the occasion, bringing a crowd of about 1,200 people:

Last night on the public square, Mr. John Jarrett was billed to make an address to the laboring element of the city. At the same place the Independent-Republican candidates were to have their great rally. The counter attraction in Mr. Jarrett necessitated the postponement of the rally. Mr. Jarrett had previously expressed to an AMERICAN reporter his fear that some wrong construction might be put upon his address. It was not in any sense political. He stated as much last night.

After he had finished the Independent orators took the stand and with the aid of fife and drum succeeded in holding many of Jarrett's audience and drawing a number of others, mostly negroes. The crowd was about 1,200 strong and was enthusiastic. Tillman, Allen, Reid and the other candidates spoke. One sentence in Judge Allen's speech that struck the reporter as rather paradoxical was his statement that he was every day gaining votes from "the ranks of the enemy," the Democrats, when he has all along claimed and still claims to be a Democrat.[86]

As noted in previous years, the existence of Black military companies in Memphis such as the McClellan Guards, the Zouave Guards, and the Hannibal Guards proved to be an exciting inspiration for Black youth in the city. They soon organized their own youthful equivalents: "The Hadden Guards, a company of juvenile colored boys armed with wooden guns and headed by a fife and drum, paraded Madison street last evening.[87] The boys had on quite becoming uniforms and went through the movements very well considering their training."[88]

The September 4th death of General Frank Cheatham, a former Confederate general in the Civil War, occasioned a large procession in Nashville on Saturday, September 6, that featured a "colored drum brigade":

Next in order was a handsomely uniformed drum brigade of colored citizens, who with muffled drums, were beating a slow funeral march.

Then came the uniformed infantry. First, the old well known Porter Rifles, who have so often represented their city in peaceful contests under the command of Capt. George Reyer. Then came the Hermitage Guards, a splendid looking body of young soldiers under command of Capt. Pres Lester. Third in order were the Langston Rifles of colored citizens. This was the largest company in line and presented a fine military body of men. They had come unexpectedly, but with warm welcome, to the place of meeting at the Capitol and offered their services in the grand funeral demonstration in honor of Gen. Cheatham. The dead man had their love also for the courtesy he had always shown their race. The dead Postmaster had built up for himself in their hearts a monument of gratitude for retaining in the postal service of this city every colored citizen who was there when he entered and who had furnished evidences of competency. The excellent appearance and soldier-like tread of the Langston Rifles excited much complementary comment upon the streets, and from the managers of the day.[89]

The Tennessee gubernatorial campaign was between two brothers, the Republican Alfred Taylor and the Democrat Bob Taylor, and became known as the "War of the Roses," as the supporters of Robert Taylor wore white roses and the supporters of Alfred Taylor wore red roses. The candidates, being brothers, attacked each other's politics but campaigned together, and the banter was fairly lighthearted. A major campaign rally in Nashville led to a parade that involved both white and Black bands, and apparently a fife and drum band: "The bands employed to attend the 'Bob' Taylor rally will report at 5 o'clock sharp at the following places: Nashville Cornet Band at northwest corner Broad and Vine streets, immediately in front of the Chief Marshal. Immaculate Band will report to Gen. W. R. Cantrell, in front of the customhouse. The German Brass Band will report to Chas. S. Ridley, chief of cavalry, corner of Summer and Broad streets. The Colored Drum Corps will report to me, on Broad street, corner of Vine. CHAS. THURMAN, Chairman Music Committee."[90] Whether the drum corps in question strictly consisted of drums, or also involved a fife, must be a matter of conjecture. Election day was November 1, and the *Daily American* in Nashville celebrated the resulting end of fife and drum bands: "To-day will end for a long while any demand for the numerous fife and drum corps that have for the past few weeks done such 'vigorous campaign work.'"[91] Bob Taylor defeated his brother and became governor of Tennessee.

"THE DRUM CORPS NUISANCE": BLACK FIFE AND DRUM MUSIC IN TENNESSEE, 1887

In July of 1887, the *Daily American* in Nashville viewed the approaching municipal election with dread, particularly because of the prominent role of fife and drum music in such campaigns: "In behalf of a long-suffering public, we offer a chromo to the city father who will engineer an ordinance through council prohibiting the march of the drum corps nuisance through our streets in the approaching municipal campaign."[92] While such ordinances passed eventually in most larger Southern cities, it does not appear that Nashville ever enacted such a law.

While fife and drum music outside of political campaigns seemed to be giving way to brass band music, one place where fife and drum was naturally still common was in the events of the Black military companies of Tennessee. Memphis had several such companies, and Nashville had the Langston Rifles, whose street parade, dress parade, and sham battle was an occasion for both brass band and fife and drum band performances:

THE LANGSTON RIFLES. Yesterday was a day set apart by the above company for a grand street parade, dress parade sham battle, etc., at the Base Ball Park.[93] In the morning the company, headed by the I.O.I. brass band and the company drum corps,[94] paraded the principal streets, and at 2 o'clock assembled at the park. A large crowd was out to witness the program. First was a match game of foot ball. The nine led by Mr. George W. Trimble were declared to be the winning kickers.[95] Next was a 100-yard foot race, which was easily won by Chas. Keill. A 50-yard race was won by Bud Dunson. Starter, Dick Morgan; judges, Capt. J. K. Knight and C. N. Clark. The dress parade and sham battle were the most interesting features of the evening, and were well executed. Capt. W. L. Irvin and his men deserve great credit for the success of the entertainment, which was given for the benefit of the company.[96]

Normally, Tennessee election campaigns were about which candidates or which parties would be retained or placed in power, but the 1887 campaign had the additional issue of whether the sale of liquor and other intoxicating beverages would be made illegal. Vigorous campaigns for and against Prohibition were made across the state. While most Black Tennesseans opposed Prohibition, there were Black fife and drum bands employed by both sides. A rally in Columbia, Tennessee, was typical: "The Square was filled with negroes last night, and they must have been filled with 'moonshine' from the hurrah they raised. 'Anti-prohibitionists' were the mottoes on their banners. They had torchlights, drums and fifes."[97] An account of another such rally in Brownsville mentioned no less than three bands:

> BROWNSVILLE, Sept. 28.—To-day has been a grand day with the antis of Haywood County. They had a big rally here, consisting of a big barbecue and speeches. They began to come out on the Square about 9 o'clock. After all had about arrived, they marched around the Square several times, led by three bands of music. Then the speakers, Hon. S. A. McElwee, D. A. Nunn and Rev. Haywood led out towards Ragland's Grove, followed by the grand procession on horseback, in buggies and wagons, all of one color. They claim that many converts have been made to the liberty-loving party. The general opinion is that it will be a close run in this county.[98]

S. A. McElwee was a Black state representative from Haywood County, and David Nunn was arguably the most important white Republican in West Tennessee, so it is evident that there was a certain degree of overlap between the Anti-Prohibitionists and the Republican Party. Whether any of the three bands employed were fife and drum ensembles is unclear.

At Lebanon, however, members of the Black community and a fife and drum band were involved with the Prohibitionists on election day, so it is evident that there were differing opinions in the Black community on the issue:

The grandest election day ever seen in Lebanon. At the opening of the polls at 9 o'clock this morning a procession of the elder men of our town, white and black, numbering 100, marched around the Square to the courthouse and voted prohibition. After voting they remained at the polls to work. At 11 o'clock the young men of the district met at Vance stable on East Main street, where they were headed by drums and fife with Frank Drake and Harvey Johnson, colored, on horseback with white helmets, with prohibition badges and an immense banner; next came the standard-bearer with a large United States flag, followed by some 200 young men.[99]

Grover Cleveland had won the presidential election of 1884, and when it was announced that he would be coming to Tennessee, cities began making elaborate preparations. In that era, presidential visits usually involved parades, and Chattanooga began making plans that initially included a Black drum corps,[100] although descriptions after the fact do not mention drummers. Memphis also planned a major parade, with a lineup that included a drum corps, the Independent Order of Pole Bearers, the Young Men's Association Band, and the Independent Order of Immaculates.[101] However, what should have been a momentous day for the city of Memphis proved to be a day of sorrow, as the man who introduced the president, Chancellor H. T. Ellett, dropped dead in Court Square after making the welcome address. The procession was also the occasion for bitter feelings, as the Knights of Innisfail, an Irish organization, refused to take part in the parade, as they had been assigned a place behind Black organizations, and the *Public Ledger* complained that the Black fife and drum band played an offensive tune: "The colored fife and drum band played the tune of 'Hang Jeff Davis on a Sour Apple Tree' while passing up Main near Jefferson. The only excuse for this performance was the dense ignorance of this band in the requirements and good taste of the occasion." The *Ledger* editor was actually being intentionally petty and disingenuous, for of course the tune in question is also "The Battle Hymn of the Republic."[102] What should have been a gala day for Memphis ended in sadness and irritability.

"WE THOUGHT THERE WOULD BE NO TAPPING OF THE DRUM": BLACK FIFE AND DRUM MUSIC IN TENNESSEE, 1888

As the new year opened, Memphis was in the middle of a municipal election campaign between what was styled the People's ticket, which was allegedly for good government, and the so-called Citizens' ticket or Chase ticket, which was largely made up of the incumbent officials of the Taxing District. Memphis still did not have a traditional municipal government, as its charter had been revoked after the yellow fever epidemics. A rally of Black citizens for the People's ticket at the Beale Street Market was the occasion for a fife and drum band, as well as an incident of political violence:

> The colored citizens had proceeded to the place of meeting almost in a body, with fife and drum, and at the head of the column a man marched with a large torchlit banner, on which was inscribed, "Meeting of the People's Ticket at Beale Street Market Tonight." The bearer of this sign was Taylor Fleck, a peaceable and law abiding citizen, who had enthusiastically volunteered to bear the banner, which was a symbol of the victory to be achieved on Thursday next. As the procession approached the speaker's stand, he was tauntingly accosted by a young colored supporter of the Chase ticket named Walter Townsend. Some hot words were exchanged between the two, and Fleck had turned to march on, when Townsend dashed at him with a long bladed knife. A friend screamed to Fleck to run, and he did so, pursued by Townsend, who made several savage strokes at him in the back. One of the slashes struck the fleeing man midway down the back, cutting his coat and making a flesh wound of several inches. Townsend fled, and, despite the efforts of those who pursued him, made good his escape.[103]

A columnist from the Fifteenth Civil District of Fayette County, writing in the *Fayette Falcon*, complained of the use of fife and drum music in connection to Black political rallies in the district, with a view toward the coming elections:

> Tap! Tap! Tap! Hark! What is that? I have not heard that noise since the 5th night of August, 1874. A neighbor just passing tells me 'tis the same old fife and drum used by the latter day saints to beat their way into office.[104] They are being unearthed in the heretofore quiet district of No. 15, and put to the same old use in exciting the poor ignorant colored man to the highest pitch before the 2nd of August next. We thought there would be no tapping of the drum and elections would be conducted quietly and peaceably, but we were not surprised when our neighbor informed us that one of those latter day saints still remained in this county and had taken up his abode near the quiet

little village of Riggstown, in District No. 15 and desired the office of Magistrate; hence the tapping of the drum from early dawn to the midnight hours.

You justly condemn the waving of the bloody shirt, but I don't think there is anything that should be more universally condemned than this mode of exciting the prejudice of the colored man against the whites. The usually selected spot to spew out their foul-mouthed venom against the respectable portion of our population, is in a deep hollow densely set with timber and overgrown with wild vines, with nothing to give them light save the starry heavens. Here they have it all to themselves, none to hinder or make afraid. One not acquainted with their mode of electioneering would think that the democrats had robbed them of their mule and forty acres of land, had insulted all their wives and daughters, had slain all their parents and grand parents, and the remaining few would have to dig from the bosom of the earth all the taxes required to run this country, unless they sent them as magistrates to the county court. In the silence of the night, how we shiver with affright, at the melancholy menace of their tone.

There is no tapping of the drum in this secret spot, for fear of attracting some unwonted for, and in days gone by it was useless to try to advance any argument with them after they had attended one of these secret harangues.[105]

Even at the late date of 1888, the Black fife and drum bands could bring forth fear, bitterness, and disgust on the part of white residents in Tennessee.

A violent encounter in the community of Shakerag in southeastern Shelby County resulted from a dispute among Black residents about which of two men was the best snare-drummer.[106] Competitiveness was a given among Black bands and Black musicians, as was the tendency for people in the community to line up as supporters of one or the other, but the resorting to violence in such a contest was fairly rare:

Justice Hughey's court-room was crowded yesterday afternoon by the witnesses and principals of a shooting and cutting scrape that occurred at Shakerag, in this county, on the night of August 1. The row originated in a dispute between two factions of negroes as to which crowd had the more expert performer on the kettle-drum. The argument culminated in a free fight. Mose Felton was cut in the back during the melee by Porter Williams, and several hard blows were given and received by other parties. There was a brief cessation of hostilities, and Dock Monroe, a friend of Mose Felton, started down the road. He and Branch Loring, a supporter of Porter Williams, became involved in a difficulty, and, after a short struggle, Losing got Monroe's head in chancery and was pounding his face to a pulp. At this juncture a pistol was fired—Loring alleges by Monroe—and Porter Williams ran up with his bloody knife and slashed Monroe several times in the back. Monroe's wounds were deep and severe, and he fell to earth apparently dead.

All the parties to the affray were arrested next day and several of them were bound over by Justice Holeman for cutting Monroe and Felton. Monroe's wounds kept him confined to his bed until yesterday, when he and Felton were brought to town and tried by Justice Hughey for shooting with intent to kill and carrying concealed weapons. Monroe is unable to bear a shirt on his back, and exhibited his wounds in court. After hearing the evidence the magistrate bound Monroe and Felton over to the criminal court.[107]

A very different account of the incident in the *Public Ledger* had appeared a couple of days before, in which the location of the incident is called Oakville, said to be seven miles from the city on the Kansas City Road. The *Ledger* attributed the dispute to the elections rather than to drumming:

Esquire Hughey to-day remanded to jail Doc Monroe and Mose Felton, who were arrested at Oakville, seven miles out on the Kansas City road, by Deputy Sheriffs Burke and Warnicke last night. Mose Felton was charged by Richard Simmons with carrying concealed weapons, and also with breach of peace, and Doc Monroe was charged by Branch Loving [*sic*] with assault with a pistol. All the parties are colored. Simmons will probably swear out another warrant against Felton for enticing Mrs. Simmons from home. Deputy Burke says the negroes near Oakville are nearly all of a most vicious character. The affray occurred the day after election and grew out of a quarrel occurring at the polls.[108]

The two accounts do not necessarily preclude each other. Shakerag was an old name for Oakville, and the snare-drumming dispute may have resulted from Mose Felton and Porter Williams having been employed on differing sides in the recent election.

In late August, a *Ledger* columnist who styled himself the "Town Rambler" wrote a fairly long editorial about Black societies, brass bands, fife and drum bands, and parades, particularly in connection with funerals, suggesting that despite Memphians taking them for granted, such processions were actually quite unique:

> As the Town Rambler was wending his way up Main street the other day he encountered the gayest procession, seemingly, that ever trod the streets of Memphis. There was a brass band in front, bursting forth in strains of the gayest music, while behind it followed a long train of negroes, with knee breeches, brass buttons, swords somewhat the worse for rust, besides a world of purple feathers and tarnished lace, so that one might have imagined that some whirlwind had blown a millinery shop to pieces and scattered its trinkets to the four winds.
>
> The Town Rambler, of course, presumed this to be a crowd on its way to a dance or a picnic but no, it was a negro funeral.
>
> To the inhabitant of a Northern city there is nothing so amusing as this love of display shown by the negroes of the South. The colored man loves loud sounds, ostrich feathers and gold lace beyond measure, but above all things he bows before the inevitable fife and drum with an Eastern devotion.
>
> There are a host of societies and fraternities among the blacks, such as the "Sons and Daughters of Jacob," the "United Sisters of Zion," and the "Sons of Ham," and their fondness for street processions is proverbial.
>
> The people of Memphis have become so used to them that we hardly notice them, but to strangers they compose one of the most interesting features of the city. Whenever the future Charles Dickens of America comes into existence, you may be sure that one of his most interesting fields of research will be among the colored people, and not the least interesting of his pages will have something about that supreme delight of a negro's desires—a gorgeous funeral procession.[109]

That the sound of Black fife and drum was hated because it represented Black political activity was made plain by an October editorial in the *Tate County Record* of Senatobia, Mississippi, which was reprinted in the *Memphis Daily Appeal*:

> We don't like to read this sort of thing. But The Tate County Record is Democratic to the core, and is anything but an alarmist or sensational. It certainly knows what it is talking about when it says that the danger of the Republicans carrying that county is imminent.

"What," it asks, "did the drum-beat mean ten or twelve years ago? It meant then negro supremacy over white men, and it means the same thing now, under the leadership of Jones and Chalmers.[110] Democrats of Tate, can you stand it? If not, up and at them in your old-time style and with your old-time vigor. The danger is imminent. They are alert and active. How are you? We repeat, the danger of losing the county is great.[111]

Fife and drum activity was also mentioned in connection with a rally at the Masonic Theatre in Nashville, where Republicans A. A. Taylor and L. C. Houk spoke to a predominantly Black audience about the doctrines of the Republican Party and the reason they supported high tariffs.[112]

The year closed with an account of a cutting fight between barbers on Beale Street, which resulted from a dispute over a bass drum: "R. F. Flippin, a barber from Jackson, Tenn., was arrested yesterday for assaulting Abe Lyles, a negro barber on Beal street, with a razor. Flippin had charge of an excursion from Jackson yesterday, which was accompanied by a brass band. Lyles, who had formerly belonged to the band in Jackson, claimed the bass drum and endeavored to take it, hence the fight."[113] As noted before, bass drums were prized possessions, and their owners were extremely protective of them and jealous about them. The drums were, of course, expensive and hard to replace.

"THE RIGHT OF WAY DOES NOT BELONG TO ANY SOCIETY": BLACK FIFE AND DRUM MUSIC IN TENNESSEE, 1889

In 1888, the accounts in Tennessee newspapers of Black fife and drum music continued to decline in frequency, while at the same time, race relations became more strained and inflamed. Southern newspapers were full of suggestions that Blacks be forced to emigrate to Haiti or Liberia, or that special areas be set apart for them. When Decoration Day came at the National Cemetery in Memphis in 1889, thousands of Black Memphians attended, but a speech by T. R. Edgington, a Union veteran and Democratic member of the Grand Army of the Republic, infuriated the crowd. Edgington suggested that the right of Black people to vote had to be restricted: "Limitations should be placed on his exercise of his right of suffrage. The limitation on his right of suffrage should be so adjusted as to secure a responsible class of colored voters whose character and standing will afford a guarantee that they will not conspire with the irresponsible and lawless white elements to seize on political power."[114] Blacks were universally outraged by the speech, but whites were largely divided. Most Republicans were deeply offended, although some stated they agreed privately; many more whites said that regardless of whether they agreed with the speech politically, they thought it should not have been given at a memorial. The *Appeal*, somewhat surprisingly, attacked the speech with some vigor, pointing out that Blacks were free citizens, and that the right to vote became inevitable once they became free.[115] On the same editorial page, the editor took the *Clay County Record*, an Arkansas paper, to task for demanding that a territory be set apart for Blacks as had been done for the native Americans:

> Our contemporary has evidently forgotten the fact that the negroes are citizens, and are not to be legislated for or about as we legislate for the Indians and the Chinese. Congress might lay off a Territory for them next December, but it could not force them to occupy it. But, even if it was so minded, what Territory could it give them that does not already contain a white population, with vested rights that could not be forced or coaxed to leave to make way for the negroes? Then, again, we could not force them to emigrate to Mexico, and if we could the Mexicans would not receive them. The same is to be said of a proposition to send them to Hayti, which has recently been circulated. Free people cannot be moved about like pawns on a chess board. To use force upon the negro to compel him to move here and there as white committees select would be to establish a precedent that might be invoked by one body of white people against another to the ruin of the very fabric of liberty. The rights of the least must be protected intact in order that the rights of all may be preserved.[116]

Despite the *Appeal's* fairly reasoned stance, the editorial fight brewing over Blacks in America was symptomatic of the ways in which race relations were deteriorating. Much of it was due to the growing power of farmers, who were organizing into the Agricultural Wheel and the Farmers and Laborers Union. These organizations were becoming overtly political and decidedly left-wing, and in the South, as was always the case with third-party movements, they were showing themselves willing to make common cause with Black Republican voters to defeat Democrats. The latter were beginning to decide that they would be better off if Blacks were gone altogether, or at least if they were no longer allowed to vote.

Black parades were also becoming a source of frustration and outrage on the part of white Memphians, as the *Ledger* revealed:

"Man, proud man, dressed in a little brief authority, plays such fantastic tricks before high heaven as make the angels weep." The LEDGER reporter would dedicate the above quotation to the various marshals of both white and colored processions, who, bedecked with sash and badge and consequent strut, stop street cars and other vehicles until their line of march is ended. If the policemen did their duty they would arrest such presumptuous imbeciles and help them learn that the right of way does not belong to any society or organization. A half dozen times has it come under the observation of a LEDGER reporter that street cars and carriages were halted on Madison or retarded on Main street because the ignorant marshals of a procession had their heads turned by the mistaken honor that had come to them.

A procession of the early part of last week made a line of street cars go at a worse than snail's pace down Main street, and notwithstanding the marshal was requested to give them right of way, he persistently refused to do so. It is not so much a question of the rights of the street cars as it is those of the passengers. No society has a right to delay their proper and reasonable transit, and we repeat, if the police would do their duty in the matter, which they do not do, the nuisance would be abated.[117]

Apparently, white frustration with such parades boiled over on June 10, and a man poured water over the head of one of the marshals of a Black procession, resulting in a hearing in police court, where the man was dismissed by President Hadden of the Taxing District:

The first case that was called this morning was concerning the emptying of some water on the marshal of the negro procession. Mr. Wurtzberger, the gentleman who handled the water, was honorably acquitted, His Honor saying that inasmuch as the water came from the artesian wells, it was too pure to work any damage. He also said: "Regularly every summer complaints are made about the manner in which these processions block the streets and obstruct both trade and traffic—especially are complaints entered against negro processions. Now, I want you police to notice this, and if you find a marshal that is too busy cavorting about on his fiery steed to properly marshal his procession, pull him off his horse and lock him up. The procession must occupy only one side of the street, and it must open its ranks for the passage of vehicles, if it does not, break it up and bring the leaders before me. Don't let the big badges scare you, they are put on with a pin and can be taken off with a pull."[118]

As white Southern frustration with Blacks grew, the Black community was no longer to be allowed unrestricted access to public social space. Elsewhere, the *Ledger* revealed that the parade in question had been sponsored by a lodge of the Black Odd Fellows and was on its way to Estival Park for a picnic.[119]

The only explicit mention of a Black fife and drum band in Tennessee in 1889 was from Fayette County, in connection with a Sunday school picnic: "The colored Baptist church gave a Sunday School picnic in the bottoms near Tucker's Mill last Friday. A drum and fife with two uniformed followers made music. They marched around town, to the amusement of the elder people and the delight of the small boy."[120] Tucker's Mill was in a bottom north of Somerville, along what today are Highways 59 and 76.

In November, five men who had been leaders in the Independent Pole Bearers applied for a charter for an organization called the "Independent Pall-Bearers" in Shelby County.[121] This would seem to be the process by which the name was changed from Independent Pole Bearers to Independent Pall Bearers. Although the assertion is encountered today that the founders intended to name the organization the Independent Pall Bearers, the preponderance of evidence to the contrary does not support that claim.

"OUR FUTURE . . . WILL BE WHAT WE MAKE IT":
BLACK FIFE AND DRUM MUSIC IN TENNESSEE, 1890

On New Year's Day 1890, a large parade and celebration of Emancipation was held in Nashville, and was attended by more than two thousand persons, including five hundred visitors from other cities. Several bands, including two drum corps, were a part of the procession, and the Honorable S. A. McElwee, formerly a state representative from Haywood County, made a lengthy and important speech to the crowd. The *Daily American* of Nashville gave a detailed account of the day:

Yesterday was the twenty-seventh anniversary of the proclamation of emancipation and was celebrated by the colored citizens of Nashville in grand style. The fact that there was to be a celebration here was widely published and over 500 visitors were in the city from Bowling

Green, Gallatin, Franklin, Columbia, Lebanon and other surrounding towns. In the early hours of the morning Nashville colored people with their visitors began to appear on the streets and by 10 o'clock, the time that the procession was announced to start, the pavements were lined along nearly the whole route of the procession. . . .

Altogether the procession contained over 2,000 people and made an imposing display, being nearly two miles in length. The Odd Fellows' band of East Nashville, Cornelius Gowdey's drum corps,[122] and the Langston Rifles drum corps also marched in the procession, which took the following route: From the Capitol to the Public Square, down Market to Broad, up Broad to Spruce, out Spruce to South Union, through South Union to Summer, out Summer to Ash, through Ash to Cherry, and down Cherry to St. Paul's Church, where it passed in review before the chief marshal and his assistants and Hon. S. A. McElwee, and then disbanded.[123]

McElwee's speech was fairly radical and militant for the era, and it raised many issues that are still discussed in the Black community today:

As a race we support all institutions and encourage every enterprise organized in the country, except our own—then wonder why negro institutions and enterprises do not prosper. We accept the advice and follow the suggestions of white demagogues, ignore the opinions and best thoughts of our people—then wonder why the race hasn't a Parnell or Gladstone. We read all white newspapers, give our best practice to white physicians, and trust our lawsuits to white lawyers—then ask why negro papers have patent hacks and professional colored men do not reach that eminence and distinction obtained by white men. We are untrue to ourselves in politics, we stab each other in the back, then ask why are our men ignored by the political parties. We occupy in politics a position that no other race occupies. We are in politics the most united and yet the most divided people in the world. In view of what has been said, I assert that unity of purpose and of action is the demand of the hour. . . . We deceive ourselves if we think that our interests, in the hands of the leaders of another race will be so guarded and protected as to give permanent success and complete victory over the opposing interests of that race. Our future is in our own hands, and it will be what we make it.[124]

As was so often the case, much fife and drum activity in Nashville was connected to political rallies and campaigns, such as an August event for the benefit of the third-party movement:

> When Hon. Joseph E. Washington completed his magnificent oration Friday night at the corner of Fifth and Woodland streets, in East Nashville, the consensus of favorable opinion from the experienced and reputable heads of families who heard him would lead an observer to suppose that Mr. Washington had spoken well, and even that his speech had carried conviction with it in respect to many important measures. Little did Mr. Washington dream that on the succeeding night he should be annihilated, crushed, swept from off the face of the earth by a speaker upon the same box he had occupied twenty-four hours previously. Yet such, in the opinion of this second speaker, was the case. All yesterday afternoon a forlorn trio of darkies disturbed the peace of East Nashville by fife and drum calling attention to a hieroglyphic banner, which experts deciphered as announcing the speaking of Joseph Wheless at the corner.[125]

In addition to the usual rallies for particular parties and politicians, the 1890 campaign also featured rallies both for and against the prohibition of alcohol. Although the Black community (and the Republican Party) were overwhelmingly on the side of keeping alcohol legal, both sides employed Black fife and drum musicians to attract attention to their rallies. This August account was for a Prohibition rally: "About 250 people were gathered last night at the southwest corner of the public square to hear Dr. Kelley, the prohibition candidate for governor, and Edward A. East speak in behalf of their party. The interest in the occasion was supplemented by the music of a negro drum and fife corps, which heralded the approaching oratory."[126]

BLACK FIFE AND DRUM MUSIC IN TENNESSEE, 1891

As in the previous year, New Year's Day in Nashville was the occasion for an elaborate parade to commemorate Emancipation Day, but in this instance, no music or bands were mentioned in descriptions of the celebration. Given that the Langston Rifles, the Rock City Guards, and something called the Mount Nebo Benevolent Society were participating, it is likely that there were drum corps or fife and drum bands present, but they were not described.[127] The occasion was also a more somber one than it had been the year before, as the election of President Benjamin Harrison had been viewed hopefully by Blacks, but Harrison had proved to be ineffective in enforcing the voting rights of African Americans. The day's speaker, the Honorable John Mercer Langston, Black congressman from Virginia, took President Harrison to task for his failure to enforce Black voting rights: "Although the President assured the persons who presented this address [on behalf of Black voting rights] that the interests of those in whose behalf it was made should not be neglected it is not known that a single case has been instituted and prosecuted with proper vigor under the act to enforce the right of citizens of the United States to vote in the several states of the Union."[128] Langston would become an advocate of Black emigration to Oklahoma and the West, and he came to be pessimistic about the future of Black people in America.

"NEITHER CHARACTER NOR STANDING AVAILS THE NEGRO": THE CURVE RIOT, THE PEOPLES' GROCERY LYNCHING, AND BLACK FIFE AND DRUM MUSIC IN TENNESSEE, 1892

The new year of 1892 was not a time for celebration for Memphis's Black community. A series of racial incidents at a community known as the Curve, in the Fourteenth Civil District of Shelby County, culminated in a police raid on the Black-owned People's Grocery Store, whose owners opened fire on the police. One of the owners, Calvin McDowell, a member of a Black militia company known as the Tennessee Rifles, stated that he and his co-owners had had a confrontation with the white owner of a grocery store across the street, and that threats had been made against them, which is why they were armed. At any rate, the news media referred to the events at the Curve (the modern-day intersection of Mississippi Boulevard and Walker Avenue) as a "riot," and blamed it on the free availability of liquor and wide-open gambling in the neighborhood, which was outside Memphis city limits. The Black defenders inside the store were arrested and jailed. On the night of March 9, 1892, a masked mob overpowered the jailer at the Shelby County Jail in downtown Memphis and seized the accused Black prisoners, shooting them to death in the Chesapeake and Ohio rail yards north of downtown Memphis.[129] In the wake of this incident, the Tennessee Rifles were ordered disbanded, and all their arms were seized. Many Black Memphis began making plans to emigrate to the West or Midwest.[130] Said a bitter James Fleming, coeditor with Ida B. Wells of the Black Memphis newspaper the *Free Speech*: "The city of Memphis has demonstrated that neither character nor standing avails the Negro if he dares to protect himself against the white man or become his rival."[131]

There were few accounts of parades or picnics, but one from Camden, Tennessee, in Benton County might have involved fife and drum music, although it is not mentioned: "The colored Aid Society gave a uniformed parade around the public square, after the picnic last Thursday, the 14th instant."[132] The parade taking place after the picnic was fairly unusual, as such processions usually occurred on the way to the picnics. Benton County had been largely Republican, and perhaps as a result, the Black community there was still allowed to parade in public spaces.

Fife and drum music was a usual feature of political meetings in Nashville, but a meeting in August in which it was heard at was somewhat unique, having been called to oppose the convict leasing system that had occasioned a violent uprising in East Tennessee known as the Coal Creek War. The uprising resulted from miners' objections to the use of convict labor in the coal mines, which effectively undercut the workers' demands for better pay and working conditions. Their response was to attack and burn down the convict camps, which led the governor, John Price Buchanan, to send militia units against the mine workers. The crisis provoked considerable outrage among working-class Tennesseans, Black and white: "The drums beat and the fife was played in front of the court-house early last night. It was the call to what was given out to be an 'opposition meeting' to the mass-meeting held at the Tabernacle several nights ago. The meeting was composed of about 500 people, 200 of whom were negroes. Dr. J. M. Lindsley was made Chairman, and a negro whose name could not be learned, arose to speak. He abused the convict lease system and scored the action of the Tabernacle meeting."[133] Governor Buchanan had not received the nomination of his party, the Democrats, despite being the incumbent, and so he was running a third-party campaign to remain in office, appealing to Republicans, the farmer-labor movement, and Blacks, hence the actions of this "opposition meeting" in endorsing his actions as governor while opposing the convict leasing system. But Buchanan's decision to employ the state militia against the mine workers destroyed his credibility with the farmers and laborers in the third-party movement.

With the Coal Creek War as a dramatic backdrop, Labor Day 1892 was extremely important in Nashville. Workers made plans for an elaborate procession, including both white and Black organizations and bands:

The bands which are to participate in the parade must report at their several starting points by 8 o'clock. The Baxter Band will report at labor headquarters on Summer street. The Great Southern Band will report to W. H. Higginbotham. Printers' Union, at the corner of High and Church streets. The Lewisburg Band will report to Charles Goodrich. Carpenters' Union, at the same place. The Phillips & Buttorf Band will report to the Machinists' Union at Mayo's drug store, on West Broad street. The Link Zouave Drum Corps will report to the Clerks' Union at Combs' undertaking establishment on Summer street. The I.O.I. Band will report to the Stonemasons' at Harding Hall, on Cherry street. The Fife and Drum Band will meet at the corner of Broad and College streets.[134] . . . SIXTH DIVISION. I. O. I Band. Stonemasons' Union, on the east side of Cherry, south of Broad. Mechanics' Art Association on the east side of Cherry, north of Broad. Colored Barbers' Union on the same side of Cherry, in the rear of the Mechanics' Art Association. Porters' Aid Association on the west side of Cherry, north of Broad. SEVENTH DIVISION. Fife and drum band. Farmers' and Laborers' Union on both sides of College, south of Broad.[135]

Governor Buchanan, having been abandoned by his own party, could only run a campaign largely in the style of Republican candidates, appealing particularly to Black voters, so fife and drum bands were a significant feature of his rallies:

Gov. Jonathan Price Buchanan spoke to fifty Democrats, one hundred Republicans, one hundred Populites,[136] twenty-five Independents, eighty negroes and twenty-five boys on the Public Square, Saturday night. A negro fife and drum band paraded the streets all day Saturday, hoping to drum up an immense gathering, but in vain. The Governor spoke on different subjects of the political issues. He said he was a Democrat of the Jeffersonian stock, and was for the people's rights. He criticized the Democratic party very severely, but whether the would-be rally gained any votes or not is to be guessed. While he was speaking, a negro was amusing a crowd in front of the Market House, singing in the tune of "Boom ta-ra-ra-boom-de-ray," a political song, one of the verses being: "poor old Buck has been led astray. November 8 is his fatal day, Then Old Pete will have full sway, Boom-ta-ra-ra-boom-de-ray."[137]

The results of the November 8 election were for the most part a clean sweep for the Bourbon Democrats, and Pete Turney, the chief justice of the Tennessee Supreme Court, became governor. Raucous celebrations broke out in towns across the state, but few of these involved fife and drum bands, as most Blacks were Republicans now, and the few that were not had joined the burgeoning Populist movement. An exception was Shelbyville, where the procession was headed by a "fife and drum corps,"[138] but whether the corps in question was a Black band is unknown. At any rate, the Democratic victories left Black Tennesseans with little to celebrate. Their rights and privileges would be increasingly eroded under Democratic rule.

Chapter 5

"NERVE-TORTURERS AND WHOLESALE DISPENSERS OF DISCORD"

Black Fife and Drum Music in Tennessee During the Nadir and Segregation, 1893–1941

The period of time beginning in the late 1890s and continuing into the early twentieth century represented perhaps the lowest point of race relations in America, an era that some historians refer to as the Nadir. During this time, Black people were summarily stripped of their right to vote and hold office, and state constitutions were rewritten to take away the franchise through poll taxes, literacy tests, and other devices. Laws requiring segregation were enacted in many states, and not always strictly in the South. Some towns and municipalities enacted "sundown ordinances," laws that forbade Blacks to remain within the city limits after dark. Lynchings and mob violence became a regular occurrence, and occasionally, large-scale ethnic cleansings took place, such as the expulsion of all Blacks from Forsyth County, Georgia, or Ocoee, Florida. Under such conditions, it is not surprising that Black fife and drum music began to be encountered less and less in the pages of newspapers. Due to segregation, whites were not visiting Black picnics, and cities were less frequently allowing Blacks to parade. The denial of the right to vote to Blacks meant that politicians were no longer campaigning to them or employing fife and drum bands to attract them to rallies. Although fife and drum activity was undoubtedly continuing in rural areas of the state, it was done in such a way as to be hidden from the larger white society.

Although there were rallies and political meetings involving fife and drum bands during this era, they were few and far between, mostly involving the Republican Party, or a few third-party efforts, such as the Populists or the American Protective Association. By contrast, the vast majority of fife and drum activity in Tennessee surrounded the Nashville minor league baseball team, the Vols, and the Black fife and drum band hired to promote them.

As early as 1901, a visit of the Cincinnati Reds baseball team to play the Nashville Volunteers occasioned a fife and drum band performance: "Nashville gave the league tail-enders as warm a welcome as the Pirates might have received. It had its martial features, for their arrival was heralded by a fife and drum corps. In windows all over town strange placards stared the Porkopolitan delegates in the face. 'Join the Reds' was the puzzling inscription."[1]

In April of 1902, the Nashville City Council took up consideration of a bill to allow businesses to advertise their products with bands or fife and drum bands, and the bill passed on three readings. As the *American* put it, "Nashville may in the future be the most musical city in the Union."[2] As it seems that businesses had been doing this all along in Nashville, it is not clear what prompted the ordinance, but in May the mayor of Nashville, J. M. Head, vetoed it:

NASHVILLE, Tenn., May 8, 1902—To the Honorable City Council—I herewith return without my approval bill No. 15, repealing so much of the digest of laws of this city as prohibits parties advertising goods, wares and merchandise by auction or otherwise by a band of music, or by fife and drum. I can but feel that the passage of this ordinance repealing the sanitary provisions of the digest upon this subject was done without due consideration and deliberation as to its effect upon the business of the city, the safety of its streets for driving purposes, and the peace and comfort of the citizens of the residence portion of the city. It occurs to me that the passage of this ordinance is a backward step, which I sincerely trust this City Council will not take.[3]

The council ultimately voted to uphold the mayor's veto.[4] The *American* was pleased with the outcome, but they wanted the ban on fife and drum and bands extended further, to ban them altogether, as they indicated in an editorial:

The American extends its heartiest congratulations to the Mayor on his veto of the brass band advertising bill. Instead of repealing or modifying the existing law, it ought to be so amended as to prohibit the march of the nerve-tearing drum corps, which goes through the streets advertising base ball games, political meetings, etc., and the park and picnic advertising by means of bands and other devices in street cars and tallyhos. This sort of business is out of date in progressive cities, and the Mayor and the Council have done well in preventing the emasculation of the present ordinance.[5]

Obviously, the newspaper's suggestion was not followed, for a few weeks later, the editor noted that "a fife and drum will give selections on the streets of our village again this morning, announcing to all who have fallen asleep in front of their stores that there will be a game of ball this afternoon."[6] The next day, they were complaining about it again.[7]

In March of 1903, a battle broke out on the pages of the *American* with regard to the Black fife and drum band that played for the minor-league baseball games in Nashville. The opening shot was fired by a letter writer calling himself "A Sufferer," complaining of the fife and drum band:

> To the Editor of the American: After waging such a valorous and successful war on the Sunday saloons, The American deserves a well-earned rest from its labors. But before it lays aside its armor and beats its sword into a ploughshare, let it gird up its loins and turn its eye to another public nuisance from which, so far, there has been no escape. The beginning of the base ball season is close at hand, and with it doubtless will come the same fife and drum corps which has blossomed in the spring in this community for the last three years. Now, in the name of outraged and suffering humanity, I wish to cry out with a loud voice against this indignity. Are our nerves to be shattered and our shoulders to be wrung again this summer by the "music" which is employed by this perspiring "band" to proclaim to the world that a game of ball is to be pulled off in the afternoon? Such an organization of nerve-torturers and wholesale dispensers of discord would not be tolerated in any other city of Nashville's size in the Union, and why they are allowed to parade the streets of this is now, and always has been, a mystery to A SUFFERER.[8]

But this time, the attack was responded to by the writer of another letter, styling himself "Reason," defending the drum corps and Newt Fisher, the owner of the Nashville Base Ball Club:

> Allow me to say: I am personally acquainted with Newt Fisher, the manager and owner of the Nashville Base Ball Club, and have in a way been in close touch with him since he started base ball in Nashville. I am in a position to know that he advertises his base ball game [*sic*] in all legitimate ways. He uses The American and all the other of

Nashville's (daily, weekly and monthly) papers and pays for the same. I have never known him to refuse to advertise his base ball game with any one who asked him. I will venture to say that "A Sufferer" never saw base ball games as rendered and conducted by Newt Fisher. The Nashville Base Ball Club has (next to the newspapers) advertised our city better than any other one thing. Nashville has won the pennant twice in succession and the name of Nashville appears in front of all other Southern cities in a base ball way as well as in many other ways. I never attend a game that my wife is not with me and I want to say that the Nashville games are conducted (as well as all the rest of them in the entire Southern League) in a manner that does not offend any one. I am glad when I see the "drum corps" around the streets announcing the game. It tells me that I can attend an afternoon's performance of merit and skill that is a credit to the players and an offense to no one. We need base ball and I am only one of the large percentage of Nashville's population who endorses it as has been conducted by Newt Fisher. REASON.[9]

However the last word was had by a man calling himself "Pro Bono Publico," who stated: "The protest of your correspondent, 'Sufferer,' against the parading of the streets by the drum and fife corps is timely and to the point. The 'music' parading the streets is not confined to the advertising of bass ball games, but is equally as much in evidence during political campaigns, one of which will soon be on. It is an intolerable nuisance and should by all means be abolished."[10] A Black fife and drum corps would remain a part of Nashville's baseball culture for many years to come.

By March of 1904, the man who had called himself "Sufferer" the previous year was writing to the *American* again, complaining of the Black fife and drum band used in connection with the Nashville baseball team. This time he called himself "A Nervous Fan":

Each succeeding year since I became a resident of this fair city in 1899 I have, through the columns of The American, registered a strenuous kick against Newt. Fisher's Drum and Fife Brigade; and though, thus far, my efforts have borne no fruit, being a great believer in the creed of "if at first you don't succeed, keep on knocking," I have decided to take up the cudgel once more in behalf of the outraged population of Nashville. The base ball season flourishes in Nashville from March until October and so doth Newt's hallelujah Band! Undaunted by the snowy blasts of winter, it bloometh forth with the crocuses each spring and remains to torture our nerves throughout the broiling summer. Does the Editor happen to know a single reason why the people of Nashville should not arise in their wrath and demand the immediate cessation of this colossal nuisance? It has caused number-less runaways on the streets of our city and would not be tolerated for a single instant in any other town in the Union. I know of no other city in the entire South in which base ball is advertised in such a village way, and it's a safe bet that if Newt would invest the coin he bestows on the "gentlemen members" of his orchestra for their services, in printer's ink judiciously scattered in The American, he would attain the desired end of drawing crowds to the park without offending our ears and outraging our nerves as his present method does. Hoping that this communication will elicit the sympathy and support of other fellow sufferers in Nashville, I am, very truly yours, A NERVOUS FAN.[11]

There was no immediate response from the editor, but in August, the *American* called for the complete abolition of fife and drum music: "While the Council is suppressing the noise-making street peddler, it should also suppress the nerve-destroying fife and drum corps."[12]

June of 1908 brought a rare letter to the *Nashville American* in praise of fife and drum music, particularly the Black fife and drum band that played for the Nashville baseball team: "To the Editor of The American: A couple of bets that Nashville will finish either second or third look pretty sick just now; but I have some consolation in listening to some of the best field music, drumming up patrons to the game, that I have ever heard—and in saying this I happened to be with the Ninth New York in the war with Spain, which was given no band. To some of us there is nothing so inspir-iting as drums and fifes well played. C. E. H. Nashville, June 3."[13] In 1909, the Nashville baseball team was still being advertised by a Black fife and drum band, which in April gathered a group of white second-liners from the Tulane Hotel downtown, which caught the attention of the *American*:

Almost every hour of the day and most of the hours of the early evening there may be seen in front of the Tulane Hotel a coterie of jolly fellows and men about town who are constantly looking for diversion. They found a few moments of amusement and distraction from their daily cares yesterday morning when the Ethiopian fife and drum corps heralding the baseball game between the Bostonians and the Volunteers approached the hotel.[14] The fifeman was blowing his best at a martial tune and the drummer was doing a rattling stunt on the snare, while the fellow with the bass drum was pounding merry hades out of that cumbersome accompaniment to band and orchestra. When the musical trio reached the Church-street entrance of the Tulane one of the coterie of noon-day loungers in front of the hotel banteringly said, "fall in boys," with which admonition he took up the march behind the fife and drum corps. Instantly ten or twelve other humor-loving fans followed suit, and before the fifeman and the drummers had turned the corner, there was a long line of enthusiastic men making merry by following the band and keeping step in martial manner. Appropriately to the local club they began to sing "I'm Only A Volunteer," which broke up the band because the fifeman got so tickled at the spectacle he couldn't pucker his lips, and the drummers stopped drumming to double up with laughter. It was none the less a funny spectacle to pedestrian spectators.[15]

Although all too rare, the above account was an example of how, approached with an open mind, Black fife and drum music might have been an opportunity for fun and racial reconciliation, rather than an occasion for racial divide and discord. The difference was likely due to the music's association with baseball in Nashville. Nevertheless, the city of Nashville had enacted a tax on baseball clubs and fife and drum bands, which in June they agreed to reduce: "The tax on baseball clubs was reduced from $100 per annum to $50 and the tax of $25 on the fife and drum band which parades the streets and calls the attention of the public to the fact that there will be a baseball game in the afternoon was removed entirely. Thomas J. Tyne appeared before the committee, representing the Nashville baseball club."[16]

Although the popular opinion seemed to be shifting to a more favorable position with regard to the Nashville baseball fife and drum group, the team itself, the Volunteers, was faring badly in both 1909 and 1910, and attendance was down, as an out-of-town reported noted:

The following represents a few remarks which Charles Dryden handed his paper, the Examiner, from the Sulphur Dell lookout:[17] "Owing to the climate here, the same kind that makes a fellow feel like boiled cabbage looks, the athletes were not keen for the pastime. Neither did the bugs break their necks in an effort to fill up the ball yard. About half the bleacher inmates came in as the personal escorts of foul balls hit over the wall in practice—and that, too, after a drum corps had canvassed the city all forenoon. The drum corps here has something on the one that drummed up trade for us in Mobile. A fife is added to the ensemble, and the coon behind it played patriotic tunes and war melodies. No use. The weather was too hot, and maybe the folks are too tired seeing the Volunteers slain by unfeeling regulars from afar."[18]

Although it was common for people to simply call them the "baseball fife and drum corps," the fife and drum band that played for the Nashville Vols actually had a name, as an April 1910 article in the *Tennessean* revealed:

Detroit, probably smarting more or less under yesterday's defeat at the hands of Memphis, will be in today and play one game with the Volunteers at the Dell this afternoon. In spite of the fact that the Turtles managed to get away with a 4 to 1 victory, as shown elsewhere on this page, the Detroit squad is generally conceded to be among the fastest and given an even break in the luck, should be able to hold its own with any of them. The game this afternoon will begin at 3:30 o'clock as usual, unless the weather gets busy again and puts a wet crimp in the ball grounds. You will be able to tell whether or not there is to be a game or not by seeing (or failing to see) those noble "Spirits of '76" on parade with the musical fife and drum.[19]

Because they loved baseball, Nashvillians had learned to accept Black fife and drum music as well.

A baseball game in 1915 between the Nashville Vols and the Chattanooga Lookouts occasioned a large parade in downtown Nashville, which included the Vols' famous fife and drum band: "Flanked on each side by crowds which packed the sidewalks, the parade moved from Capitol Boulevard, down Union street to Fifth avenue, but we almost forgot the biggest scream of the whole affair. An old open carriage that the Vols' ragtime fife and drum corps, drawn by the largest horse in town hitched to a tiny donkey, with a pair of Shetland ponies in front, hauled Harry Connors and some more of the elephantine directors of the Vols."[20] So well-known was this fife and drum band in Nashville that organizations began hiring it for events other than baseball games, including an October 1916 rally for women's suffrage in Nashville:

A fair-sized crowd attended the federal amendment day demonstration of the equal suffrage league, held in the courthouse yard Monday afternoon. All the speeches were well received and it was declared by the members of the league that a good impression for their cause was made. Mrs. W. J. Morrison presided and all the speakers scheduled were present. The demonstration was held on the east side of the courthouse, Mrs. D. T. Kimbrough, Mrs. E. B. Williams, Dr. J. P. Gray of Peabody college, Mrs. Leslie Warner and Mrs. Miller Dismukes were the speakers. The demonstration was called for 3:30 and several were present at 3. The fife and drum corps, so long identified with the base ball games, held the gathering until the speakers arrived.[21]

By 1917, the baseball fife and drum band was also being hired for many other events in Nashville. With the entry of the nation into World War I, many patriotic rallies and parades were held, and Tennessee was no exception. The visit of General Leonard Wood to the city occasioned a large parade in his honor at which the fife and drum musicians were engaged to play:

Registered men of the Ninth ward intend to turn out in large numbers for the parade in Gen. Wood's honor Saturday. A meeting of all enlisted men in that ward is called for tonight at 7 o'clock at Taylor's drug store, Fifteenth avenue and Church street, where all arrangements will be completed for the parade. The meeting is called by W. Turner Henderson, J. L. Hill, Chas. B. Hardly, Chas. Davitt, W. F. Dunbar, Rhos. Lellyett and Jordan Stokes Jr. In order to get out a large crowd for the meeting tonight the committee has engaged the baseball fife and drum corps and this will parade the streets of the Ninth ward all day today in order to thoroughly advertise the meeting. All men are requested to bring their registration card and honor badge with them.[22]

The same band was also employed by the Nashville Rotarians when they headed to Atlanta in June of 1917 for the International Convention of Rotary Clubs: "The baseball band was taken along and the shrill blasts of the fife and drum corps will be heard all during the convention."[23] On the next day, the newspaper reported the parade of the Rotarians in Atlanta with the fife and drum band, which of course made a big impression: "Atlanta and the International Association of Rotary clubs was given to understand that Nashville Rotary club was at the convention in true style tonight when every member of the Nashville delegation paraded the uptown streets. The Nashville body was headed by the fife and drum corps. Marching single file and with the beautiful Nashville ladies at the head, they paraded the various business streets that were lined with people. Everywhere they appeared they were greeted with applause. They also visited all the hotels in the city and gave a serenade."[24] On the last night of the convention, the Nashville members of the Rotary Club paraded around the East Lake Athletic Club in Atlanta with their fife and drum band, and then went inside for the final night of social festivities before they returned to Nashville the next day.[25] There was no more news regarding fife and drum music until September, when the *Tennessean* asked, "When the baseball season and the municipal campaign have ended, what will become of the brunette drum corps?"[26]

As late as 1920, the Nashville Vols baseball team was still employing a Black fife and drum band, and after a particularly big pair of wins in Birmingham against the Barons, the Vols were welcomed home to Nashville with a huge parade:

> Get out your horns and other noise producers, for those triumphant Vols are returning home today, after twice soundly thrashing Moley's Barons to open the season at Sulphur Dell against the aforementioned Barons. The triumphal march in celebration of the first two victories as well as the formal opening of the baseball season in Voltown will begin promptly at 10 o'clock this morning, at which time all local baseball bugs are supposed to turn out to welcome the Ellamites. Tony Rose's band will head the parade and furnish its share of the noise and music. Immediately behind the bass drum will be the Vols and the Barons in their fighting togs. The original African fife and drum crops [*sic*] will join in the procession with its familiar sign relating to a baseball game down in Sulphur Dell. After the Vols and Barons have paraded up and down the streets long enough to get up a healthy appetite, they will allow the band to do the parading by itself while they primp up for the feed which the Kiwanis are giving them at the Commercial Club at noon. About 3 p. m. this band, which has been raining all the disturbance in the business section, will follow the crowd down to the Dell to see what is going on. There it will keep up its racket until the old, familiar strains of "Play Ball" will start the local baseball season on its 1920 journey.[27]

Despite the long tradition and evident popularity of the Black fife and drum corps in association with Nashville baseball, 1927 brought the shocking news that the band's run with the Nashville Vols might be coming to an end:

This here community is standing on tiptoe awaiting the decision of home moguls as to whether or not they will once more employ that celebrated Senegambian fife and drum corps to inform the natives there will be baseball in Sulphur dell. "Rippydedee's" band has come to be an institution not only in our town but throughout the length and breadth of Dixieland.[28] The fife, the big bass drum and the son of Ham who carried the banner chronicling the names of combatants in the dell is to home baseball what books are to eyes, what life is to limb, what blood is to thunder and Santa Clause to Christmas. As well split asunder the Siamese twins, shoo Mary's lamb away from its proximity to her, chase Captain Kid from the pirate story books, or fasten the door of the cupboard to Old Mother Hubbard when she goes to look for a dog bone. Let the woodmen fail to heed the warnings to spare that tree.—But save the fife and drum corps for the Vols.[29]

Four days later, still no decision had been made regarding the Vols and the Spirit of '76 fife and drum band, so the *Tennessean* addressed the issue again, and heard from Yeatman Milan, the manager of the band as well:

After anxiously awaiting to hear some whisper of approval over our suggestion that the "spirit of '76" again be pressed into service to daily inform the populace whether or not Those Vols will be staging a baseball war in Sulphur Dell we have finally discovered at least one endorses for the suggestion. The fife and drum corps itself is heartily enthusiastic over the idea. In a quaintly worded communication from Yeatman Milan, dusky manager of the singular band we are gravely thanked for our efforts to have these Senegambian Sousas tooting through the public thoroughfares this summer. Here's the epistle he sent: To the reporter on the Tennessean, we the Nashville Base Ball Drum core [sic] are well pleased of your writting [sic] up the Drum core in the Tennessean. We have tried for years to satisfied [sic] the public and also the Base Ball fans. We have also had the pleasure of joining with the Rotairing Club [sic] to Atlanta, Ga., and Paducah, Ky., also rendered serface [sic] for City Orficials [sic] for years / I Sincerely thank you for the write up. Yeatman Milan. Managr [sic], Mooney Fruit stand. Cedar and Fourth.[30]

The man in question, Yeatman Milam, had a fairly tragic life, to say the least. He is first mentioned in the *American* in 1896, when he was arrested by the Nashville police on charges of fraudulently selling a woman's property for his own benefit.[31] How the case was disposed of is never mentioned, but in March of 1899, Milam married a woman named Maud Holt.[32] Little more than four months later, she was dead after being brutally attacked by a madame named Grace Chester. Holt had been pregnant at the time, and the attack killed the couple's unborn child as well.[33]

From the 1900 census, we learn that Yeatman Milam had been born in Tennessee in 1870 and was living in the Fourth Ward of Nashville.[34] In 1918 he was listed as a member of the orchestra of a Black motion picture theater, the Bijou: "The Bijou is also very fortunate in having assembled and kept intact a faithful and efficient corps of house attaches and employes. Mrs. S. B. Carter is the cashier. She has served faithfully and efficiently and has created a host of friends in her present capacity. She is ably assisted by Miss Allen Streator. The orchestra is capably directed by Mrs. Maggie Christopher. Others in the orchestra are A. D. King, Robert Thompson, and Yeatman Milan [sic]."[35] Although the article does not mention instruments played, it seems likely that Milam was a drummer.

In November of 1947, buried in a list of obituaries was one announcing the death of Yeatman Milan [sic] at a local hospital in Nashville. The brief notice stated that he was survived by two daughters, several grandchildren, and a host of relatives. His long career in music was not mentioned at all.[36]

The *Tennessean* never reported the outcome of the debate about Black fife and drum music and the baseball team in 1927, but at some point the decision was evidently made to rehire the Spirit of '76 band, because by 1929 they were again parading the streets of Nashville and announcing games:

> If this paper was the fife and drum corps that parades about our streets to announce such momentous affairs as wrestling matches, baseball games and shoe sales, it would have come up on your porch this morning with a sign which said in big red letters—BASEBALL TODAY VOLS VS. MILWAUKEE At SULPHUR DELL AT THREE O'CLOCK. There would have been no surprise in the announcement that the Vols are going to play Milwaukee at 3 o'clock. But the fact that they are going to stage the affair in what has been a swimming pool and fish pond for so long and at a respectable hour is something that will more than likely leave the populace all agog.[37]

In January of 1948, the *Tennessean* reported that Emmet Sims, the last surviving member of the fife and drum corps that advertised Vol baseball, was employed as a porter at a Third Avenue jewelry store in Nashville.[38]

With that brief notice, the major newspapers in Tennessee went silent with regard to fife and drum music for twenty years. Although the music undoubtedly continued at rural Black picnics, it was no longer in the public eye, where newspapermen could encounter it.

Chapter 6

"LIKE A MUFFLED, RUMBLING HEARTBEAT"

The Rediscovery and Disappearance of Black Fife and Drum Music in Tennessee, 1942–84

By 1942, Black fife and drum music was largely invisible to the larger society. Unmentioned in newspapers and magazines, unrecorded by record labels, the genre had an ephemeral existence in rural Black communities at funerals and picnics. Things might have remained that way forever, but a number of factors came together in postwar America that resulted in the rediscovery of the Black fife and drum tradition. One factor was the activities of folklorists and musicologists such as Alan Lomax. In 1942, he and Louis Jones were commissioned by the Library of Congress to go to the Mississippi Delta and make field recordings. While most of these recordings were made in Clarksdale and Coahoma County, one session was made near Sledge in Quitman County—of a fife and drum ensemble led by Sid Hemphill. Of this fife and drum music that he had uncovered, Lomax later stated: "It dawned on me that on that dust-laden summer afternoon in Po Whore's Kingdom [a picnic grounds] in Mississippi,[1] I had stumbled onto an outcropping of African music in North America."[2]

THE YOUNG BROTHERS AND THE SOUTHERN FIFE AND DRUM CORPS

The recordings that Lomax and Jones made in Quitman County, Mississippi, in 1942 were for the Library of Congress, and as such were not disseminated at the time they were made. But Lomax returned to Mississippi in 1959 to revisit some locations and make new recordings, against the backdrop of an America whose popular culture was changing rapidly. The end of World War II was followed by the birth of an independent recording industry and the proliferation of radio stations, record labels, and record stores. In addition, a burgeoning folk music scene was growing, beginning in New York City and spreading to other cities and college campuses. As Lomax was returning to Mississippi, blues researcher Samuel Charters was in Memphis, looking for the 1920s bluesman Furry Lewis. The early 1960s brought many discoveries and rediscoveries—Sleepy John Estes, Yank Rachell, Mississippi Joe Callicott, Nathan Beauregard, Bukka White, Gus Cannon, and Willie Borum. Many of the classic blues recordings of the 1920s and early 1930s had been made in Memphis, and so a number of young Americans (and even Europeans) interested in the blues descended on the Bluff City.

On his 1959 visit to Mississippi, Lomax discovered a new band in the Tate and Panola County region, a fife and drum band consisting of fifer Ed Young, his brother Lonnie on the bass drum, and their other brother G. D. on the snare drum.[3] Although this ensemble was clearly a Mississippi fife and drum band, it came to have special significance in Tennessee, because Ed Young ended up moving to Memphis and becoming the janitor of Porter Junior High School.[4]

By 1968, the folk renaissance was in full swing, and white young people were at least temporarily enthused by unique homegrown musical styles. Ed Young's band, now dubbed the "Afro-American Fife and Drum Band," was invited to play the Smithsonian Institution's Folk Festival during the Fourth of July weekend, and the band of Mississippians was dubbed "an Afro-American fife and drum group from Memphis" by the office of Senator Howard Baker of Tennessee, which was, of course, not entirely accurate, even if Ed Young was now living in Memphis.[5] The band was said to be "a hit" at the festival.

But they were soon heading for another festival, one in Ed Young's new hometown. The interest in uncovering and rediscovering old bluesmen had attracted a number of serious researchers, enthusiasts, musicians, and hippies to the city of Memphis during the early 1960s, and some of these had formed an organization called the Memphis Country Blues Society. Among the leaders of the society were Bill Barth, a New York City native who had helped locate Skip James in a Tunica, Mississippi, hospital in 1964,[6] and Robert Palmer, who later wrote the book *Deep Blues* and was involved with the Fat Possum record label in Water Valley, Mississippi.[7] In 1966, the Memphis Country Blues Society launched the Memphis Country Blues Festival at the Overton Park Shell, an outdoor venue in Memphis's largest park. The out-of-towners who had moved to Memphis found kindred souls in local musicians like Jim Dickinson and Sid Selvidge, who had been organizing folk events at local coffeehouses and other venues, and who would become enthusiastic participants in the blues festivals. With each year, the festival, which had started in a small and low-key fashion, became a bigger and bigger function, and the 1968 festival announced that one of the performers would be something called the Southern Fife and Drum Corps.[8]

Although it would seem that Ed Young and his brothers had used the Afro-American Fife and Drum Corps name when they played the Smithsonian Festival, in 1966, they played the Newport Folk Festival in Rhode Island, where they were billed as the Southern Fife and Drum Corps.[9] It seems that the ensemble used both names for a period of time, with the Afro-American name more common in later years. Although the newspapers mentioned the band consistently in the days leading up to the 1968 Memphis Country Blues Festival, after the event was held on July 20, there was no review of the concert or description of the performances, and despite the festival being recorded by Sire Records, the resulting album, *The 1968 Memphis Country Blues Festival*,[10] did not include any fife and drum band recordings. A similar record was made in Memphis studios by the Blue Thumb label, entitled *Memphis Swamp Jam*,[11] consisting primarily of performers that had played at the festival, but it chose to use Napoleon Strickland, Johnny Woods, and Otha Turner, who likely did not play at the festival,[12] rather than the Southern Fife and Drum Corps, which possibly did. No surviving recordings or films of their performance in Overton Park seem to exist.

The next year, the Memphis Country Blues Festival got subsumed into the city's Sesquicentennial, becoming co-branded as the W. C. Handy Music Festival. For a short time, the Rolling Stones were expected, and the venue was changed to Crump Stadium, as the Overton Park Shell was not thought to be adequate for the crowds that would have turned out. But eventually the Stones pulled out, the city funding that was promised dissipated, and the event was held at its usual location in Overton Park. The Southern Fife and Drum Corps was again the only Black fife and drum band billed as part of the event,[13] and unlike the previous year, in 1969, two different sets of film crews documented the festival. The cameramen from WNET, a public broadcasting station in New York City, were in Memphis filming the event for a nationwide PBS program called *Summer in America*, which delivered a truncated version of the day's music to homes nationwide. However, this crew ran into a problem when their cameras started to overheat due to the hot weather. The other crew, hippie enthusiasts from Eugene Rosenthal's record label Adelphi in Maryland, had no such problem, and they apparently recorded the entire lineup of performers. Unfortunately, neither of the two sets of footage are readily available to the average person. Both the *Summer in America* footage and the Adelphi footage (which was later sold to Fat Possum and prepared for release under the name *Memphis '69*) have been screened publicly in Memphis, but neither is available for streaming or purchase. The *Summer in America* program did not include any fife and drum music, and it is unclear whether the *Memphis '69* footage does. Both the DVD and a three-LP soundtrack are ultimately scheduled for future release, so it is likely that the full scope of these films and recordings will become apparent.

There was little mention of the Southern Fife and Drum Corps or the Young Brothers after 1970. Lonnie Young passed away sometime before 1976, and his death led to Lum Guffin of Bartlett being placed on the American Old Time Festival Tour in his place,[14] but the Afro-American Fife and Drum Corps name strangely appeared one more time in 1977, in connection with the second annual Grassroots Days, a Tennessee folk festival held in Nashville's Centennial Park in September. One of the featured performers was said to be an "Afro-American fife and drum blues band from Fayette County."[15] Ed Young was never from Fayette County, and it is possible that the reference is to some other band than the Young Brothers. There were actually two Black fife and drum bands in Fayette County—the Broadnax Brothers Fife and Drum Band in Brewer, and the Fredonia Fife and Drum Band from the Fredonia community near Stanton—but there is no evidence that either band ever played in Nashville. After 1977, it was common for the Tennessee folk festivals to book the Rising Star Fife and Drum Band from Como, Mississippi, as there were no longer any well-known fife and drum bands in Tennessee.

THE BROADNAX BROTHERS FIFE AND DRUM BAND
IN THE MASON, TENNESSEE, AREA

Aside from the Young Brothers, who were actually a Como, Mississippi–based fife and drum group, it would seem that the first Tennessee fife and drum band to be discovered by outsiders was a group led by Ossie Broadnax in a Fayette County community called Brewer, located just across the county line from the Tipton County community of Mason. One of the blues enthusiasts who had come to Memphis in search of old bluesmen in the late 1960s was a Swedish researcher named Bengt Olsson. He had come to Memphis in 1969 and for a time was living with Bill Barth, one of the founders of the Memphis Country Blues Festival. By 1970, he had a brief published book entitled *Memphis Blues*. Although a slim tome, it was the first book about its subject to be published, and it remains an indispensable guide for the Memphis music researcher. But Olsson remained in West

Tennessee, doing cutting-edge work in the rural areas outside of Memphis and uncovering information about blues musicians who otherwise would have largely been forgotten.

In 1971, Olsson met Ossie Broadnax at a house on Highway 59 in Fayette County, near Longtown. In his writings, Olsson gave a detailed description of Broadnax's house, but he consistently referred to this man as Othar Broadnax, apparently confusing him with Othar Turner in Senatobia, as both men were fife players.[16] Nevertheless, we can tell from both census and death records that the man's name was Ossie Broadnax (pronounced "O-cee" according to Mason historian John Marshall), and that he was born on March 12, 1885. His wife was named Katie Broadnax, and he had a son named John and daughters named Lula and Louise. But there was some question about both the spelling of his name and his age, as he appears in the 1910 census as "Ocie Brodnax" with a birth date of 1890, and in the 1930 census as "Ocie Brodnax" with a birth date of 1888! However, from the 1930 census it is clear that this is the same man, as he has a son named John H. Brodnax in both the 1930 and 1940 censuses. The confusion over spelling comes as no surprise—there had actually been a white woman in Mason, Tennessee, named Ocie Brodnax, and it may have been a result of that fact that the musician changed the spelling of his name to "Ossie." Also, as a rule, the white Brodnaxes spelled their name "Brodnax," while the Black families of that name added the extra "a," but there must have been some confusion about this in the 1890–1930 period, or perhaps the census enumerator wrote it down wrong. At any rate, we know from Social Security death records that Ossie Broadnax died in Gallaway, Tennessee, in Fayette County in 1981, at the age of ninety-six.

It is unclear exactly how many different musicians played with the Broadnax Brothers, but in an interview, Annie Humphrey, the daughter of Bennie Thompson of the Fredonia band, stated that the nucleus of the Broadnax band was two brothers, Ossie Broadnax and Jethro Broadnax.[17] Fife player Ed Harris, when interviewed by Robert Jeffrey for the Tennessee State Archives' Folklife Collection in 1980, also mentioned these men.[18] Other known members include snare drummer Plez Rivers (mentioned by both Humphrey and Olsson), who was the father of Chicago blues musician Homesick James, and R. Lee Taylor, mentioned by Ed Harris as a "lead drummer," probably a snare drummer.

The Broadnax band played an important role in the music and social history of the countryside in and around the Tipton County town of Mason, Tennessee. In October of 2018, at the annual Mason Unity Fall Festival, a young woman who said she was a granddaughter of Ossie Broadnax recalled her grandfather playing for Trade Days in Mason, the Monday gatherings when people came to the square to buy and sell fruits, vegetables, and goods.[19] The square in Mason was along Front Street and the railroad, fronted by a row of juke joints that were euphemistically called "cafés," as Mason was supposed to be a dry town, although liquor flowed freely there well into the modern era. She also recalled the Broadnax Brothers playing at horse races at a place called Booster Peete's, which was located in the countryside north of Mason along the Tabernacle Road. Although horse racing was and remains illegal in Tennessee, the races at Booster Peete's and those at another nearby spot called Dyson's were on private property, and thus could occur without interference from the authorities. The fife and drum music was used to advertise and attract crowds to these events and picnics. A man nearby in front of the Log Cabin, one of the last Mason cafés still standing, mentioned that he could recall the Broadnax Brothers being driven around the backroads of Fayette County in a wagon, beating the drums. "That's how they would advertise a picnic. They would ride around all Friday afternoon and evening, playing on the back of the wagon, and you knew there was going to be a picnic that Saturday."[20] He also recalled that although the Broadnax brothers were from the Brewer community,[21] they had eventually moved to a house close to Highway 14 between Mason and Covington.

The tendency of the Broadnax Brothers to play in a wagon pulled by mules is mentioned by many who recall the band, and may be referred to as far back as the 1930s. In a letter to his friend John Flowers Taylor, Louisiana historian and Mason native Joe Gray Taylor wrote about Black Fourth of July parades and picnics that may have included the Broadnax Brothers band: "Do you remember those black Fourth of July parades and celebrations? Before the depression they had a band of sorts from Memphis leading the parade, but when I vividly remember they had to be content with a bass drum in a wagon. I used to wonder why only black people celebrated Independence Day, and many years later I learned that white southerners quit celebrating after Vicksburg was surrendered on the Fourth of July, 1863. I don't think I remember hearing a firecracker in July until after World War II."[22] In addition to playing for picnics, horse races, and trade days, the Broadnax Brothers band was also in demand at rural juke joints, particularly in the Brewer area, such as one that Ossie Broadnax had taken Bengt Olsson to, the Dew Drop Inn: "The Broadnax Band used to get hired regularly by backwoods cafes in Bruels [sic] during weekends. They were actually hired as a blues band, a band to provide dance music, and so was the Longtown Band and Fredonia Band."[23] Although it would seem that the Broadnaxes played more often in Tipton County than they did in Fayette, Myles Wilson, former superintendent of Fayette County Schools, and a co-owner of the legendary blues club Tay-May in Mason, recalled the Broadnax Brothers playing for picnics at a place called Buford Evans' on the corner of Highway 59 and the Oakland Road.[24]

Although Ossie was apparently also a drummer, the band's snare drummer Plez Rivers had a certain degree of recognition in the early 1970s as the father of the Chicago musician Homesick James. Bengt Olsson went to visit him "at the end of a dirt road, way out in the woods near Bruels [Brewer]." Rivers told Olsson:

> We never played in Somerville—you better not stomp your foot there. They put you in jail for nothing and when they do you don't know much about it 'cause they done mashed that blackjack on your head. But we *played* in Mason. That was our town, played right there in the center of town in front of Mr. Taylor's drug store on trade days. We used to play, that's what we liked the best. We had everything they ever wanted with them drums, Charleston and "Steppin' On A Puppy's Tail." Al Stanback from Mason recorded us[25] and after that people from all over who'd never heard of us booked us.[26]

Plez also told Olsson about Mason's violent history. The little town could be quite rough, and fights and shootings were common:

> According to Plez Rivers, there were many violent deaths in Mason. Plez played there with the Longtown Band (Bob Swift played the fife) and once there was a shoot-out involving several people. Plez prided himself on being the best runner in "our parts." He said one secret was to keep your mouth closed when running. Plez left Mason running when the shooting started and ran all the way home with his drum strapped around his neck, banging against his body. "The drum had been busted all to pieces when I reached home." He was running from bullets *and* the police.[27]

In March of 1974, the film crew of the Super 8 Film Company from New York came to the Mason, Tennessee, area while working on the documentary film *Tell the Angels*. The crew consisted of Mark Mikolas and his wife Judith, a researcher and interviewer, and Bill Barth. Bengt Olsson seems to have been their tour guide, leading them to people and locations that he and Barth thought should be filmed. He had brought Lum Guffin with him from Bartlett, and they stopped at the Dew Drop Inn in Brewer,[28] "the kind of cafe that only a decade earlier used to hire drum and fife bands for Saturday night dances. Owned by [a] black man, [it had a] jukebox, a few metal tables, beer cases kept in shed."[29] Hallie Massey [Manson] of the Fredonia band was there as well, and Ossie Broadnax, whom Olsson remembered moving from side to side as he beat the snare drum, while youngsters did a dance called the Robot to the music, some of them humping the ground, a style of dance that had also been noted at fife and drum picnics in Senatobia. Olsson recalled:

> When I asked Lum what song it was they just played, Lum whispered to Plez and said "We ain't gonna tell you!" and laughed. Lum thought Massey's music was "wild" and "out of control," like someone who could read music meeting someone untrained. Lum's band played "Dixie." Two men in front (drums), man at far front had sword with which he directed the second-line behind the band,[30] made them part, then came together again, etc. Fife blew a start-up signal twice, then the marching started, or shall we call it trucking. [They] played "When The Saints," "In Your [sic] Sweet Bye and Bye," and "Glory, Glory Hallelujah (When I Lay My Burdens Down)."[31]

In a July 12, 1974, letter to Dr. David Evans, Bengt Olsson gave a considerable amount of information regarding the Broadnax Brothers band. He stated that the band consisted of "Other Broadnax" (Ossie Broadnax), who played fife and snare drum, and three brothers: Fred, who played fife and snare, Jeff, who played bass, and Aloshua, who played fife. Their father Elijah led a fife and drum band that played almost only religious music and a few marches, and this band occasionally added brass instruments, such as a trumpet and trombone.[32] Olsson quoted Plez Rivers, later a snare drummer for the band, with regard to its versatility: "The blues was all of us, but we'd play church songs for church people, 'cause it made 'em happy. We had anything they wanted with them drums. No, they never did no marching to our band. They did the Charleston and Steppin' On A Puppy's Tail, no marching."[33] He also noted that the band played in Ripley, Tennessee, Red Banks, Mississippi, Como, Mississippi, and for annual Pole Bearers' picnics in Brunswick, Tennessee, and Grand Junction. Ossie Broadnax's first fifes had been made of cane, but later he had fifes made of rosewood and walnut. Eventually, he was given a metal fife by a white man in Mason.[34]

Sadly, not much remains from the film team's venture into the Mason area. Mark Mikolas, in an email, recalled that Plez Rivers had developed a kind of coded language that he used, such as "I was having a smile when George came in with the stuff," by which he meant that he was having a drink when the sheriff came in with a gun.[35] His ex-wife Judy Capurso stated that they had not captured Plez Rivers on film, but merely taken slide photographs of him and interviewed him.[36] All of the resulting tapes and slides were donated to the Center for Southern Folklore in Memphis, but the center has moved several times, and the items sadly seem to have been lost. The movie they were making, *Tell the Angels*, which included footage shot in Memphis and Hughes, Arkansas, won some awards in the early 1980s, but has also been lost.

Bengt Olsson did record Ossie Broadnax alone in the summer of 1971, apparently around the same time he discovered Lattie Murrell. The six minutes of recording comprise seven short pieces where Broadnax sings, accompanying himself with either the fife or the snare drum. Two selections are blues songs: "Don't the Peaches Look Mellow" and "Ain't Gonna Be Your Dog." The remainder of the songs are either untitled instrumentals or spiritual tunes, including "Tell Heaven I'm Coming," "Some Call Daniel a Baptist Man," and "I Found Jesus." Of these, only "Don't the Peaches Look Mellow" saw release on the *Old Country Blues* album, credited to "Othar Broadnax." It was reissued on CD in 1993 as part of the *On the Road Again* compilation, still credited to "Othar Broadnax." In a 1972 letter to David Evans, Olsson suggested that the "sanctified" pieces were similar to the repertoire of Elijah Broadnax, Ossie's father. He also associated "Ain't Gonna Be Your Dog" with the Fayette County bluesman Johnny Wilson, although the lyrics are traditional and are found elsewhere.[37]

The death of Jeff Broadnax and the illness of Ossie Broadnax brought the Broadnax Brothers band to an end in the mid-1960s. Although Ed Harris tried to continue a rump group of former members of the Broadnax and Fredonia bands, by 1981 that too seems to have come to an end.

BENNIE THOMPSON, HALLIE MANSON, AND THE FREDONIA FIFE AND DRUM BAND

The other primary fife and drum band in the Mason and Stanton area was called the Fredonia Fife and Drum Band, which was unique due to its significant age and its affiliation with a lodge of the Prince Hall Masons. Dr. Dorothy Granberry, a local historian in Haywood County, suggests in an article that the band might have been founded by a man named Penn Jones sometime in the early 1910s.[38] The Fredonia community, for which the band was named, straddles the line between Fayette and Haywood Counties, but is closer to the Stanton and Douglass communities in Haywood County.

Granberry describes the band's heyday as the 1940s and '50s in the Stanton area and gives an account of the context in which the music took place:

> If you were in Stanton during the 1940s and 1950s you knew about the Fredonia Lodge Drum and Fife Band. This four-man ensemble was a standard feature of summer picnics. In the days when there were few telephones, rural people were called to outdoor picnic parties by the booming bass drum beginning around one or two on hot Saturday afternoons. In the 1940s, the band consisted of Hallie Manson on the bass drum. This drum bore the group's name, the Masonic symbol and the lodge number (139). Leon Thompson and Eli (Buster) Harwell were both fife players. Leon's brother, Ben Thompson, played the snare drum. When the group played, the players danced and shuffled about to the rhythms produced by their instruments. All of the men lived in the greater Fredonia community (some in neighboring Fayette County and some in Haywood) and all were lodge members.[39]

The man she refers to as Hallie Manson was the man Bengt Olsson called Hallie Massey, the same man that Olsson and the film crew were enjoying in 1973 at the Dew Drop Inn in Brewer.

According to Olsson "Halley Massey [sic] (bass drum) first had his own band. Later, parts of his own band and part of the Fredonia band joined forces. He had a jug in his first band—this was around 1915. . . . Massey [was] very flamboyant, [a] showman, clown, entertainer. He lived in the Oak Grove community outside of Somerville."[40]

We can confirm from census records that the man's name was Hallie Manson rather than Hallie Massey, and that his father and mother were Henry and Loula Manson, living in the Fourth Civil District of Fayette County, Tennessee, in 1900, when Hallie was five years old. From the 1920 census, we learn that Hallie was born in 1894, that he was married to Lizzie Manson and had one daughter, Lulu Manson. He was still living in the Fourth Civil District, where his parents had lived twenty years before. By 1930, he had moved to District Five of Fayette County, where he was living with his wife and four children. He died on November 10, 1988, in Memphis, at the age of ninety-four years.

In an interview, Ben Thompson's daughter, Annie Humphrey, revealed that her father was the leader of the Fredonia band, playing the bass drum, and his brother Leon was the fifer. She stated that the snare drum was played by "Hallie Massey," who was of course Hallie Manson. "They played mostly for picnics, sometimes for schools and field days. . . . Fields School in Mason, Bernard School in Fayette County, the Fredonia School, the Pleasant Grove School. Douglass community [in Haywood County] had a picnic every August." Ms. Humphrey also recalled her dad playing for horse races at Williams's Horse Track, which she recalled as being about a half mile from Fredonia Church in Fayette County. Like those at Booster Peete's or Dyson's, these races were probably able to go on because they were being held on private land. And at the Belmont Picnic, which was held at Belmont CME Church south of Mason, she stated that both her dad's Fredonia band and the Broadnax Brothers band would play.[41]

Unfortunately, while pictures have surfaced of the Fredonia band, there is no documentation of what this ensemble sounded like. By the time that Bengt Olsson and the Super 8 Film Company crew came to Brewer in 1974, the Fredonia band had broken up due to illnesses or deaths, and what Mark and Judy Mikolas, Bill Barth, and Bengt Olsson documented in March of 1974 was actually a rump group of musicians from different bands who were brought together for the documentary project. Halley Manson was a veteran of the Fredonia band, while Plez Rivers had taken the late Fred Broadnax's place in the Broadnax band, and Lum Guffin of Bartlett was the leader of the United Sons and Daughters of Zion Fife and Drum Band. Although this was not the original Fredonia band, the researchers filmed and recorded it under that name. None of the film footage, or the fifteen hours of taped interviews, have surfaced, but one reel of recordings was found in the personal collection of Dr. David Evans, which was apparently sent to him in 1975 by Judith Mikolas. The tape contains roughly eight tracks of interviews and fife and drum selections.

A check of the eight tracks on the March 15, 1974, tape shows all of music recorded to have been religious in nature:

1. Interview & There'll Be Glory
2. Interview, Practice & Fife and Drum Piece No. 1
3. Fife and Drum Piece No. 2, Interview & The Battle Hymn of the Republic
4. Glory, Glory Hallelujah & Interview
5. Do You Know Him & Interview
6. The Dead Lick, Interview & Will the Circle Be Unbroken
7. Will the Circle Be Unbroken (continued)[42]

The location of these recordings is somewhat confused, to say the least. Bengt Olsson, in his unpublished manuscript, seems to suggest that the location was the Dew Drop Inn (the juke joint in the Brewer community of Fayette County), and he in fact gives a detailed description of the place.[43] However, Judith Mikolas, in a letter to Dr. David Evans discussing the reel of tape she had sent him, states the following: "Lum plays fife, Plez beats snare, Hallee [sic] beats bass drum. They play at the relatives' of an ex-member of Hallee's band (Leon Thompson).[44] This family owns the bass drum that Hallee is playing. This is where the selection starts. In the beginning, there is considerable wind distortion, which disappears when they move behind the house."[45] Given that Olsson's memory was written thirty-three years after the fact, it seems likely that Judith Mikolas's location is the correct one, although with five hours of footage, they may have shot at the Dew Drop Inn as well.

One of the difficulties of the recording is the inability to determine which of the three men is speaking in the interview sections. They mention the sound of the drum carrying for "twenty miles" or so, the number of years they have been playing, and different bands they had played with, such as Tom Skipper's, Jack Raine's and Kane Skipper's. One of them mentions going down to teach drums to the "Bledsoe boys," and another mentions going to play for the Fourth of July at Mount Olive in 1967.[46] Two of them mention having not played drums in four years, but one of them points out "It don't take long to get back." They also mention Robert Taylor's band and the Miller band, refer to the Skipper band being from Longtown, and discuss going down to Union Hill in 1973 to play for Boston Bledsoe,[47] but failing to round up any young people willing to play drums for them, which opens a window onto the way that the tradition began to unravel in the early 1970s. The drummers also discuss and demonstrate for the Mikolases the "dead lick," the beat that was used to announce that someone in the community had died.[48]

The musical tracks recorded are interesting as well, although they highlight a vast difference in style between Lum Guffin and the two Fayette County musicians. The drumming styles of Plez Rivers and Hallie Manson show similarities with the Mississippi style. Both the snare drum and bass drum parts are highly syncopated and feature irregular accents that suggest polyrhythms, while Lum plays in a pentatonic style that resembles an older military tradition. Perhaps nowhere is the difference highlighted better than when Lum suggests that they play "Glory, Glory, Hallelujah." He sings what he is suggesting, which is the "Battle Hymn of the Republic." Manson and

Rivers do not know that version, and make it clear that what they know as "Glory, Glory, Hallelujah" is in fact "When I Lay My Burdens Down," a tune well known in the Mississippi fife and drum tradition. They go on to play and sing that version, but Lum does not know it, and struggles to fit in with them. Ultimately, Lum referred to Manson's music as "wild," whereas Manson saw Lum's music as "disciplined, like a drum and bugle corps."[49] A comparison of the recording of "Do You Know Him?" from this reference tape and the version on the *Old Country Blues* album on Flyright shows them to be the same recording, and it does indeed sound "wild."

In his July 12, 1974, letter to David Evans, Bengt Olsson gave significant information about Hallie Manson, whom he consistently referred to as Hallie Massey:

HALLIE MASSEY: 80 years old ["Feel better now than I did twenty years ago"]—witty—curious—bushy white mustache—always on the move. . . . Before we located him, everyone told us Massey was "a real clown who could do all kinds of tricks with his bass drum." They were right. Around 1905 he went to a drum & fife picnic by the water-mill at Somerville.[50] The band members were fairly old according to Hallie [probably in their 50s] and Jim Hose, the snare drummer, took an interest in Massey, who at the time was a fine guitar player [using knife and bottleneck] and also could play piano, harmonica and jew's harp. "He told me 'It seems like you can do anything but play a drum!' and hung the snare around my neck and from that moment on I could play." I wish I had more details but on the two occasions we saw he always had to be somewhere else before long. He held his band—which included a jug—together until around 1920, when they split up. At about the same time the Fredonia band [named after a church nearby—but not closely associated with church like Lum; just called band after the center of the community] parted ways, so the remainder of the two bands teamed up—fife/2 drums/kettle drum. They continued to be known as the Fredonia band. Massey was also in demand as a solo artist—just he and bass drum—due to his clowning! He'd run through the repertory of his tricks, collect the dollars and leave his [mostly] white audience laughing. "After they got home from work most people went to sleep. We would be out there with the drums and wake 'em up. They just couldn't stay in bed; they had to get up and go partying. Sometimes they could hear us as far away as twelve miles!" If he had his choice they would just play church music, but if they got requests for blues and jazz they could play that too. Funnily enough, the one song no one saw much harm with was "Sally Got a Bigger Leg Than Anybody Else." When I asked Lum what he thought of Massey's and Plez's music he said "It's alright, but kind of wild," whereas Massey, upon hearing Lum play the snare, thought it almost sounded like drum and bugle music.... One of the fife blowers—regarded as the best in the area—Leon Thomas (Thompson), who occasionally played with Massey died around 1960 and was buried with his fife.[51]

"SALLY'S GOT A BIG LEG": LUM GUFFIN, THE UNITED SONS AND DAUGHTERS OF ZION NO. 9 FIFE AND DRUM BAND, AND THE BRUNSWICK PICNIC

Although the Broadnax Brothers and the Fredonia bands were undoubtedly the first Tennessee fife and drum bands to be documented in the modern era, and while one of these two was likely the "Tennessee fife and drum band" that Dr. David Evans mentioned in his 1972 article,[52] by far the best-documented Black fife and drum band in the 1970s was that of Columbus "Lum" "Lucky" Guffin of Bartlett, Tennessee, an ensemble known as the United Sons and Daughters of Zion No. 9 Fife and Drum Band.

In November of 1882, a brief notice in the *Memphis Daily Appeal* told of a charter application for something called the United Sons and Daughters of Zion, No. 9, filed by Lovett Bell, B. L. Griffin [*sic*], J. J. Jackson, B. Scruggs, and Hampton Kirk. Although the article referred to one of the founders as "B. L. Griffin," we can recognize him as Butler Guffin, the grandfather of Lum Guffin.[53] From census information, we learn that Butler Guffin was born in South Carolina in 1841, and in 1910 was living in the Seventh Civil District of Shelby County, which included the town of Bartlett. According to Bill Barth, Butler had acquired eighty-five acres of land immediately after the Civil War, and this was the land on which Lum Guffin still lived in 1969, on the Old Brownsville Road near Bartlett.[54]

Much about Lum Guffin's life is uncertain, but census records help us fill in some of the gaps. Columbus "Lum" Guffin was born in 1902, the son of Columbus Guffin and Tennessee Guffin, and in 1910, at the age of eight, he was living in the Seventh Civil District of Shelby County, Tennessee. In 1920, at the age of eighteen, Lum was listed in the census as a "boarder" in a house at 872 Olympic in North Memphis with six other people, ranging in age from nine to thirty-nine, most of whom were named Taylor. By 1930, Lum was back living with his father and mother in the First Civil District of

Shelby County. Although not a blues musician, Lum's father Columbus had a string band and played the banjo.[55] He must have also been a fife player, as Bill Barth mentioned that Lum had his father's fife made of rosewood with silver tips.[56] Olsson mentions that Lum had visited Beale Street to check out jug band performers,[57] and Barth mentions a stint as a hobo: "Lum tells of riding trains to California to stay with a brother who lived in Oakland, hopping freights, riding the M & O, the Southern Pacific, and the Illinois Central. He says of his experiences 'you gotta stay with it, that's what hoboin' is.'"[58]

But Lum Guffin ultimately returned to Bartlett, to the rural area near Prosperity Missionary Baptist Church where he had grown up, and he became a well-known performer in the area, though unknown to the larger world outside. However, a chance meeting of Guffin with a Mississippi blues researcher and musician named Bobby Ray Watson in 1968 led to Guffin being invited to perform at the 1969 Memphis Country Blues Festival at Overton Park in Memphis. That performance evidently made him a hero in his rural community: "In the local grocery store there was a newspaper clipping proudly pinned to the wall, showing Lum on stage."[59]

After his introduction to a larger public, many others beat a path to Guffin's small wooden shack along the dirt track known as Guffin Lane; blues researcher Steve LaVere visited, and in 1972 he led Stephan Michelson to Guffin.[60] It would seem that Bill Barth took his friend Bengt Olsson to see Lum as well, either in 1972 or 1973, and that Olsson made the recordings that led to the *Walking Victrola* album, ultimately released on the Flyright label in the United Kingdom, a subsidiary label of the Interstate Music Company Ltd. The field recordings that made up the album were all of Lum singing and playing the guitar, but the liner notes, written by Bill Barth,[61] described a fife and drum picnic in 1973 at Prosperity Church near Bartlett on the occasion of the anniversary of the founding of the United Sons and Daughters of Zion No. 9:

> In 1880 Butler Guffin and some neighbors formed an organization called the United Sons and Daughters of Zion, with various chapters around the east Shelby County area. He became secretary of Chapter No. 9 and today his grandson Lum is the President of this Chapter. Officially chartered by the State of Tennessee, on March 5th 1882, the U.S.D. of Zion was formed as a non-denominational charitable organization, whose purpose was to take care of its members in time of need, to play music at various functions, and to observe each year the anniversary of the organization's founding, with a picnic with

music, not country blues, but rather the playing of drums and fifes in the earliest traditions of black music. Each year up till the present time this tradition has been carried on by the present members of the organization.

This year March 5th fell on a weekday, so on Saturday March 3rd, the annual meeting was held. The day was sort of damp, and a grey haze hung over the countryside. I had spoken to Lum earlier that week, getting a bit of biographical data, and he had invited me to the picnic that weekend.

Lum was playing snare drum (marching drum), and later alternated on bass drum and fife, with the other players, and the music was incredible.

After driving through the damp haze to the old church where the picnic site was, I felt as though I had entered another era, thought by most people to be extinct, but yet there it was. Lum asked me to help hold the bass drum and it was like holding thunder, the music booming out, with two snare drums, bass drum and fife all going at once. Strangely enough they played no blues as do some other survivors of this tradition, but instead played dance tunes, which wouldn't have seemed out of place in a black or white string band like the Mississippi Sheiks or the North Carolina Ramblers, country songs. The drummers would stop and keep time by hitting their sticks against the wooden edges of the drums while the fife lined out the tune, then all joined in with the drums accenting the fife notes.

The barbecue served was delicious, and as I stood and ate I though of what I was witnessing, a tradition of black music which has hardly changed in over 100 years, kept alive through organizations like the one started by Lum Guffin's grandfather and his contemporaries, a tradition which had seemingly vanished in terms of modern music, or even in terms of old-time country blues was there before me, alive and well in east Shelby County.

Lum said later that most young people consider that sort of music "old-fogeyism" and so it is fading, though not quite as fast as was thought.[62]

While most of the interest in Lum Guffin was in regard to his guitar playing, he also played the snare drum, bass drum, fife, mandolin, and piano.

In an interview, Rev. Arthur Becton from the Bartlett area described some of the community functions at which Guffin's fife and drum band often performed:

We have a group there we used to call SBS No. 4 society, which, once a year annually, we would have a picnic at the Easter Brown Grove, and the group that would come over and play the music was Mr. Lum Guffin, and if I remember correctly, Mr. Henderson Owen; they had the drums, fifes. They would play there, and plus, they would play at the IPB No. 6 Society picnic. . . . The IPB was "Independent" something or other, but the SBS No. 4. was considered the Social Benevolent Society, and what the group was, it was a group that we had, a community group that did community service for people that was a member of the society.

I was a member for twenty-six years. I got in there, my mom and them put me in there when I was sixteen years old. What we had to do was, when peoples in the community that was a member of the SBS No. 4 society, we would have to go visit them, and if there was a man, he was sick, and the family had been sitting with him all this time and they had nobody else, the society would appoint two men per night to go sit up all night and take care of him, and if he was sick and winter time came, the society would appoint like six men to go into the woods and cut his winter wood and haul it to his house, to make sure he was protected. When it come down to the women, they would appoint two women to go during the day, to help the wife clean the house, cook and all of that, and at night they would appoint two to go sit with her during the night session. . . . It was all about helping those when they were down. . . . That is what the IPB 6 was too. They did the same thing.

But they held like a fundraiser, the SBS No. 4. They would have a picnic on the Ellendale Road that we called the Easter Brown Grove, and Easter Brown Grove was my great aunt's property, which my granddad bought, and they would have picnics there . . . as fundraisers. IPB 6, they would have theirs at Brunswick; we used to call it the Gravel Pit Picnic . . . and IPB. No. 5, which was Oak Grove on 64 highway [sic],[63] had theirs at Oak Grove, just where Oak Grove Baptist Church is.

We would always see Lum Guffin play, and if I remember correctly, Henderson Owen would always play, had a big old drum that took two men to hold that thing; and they played this drum, and the fife . . . he had one that was metal, and then, just being a kid, I seen him play one that looked like a fishing cane. I don't know what he made it out of. But he would play that thing and they would sing, and they would play that little old fife and play the drum. I was probably ten or twelve years old when I first heard them at Easter Brown Grove, and that would have been in '51 or '52. And when I went to junior high school, about 1952 or 1953, that is when they had the big picnic, the Gravel Pit Picnic. That was the one at Brunswick Road and Highway 70. And what they would do, they would leave their society hall, across the street from the school, the one that is still there, and they would march down to the picnic area when they opened up the picnic for that weekend, and they would start.

Then the drum and fife music would come in one night, and they would play during the day, and people would just stand around and watch them play, and they would dance there in that dust and stuff. . . . That picnic would start on Thursday evening, because we were going to school, and we would see them going down there on Thursday evening, and they would go Friday and Friday night and Saturday, till Saturday at night, early part of the night, they would close, because of church on Sunday.

Sometimes they would have two fife and drum bands play there, but I don't know who the other band was. I just recall Lum Guffin and Henderson Owen. Henderson Owen was from Bartlett. That's where he was from, and he has family that lives on Shadowlawn Road, that's where his son lives, across from Shadowlawn School. They would play the music, and that was the only music there until the early part of the 1960s. That's when they just about quit playing, because they started bringing in music from jukeboxes and things. Before then, there wasn't no lights, there wasn't no electrical nothing, just that music. That's what the drum was.

In our society, we had one of those big old drums, about that size, and that used to be a way that they would notify members when they need to meet. For instance, in SBS No. 4, we had this drum, and we had men called marshals. And what they would do, they would appoint marshals to visit . . . and one marshal would be responsible for so many members. If you were sick, the marshal would visit, and appoint people to go sit with you. But when someone would die in the society, at sunrise, the drummer would go out and alarm the drum. That thing would carry from what we now call Kirby-Whitten Road and Ellendale Road, now Egypt-Central Road, Easter Brown Grove, that sound would carry from there all across Shadowlawn Road into Germantown Road, which we call the Horton subdivision. You could hear that drum. And they would do it in the early morning, just before sunrise, and they would do it in the early evening, a half hour before sunset. Once you heard the drum, the marshals was to go to the drummer and get the news. What they called ride, years ago they rode horses, but they would have to go around to all the members and let them know what the alarming of the drum was for, and tell them that there was a death in the society. And once he do that, he had to go and make sure that everybody know that was in the society what day and time the funeral was. And everybody had to go that was a member; they would fine you for not showing up. And the men, I being the youngest member at sixteen years old, they would appoint three or four men to dig the graves, digging with shovels.

The musicians didn't play at the funerals, only the picnics. They would play that music and sing, and I remember one song that Lum Guffin sang, he would be singing that song about "Sally Got a Big Leg." That's the one I can remember. "Sally's got a big leg, anybody else want to go to heaven, got to go by themselves"—that was one of the lyrics of the song. And Lum never came to the picnic dressed down, you saw him as the kind of man with white shirt on, black pants, even in that dust, and suspenders . . . kind of different, but he played that drum and played that music.

One time I tried to make a fife out of fishing cane, but I didn't know what I was doing, and it wouldn't blow. I never did try to play the drums, but we kept that drum, SBS Society, until the 1970s. I don't know what we did with it. They didn't use it, they didn't alarm it anymore, because everybody had phones. But that was a way to do it when there were no phones.

At a picnic, there was food, music, fellowship, and plenty of dust; and the band playing, people dancing in that dust to the music. These older people would dance, I don't know what kind of dance they called it, the shuffle or something like that, but they would dance to that music. They would barbecue, they would have whole hogs on the pit, fish, watermelon, drinks. At that time you couldn't hardly get up Brunswick Road, because they was on both sides of the road, and all the way down in those woods, with stands, each one of them had their stand, selling food, and people were just back and forth across the road to that stand. They had games set up.

After that older group passed on, younger people just didn't do it, plus the music changed. After '63 or '65, that was the last one, the Gravel Pit Picnic. And they stopped it because music changed, they had jukebox in there, lights all over the place. They had just had little ball lights before that. That was the way it was at Easter Brown Grove.

They just had ball lights. One time somebody had a generator, and they had lights, but it was dusty—dust would be over your shoe.[64]

Bartlett-area historian and landowner Ellen Davies-Rogers was descended from an early family in West Tennessee, and in her book about Arlington, *The Holy Innocents*, she included diary entries by an ex-Confederate captain, Kenneth Garrett, that mention the Independent Pole Bearers' picnic at Brunswick: "Friday, July 28, 1905 . . . Charlie [apparently one of Captain Garrett's employees] had a holiday—went to a picnic at Brunswick." And "Friday, August 2, 1907 . . . Roland [another employee] went to Pole Bearers Picnic at Brunswick."[65] In a footnote, Davies-Rogers gave the following information about the Pole Bearers: "Independent Pall Bearers, a fraternal insurance organization for Negroes, one of the oldest and most highly respected societies in the Brunswick Community. Drum beating at the funeral of a deceased member could be heard for miles around. The Hall is located on Brunswick Road at Craven Road. The Picnic is still an annual event."[66] From these diaries, carefully preserved by Davies-Rogers, we can prove that the Brunswick or Gravel Pit Picnic went back to at least 1905.

Roy Brewer, the current president of the Independent Pallbearers Society No. 6 at Brunswick, spoke in an interview about the role that drums played in his organization:

Back then, people did not have telephones. But word traveled fast; at that particular time, there was a big bass drum they would beat. They would start right in front of the society hall. When there was a decease in the Independent Pole Bearers, that big drum was beat. You could hear it, I bet, about fifteen miles away. On a windy day, it would carry twenty miles. The drummers that we had . . . John Mitchell, he used to play the fife, drums; Melvin Kilpatrick, he used to beat the big bass drum. The picnics . . . they used to start before Labor Day—they would start on Thursday, right in front of the hall, beating the drum. They would start dancing and going down for the picnic. Back then, when people were working on people's places, Mrs. Davies and others, they accepted that and gave people that weekend off. People would come from miles and miles away, from everywhere. There would be traffic on both sides of Brunswick Road, all up and down 70 Highway. There would be so many people that in two or three hours it would be dusty. They would get down there and play the song about "Big Legged Woman," blowing the fife and dancing, drinking beer, partying, barbecue. That went on. This picnic would run from Thursday to Sunday, about 1:30 to 2:00 in the afternoon. It would be three or four fife and drum bands playing, but I can't remember all their names. They would have the big old bass drum, and then the little round drum with the sticks, like you see in the military, and then a man would be blowing the fife. At that time, I think they had a cane fife. There were also picnics out on 64, and I imagine that Fullview had a picnic, but all of the societies would come together for this big picnic here. They would have stands and stuff, and sell barbecue for their societies, beer, whatever they had. But, as things progressed and time passed, young people got up in it, drug-related, and it just cut out.[67]

In the liner notes to Flyright's compilation of Bengt Olsson field record-ings entitled *On the Road Again*,[68] Olsson gave a description of the Bruns-wick Picnic, an event he may in fact have witnessed in either 1972, '73, or '74:

Lum . . . became leader of the fife and drum band. The band only came out twice a year: To celebrate the anniversary of the chapter's found-ing, March 5th, and for the Brunswick picnic sometime in mid-June as I recall—where the members and bands from all the different orga-nizations got together for a feast . . . barbecued hogs, lamb, chicken, watermelons, drinks . . . a man from another part of the country brought in his "Flying Jenny" the merry-go-round. . . . Everyone agreed that the Brunswick chapter, No. 6 had the best band, led by Karo and Will Baxter. Though they did not belong to the organization, the Broadnax Band played at the Brunswick picnic each year. They arrived in a wagon pulled by mules, and, as they travelled, played from the wagon, attracting crowds along the way, and by the time they arrived at the picnic site they had a long line of people following them.[69]

In his unpublished manuscript of the revised *Memphis Blues*, Olsson gave a much more detailed description of the involvement of the Broadnax Brothers band in the Brunswick Picnic: "[The] Broadnax Band went to the Brunswick picnic on [a] mule-drawn wagon and played on [the] back of [the] wagon on [the] way to [the] picnic. People could hear them coming from far away, and stopped working in the fields to watch them drive by, playing their music. 'They'd be out in the fields doing the Grizzly Bear and the Mule as we passed by.' Other [Ossie] Broadnax told about the band arriving in a wagon pulled by mules. . . . 'The Broadnax Boys! Everybody knew about the Broadnax Boys Band!'"[70]

While Roy Brewer attributed the demise of rural events like the Brunswick Picnic to the advent of drugs, Lum Guffin gave Bengt Olsson a far more prosaic reason: "1974 was the last year Lum got together the band for the annual celebration. Everyone today is buying insurance and there is no longer need for an organization like the United Sons and Daughters of Zion."[71] We do not have much background information about Olsson's field recordings, such as dates or places, but at some point in the early 1970s Olsson recorded Lum Guffin's United Sons and Daughters of Zion No. 9 Band performing "Sally's Got a Big Leg." Judging from the laughter and talking in the background, it seems likely that this recording was made at a picnic, and it is possible that it was recorded at Brunswick.

Perhaps due to that recording by Olsson, Lum Guffin's United Sons and Daughters of Zion No. 9 Band was invited to be part of a national tour of something called the American Old Time Music Festival in 1976, under the direction of Mike Seeger, son of musicologist Charles Seeger and half brother to folk singer Pete Seeger. Newspaper articles mention Guffin and his drummers in several of the cities that the tour visited. Unfortunately, many of the newspapers engaged in the wildest speculations about this music, and occasionally identified Lum Guffin and his drummers as being from Mississippi, perhaps because that state's fife and drum tradition was so much better known than that of Tennessee. Nevertheless, the tour garnered critical acclaim and resulted in the only video footage that exists of a Tennessee fife and drum band.

The earliest mention of Guffin in connection with the American Old Time Music Festival comes from a March 1976 article in Canada's *Calgary Herald*, which gave some fairly inaccurate information about Black fife and drum music: "Lum Guffin and his band play Afro-American cane fife and drum music. If an 'endangered species' list existed, this music would be on it. The Guffin style of fife and drum music is extremely close to the instrumental sounds of West Africa. One reason this music is rare today is that drums were outlawed during slavery because they served as a means of communications to the slaves. The music now survives among a handful of musicians in the deep South."[72] Although it is true that Southern states banned drums among slaves for the reasons the article indicates, as we have seen, the laws were not enforced with regard to the use of drums by Blacks for the militias, which would seem to be the basis for Black fife and drum music in the South. And far from being rare, the music proliferated in the South during Reconstruction. The rarity was rather the result of city ordinances forbidding such bands in the bigger cities, the movement of Blacks away from rural areas to the cities, the movement of Black people away from the societies toward life and health insurance, and the availability of recorded commercial music, radio, and eventually television. However, such theories as those in the *Herald* article are often encountered. The after-concert review was written by free-jazz musician and critic Eugene Chadbourne, who was living in Canada at the time to avoid the Vietnam War and gave a much more knowledgeable assessment of the genre:

> Things started off with a fife and drum band led by Lum Guffin, a replacement for the late Lonnie Young. I heard my first traditional black fife and drum music about seven years ago and have been enchanted with it ever since.[73] It connects directly with African music perhaps more than any other Afro-American folk style, but then again there's something distinctly American about it. It was a pleasure to see how quickly it communicated with the audience; when the group returned to close off the concert, pied piper Guffin was in such control over the crowd that he could have led them anywhere.[74]

A few days later Guffin and his drummers, brothers John and James Mitchell, were in Salt Lake City, Utah, where they also made a favorable impression, although the local reviewer was mistaken about where the musicians were from: "From northern Mississippi, Lum Guffin and John and James Mitchel comprise one of the last existing fife and drum bands. The trio of old timers marched in through the audience with a bass drum, snare and a shrill fife, pounding and wailing away. It didn't matter that the songs were all in the same key with nearly the same tune; the important thing was that the three were making a joyful noise for all they were worth."[75] Presumably, the better-known Mississippi bands of Napoleon Strickland, Sid Hemphill, the Young Brothers, and Otha Turner led the reviewer to believe that Guffin and his drummers were also from that state.

The next week, they were in San Francisco, and again, the *Examiner* reviewer had only positive things to say:

> The most attractive aspect of the AOTMF [American Old Time Music Festival] is its format, pacing and variety of music. Last night's events began and ended with Lum Guffin, fife-player, and the drumming brothers John and James Mitchel [*sic*] playing blues marches and hymns as they marched through the tables at the Great American Music Hall. Fife and drum music, with obvious roots both in African and European cultures as well as American pre-Revolutionary and

the earliest of "jazz" forms, is classic stuff and was sensitively, indeed beautifully, played by Guffin and the Mitchels, all elderly.[76]

In addition to the dates we have reviews for, we know that Lum Guffin and his musicians were in Seattle, Washington, on April 5, 1976, at the University of Washington, because they were recorded and filmed there by the ethnomusicologist Robert Garfias, making the United Sons and Daughters No. 9 Band of Bartlett, Tennessee, the only such band from the state known to be documented on film.[77] The extant video is quite interesting. It documents four untitled songs, of which the second is "Sally's Got a Big Leg," which can be clearly deduced by comparison with Olsson's recording of that song from the *On the Road Again* compilation. The four songs are largely modal, have hints of pentatonicism, and in contrast to many extant Mississippi recordings of fife and drum music tend to have a major tonality. The overall musical style is also far more militaristic than most Mississippi groups; indeed the first selection played alternates sections in 6/8 and 4/4 time, which is never the case in Mississippi fife and drum (see photo section). The men are also dressed formally. Lum Guffin is wearing a full suit with coat and hat. The two Mitchell brothers are wearing collared shirts and sweaters, and all have on dress shoes, which is also in stark contrast to the usual appearance of Mississippi-style bands. Lum is playing a metal fife, and one Mitchell is playing a deep wooden military snare drum, while the other is playing a more modern and fairly small bass drum. Although Olsson stated that Lum's music was from a closed society, the church, the music played in the video does not seem to be religious, and no familiar hymn tunes are heard. Rather the music seems to be marches and rural dance tunes from the late nineteenth or early twentieth century. There is very little blues in it; only the tendency toward pentatonic melodies and the occasional polyrhythmic accent in the drums suggest that we are hearing a Black band. This perhaps was a musical tradition little changed from the 1800s.[78]

After spending a fair amount of time on the road, by October 1976 Guffin was back in Tennessee, where he took this same band to the inaugural Tennessee Grassroots Festival in Nashville.[79] Unfortunately, no films or recordings were made of the first few Tennessee Grassroots Festivals, so it seems we have no documentation of this performance. However, this was the same band that Guffin had taken to Seattle, and we can assume that the performance in Nashville was similar to the one documented on tape and film.

In a July 12, 1974, letter to David Evans, Bengt Olsson listed a number of drummers whose names were associated with various benevolent societies in Shelby County. From the United Sons and Daughters of Zion No. 9 he listed Jimmie Kirk and Willie Taylor, who each played both the snare and bass drums. He added the information that Taylor was over eighty years old and "very fragile."[80]

After 1976, it does not seem that Lum Guffin brought out the United Sons and Daughters of Zion No. 9 Band much; if he did, it was perhaps only for picnics held on his own land on Guffin Lane. The experimental filmmaker and musician Tav Falco and the Italian musicologist Giambattista Marcucci visited Lum Guffin on August 8, 1978,[81] and filmed and recorded him. Falco's footage became a black-and-white documentary film called *Key to the Highway*, while Marcucci's field recordings were released on several LPs by the Italian label Albatros, and later, more thoroughly and in the way Marcucci intended, on his own Mbirafon label as part of the excellent Blues at Home series. None of the footage or recordings involved fife and drum, but some of Lum's young white friends and admirers must have been aware of his history with the genre. The blues musician Steve James, who lived near Lum on Ellendale Road in the mid-1970s, recalled that Lum kept his drums under his wooden front porch.[82]

Lum continued to perform throughout the 1980s, at least on guitar. Dr. David Evans recorded him downtown on the Mid-America Mall in Memphis in 1980, and he played live on the air from radio station WEVL in 1987. Yet time eventually took its toll. Columbus "Lum" Guffin died on November 27, 1993, and was buried at his beloved Prosperity Missionary Baptist Church, where the United Sons and Daughters of Zion No. 9 chapter had been founded. He left eight children.

According to Roy Brewer, the Brunswick Picnic also died, about 1978 or '79, after there had been a marked increase in people attending who were under the influence of drugs or alcohol. The Independent Pallbearers Society owned the land on which the Brunswick Picnic was held, and began to feel that if something occurred, such as a shooting or a fight with injuries, the society could be held legally responsible, so the event was reluctantly discontinued. The picnic site is now an overgrown woods at the intersection of Brunswick Road and Highway 70. Only a row of old wooden whitewashed poles suggests that the spot was once something more.

THE INDEPENDENT POLE BEARERS SOCIETY NO. 9
AND BLACK FIFE AND DRUM MUSIC IN CAPLEVILLE
AND OAKVILLE

Until the early 1970s, the Capleville and Oakville communities along Highway 78 (formerly the Pigeon Roost Road) were predominantly Black rural areas just to the north of the Mississippi state line in southeastern Shelby County. Oakville had once been called Shakerag and was the scene of an early violent fight that was said to have resulted from a dispute among Black residents about which of two men was the best snare drummer, so it would seem that Black fife and drum music had deep roots in the community. The Oakville Missionary Baptist Church was founded in 1871, and an Oakville cemetery called Payne's Cemetery is one of the oldest Black cemeteries in Shelby County. Capleville was the location of a large, consolidated Black elementary and high school, but otherwise was predominantly rural and agricultural. In this community, in 1889, Black tenant farmers and sharecroppers founded what they called the Independent Pole Bearers Society No. 9.

This chapter eventually established a cemetery and lodge hall on Tchulahoma Road in the southeastern portion of Shelby County, and was the subject of an in-depth article in 1976 in the daily Memphis newspaper the *Commercial Appeal*. In the article, the chapter president Jessie James Smith described how the society was formed due to the lack of life insurance for Black people at that time, and how special signals on the drums were used to indicate when a member of the society had died or was sick. He also displayed the chapter's banner, black on one side for funerals and red on the other for picnics and other festive occasions. He mentioned that the drums would play for the picnics, occasionally accompanied by a fife, which was still occurring at the time the article was published.[83]

In 1984, folklorist Dr. David Evans of the University of Memphis interviewed a man named "Chicken" George Walker, drummer for the Blues Busters, a Memphis blues band that had recorded for High Water Records, the record label that belongs to the university. Perhaps somewhat unexpectedly, the interview took a turn toward Black fife and drum picnics in the Oakville community:

Evans: When did drums come into blues? When you were first starting out, I guess they had drums. You said this Junior Buttcut—
Walker: No. I don't know how the drums managed to come. I think the first time I ever thought about getting some drums putting into, we was out there at something like a picnic on Shelby Drive, and this

dude had a whistle, a stick. He had a whistle, a cane. He was blowing that cane. And this dude had a snare drum behind him beating it, and another dude had a bass drum back there beating on it. This dude right across here named Goodman [?], stay across the walk there, he was one of the dudes beating on these drums. Right there off Shelby Drive, down there across Getwell. They used to have picnics down there on the side of the street.[84] They would walk through there beating that thing and that man be blowing that cane.

Evans: When did you see this?

Walker: Back when I was a little bitty boy. I would go to these picnics. My people would carry me to the picnics with them. They would blow them things, and I used to dance when I was a little bitty boy. Me and my sisters would win all kinds of contests dancing. Went out here and danced at Kennedy Hospital for the soldiers and stuff when I was a little boy.

Evans: Did you ever play that kind of drum at the picnics?

Walker: No. I was too little. I couldn't tote that stuff.

Evans: They never had picnics like that around Oakville?

Walker: Right outside Oakville. That's where it was, right up there on Shelby Drive. That's Oakville right there. Up there on Shelby Drive, they call that Capleville.

Evans: Would you say that your style of drumming is influenced by that kind of drum beating that you saw at the picnic? Would you say that you picked up on any of it?

Walker: Yes, I picked that up from them playing them drums out there at the picnic. Seem like that man blowin', they go wup ta ta ta, wup ta ta ta, like that behind him, and they were keeping time with themselves. And then I was thinking, well, we were playing them guitars like that too, making them funny sounds. What made me really start playing drums, they started selling them pick-ups and putting them on them boxes. That made them a little louder. So that way I wanted to get a set of drums. I knowed if they didn't make the guitar louder, I couldn't play the drums, because it would have been too loud over the guitar. We used to get in the dust. Set them drums right there in the dust. Man, there'd be so much dust, and we'd jam right there, me and Will Roy. Will Roy could sing then, man.

Evans: So you were kind of inspired by seeing those picnic drummers?

Walker: Right.

Evans: Would you say you got some of that beat in your style of drumming?

Walker: Right. If you kinda listen really close to the way I play, I play nearly 'bout what the dude be singing, on the drums. I picked that up from them, because they following that dad-gummed cane man good on the drums. I picked that up from them. I have run up on a bunch of drummers, man, I know they can beat me drumming, but I'm timing. I'm playing the song. I'm timing. I ain't trying to show out. I ain't trying to bring nobody out from under nothing. I'm playing the song. I'm playing the blues.

Evans: I've talked with some of those old drummers that play the picnic drum. That's what they say. They play the song.

Walker: Yeah, they play the song, man. All that rolling and shit, when you do that roll, somebody's supposed to come out from behind something running or something, the way I feel about it. Ain't no rolling in no blues. That rolling shit ain't in no blues. If he call himself a blues drummer and he doing all that roll.... Now he can throw a few bombs. But ain't no rolling in no blues. He ain't playing no blues with me.[85]

Jessie James Smith was the man whose interview was prominently featured in the 1976 *Commercial Appeal* article, and in 2019, his daughters Sandra Stepton and Elizabeth Harmon gave interviews regarding the Independent Pole Bearers No. 9 and the picnics which that chapter used to hold. Ms. Stepton stated:

One thing that I can remember about the picnics is that it was something like a fundraiser. My recollection is that my dad would have handbills struck, and he would put them on poles around the community to let everybody know when Number 9 picnic was coming up. My mom would immediately start to catch fish, fry fish; that's what they did, they fried fish, they made different types of sandwiches or whatever, and they had what was called a stand. Number 9 might have a stand, and my mom and my aunt . . . would work the stand. And so there would be aluminum tubs of ice and drinks and everything, and they sold those things. And so Mom would wash fish all night the night before, and then they took it out and it was in this big tub, and it got breaded, and she dropped it into the hot oil right there on a charcoal burner, and made like buffalo fish sandwiches and those types of things. I don't remember much else being sold than fish, but I was a little kid. People would come from miles around. People who had moved away from the area, at least as far as my family was concerned, would try to make their vacation time in order to come back for Number 9 picnic. Imagine those trees over there on the other side. Each one of those was somebody's stand, and they would like put boards up, and make like a little tray area or serving counter, or whatever, and you would be over in the stand preparing food for the people. Sometimes they were two- and three-day picnics. Mama didn't let us go to it every day. Rather than somebody hooking up an iPod or whatever, or a DJ, the guys would play their drums. My dad played the snare and the bass, and all of his cousins were drummers. People would dance. My grandma . . . she sat most of the time that I recall, because she was rather old, but she would get up out of that seat, and we called it a Tennessee two-step, I don't know what it was, but once they started . . . the fife would start first. Mr. Cecil, he would make his own fife out of like bamboo things or whatever, and you could see him over there burning holes in them. And then, because some of them weren't any good, and he would give them to the kids, he couldn't get the sound he wanted out of them, and what was that song he would do? [imitates sound of the fife] . . . and he would start out, and then he would play a note and then the bass would start [imitates the booming of the bass drum], and then the women would start gathering behind them, and they would march all around this place, wherever it was. It would be like a parade. There was a lady, we called her Miss Sue Black. She kept a white baseball cap on her head, and she wore white slacks all the time, she would be totally white. She had a cane, and she would lead them, like the drum major. It was awesome.[86]

Ms. Stepton's sister Elizabeth Harmon, whose son Errol Harmon is the current president of the IPB Society No. 9, recalled where picnics were held:

One place was here [the No. 9 Cemetery on Tchulahoma Road], but then, up on Shelby Drive before you get to Malone Road, there is a section over to the right, and that is where all of the picnics were held. Those are Jacksons that live on that land now, and their grandfather, he got Jackson Pit;[87] for a Black man to have that back in that day, he had to be a very prosperous man, so we would have picnics on his land. There wasn't a name for the place; it was just his land. Butler Jackson. There's about three houses up there now. Another place was Faulkner Grove . . . if you know where there is a McDonald's on Shelby Drive, it's behind there . . . it's still there, it's a picnic grounds; the family there has developed that into a picnic grounds. There was on their calendars every year a time for the picnics, usually in August, but it could have been September. People knew when it was going to happen, and they would come from near and far. My father, he would go to Brunswick and several other picnics. We would never go out that far, because he would have to carry his drums on the back of a truck, and Mama wouldn't let us go out that far. But the Burdette chapter [on Malone Road], we would always join with them and have picnics together. My dad's father Linwood Smith played the drum, his uncle Jeff Smith beat the drums, his uncle Doc Smith played the drums, then their children played the drums: "Too Tight" Smith, his name was Willie James Smith, Sammy, Jeff David, and then later on, a young man about my age, my cousin, he started playing drums with my father. Even my baby brother played the drums with my father. Because most of them had died out by the time they came along, and Daddy would get them to play drums with them. And he would go to Benjestown; that's where he would take them to play the drums. And then in later years, we had a few picnics here on the grounds [at the cemetery and lodge hall] under that old tree there. And we would have a stand where you could stand and eat, and they cooked on the inside of that, and it was around that old tree. The drumming and picnics began to disappear around the latter part of the seventies. The older guys, they had stopped being able to play the drums, so you would have to get somebody else to play. Then you would have to find younger women that would stand in a place and fry fish all day. So I would think the last one we actually went to would have been in the middle eighties, about 1985.[88]

The Independent Pallbearers Society No. 9 remains an active chapter, with about two hundred members. Unfortunately, on Christmas Day 2018, the lodge hall, located on the cemetery grounds at 4819 Tchulahoma Road in Memphis, burned to the ground. Errol Harmon, the current chapter president, who is a Memphis attorney as well as a football coach in the Shelby County Schools district, has overseen the building of a pavilion to replace the lost lodge hall, and is actively involved in researching the history of the Independent Pole Bearers/Independent Pallbearers in the Memphis and Shelby County area.

MOUNT PISGAH, CORDOVA, AND
THE INDEPENDENT POLE BEARERS SOCIETY NO. 12

One Sunday afternoon, while driving around eastern Shelby County looking for blues musicians, Bengt Olsson ran into brothers Steve and Lincoln Jackson on the Pisgah Road between the now-extinct town of Lenow
and the Black community, school, and church known as Mount Pisgah.[89]
Although Lincoln had been a guitar player, and Olsson's interest was primarily guitar-based blues, the man and his brother lived in an area of Shelby
County where fife and drum music was common. Olsson soon moved in
with Lincoln Jackson for a period of time.

Olsson, being from Sweden, did not always understand what his rural
Black friends and informants were telling him. He soon was being told
about "Pole-Ball" picnics—or at least that is what he imagined was being
said. "I'm not quite sure what 'Pole-Ball picnics' meant," Olsson wrote in
field notes that ultimately became part of his unpublished manuscript revision of *Memphis Blues*. "Seems like the one in Brunswick was one of them,
Lincoln says band used to be called Pole-Ball Society, No.12, yes, that was
the Mount Pisgah band."[90]

At some point, Olsson eventually got the correct name, for he asked
Lincoln's uncle Andrew Jackson to explain the origins of the "Pole Bearers"
name: "I had often wondered how the Pole Bearers got their name, so I once
asked Uncle Andrew to explain it. 'Why, we called ourselves Pole Bearers
because we used to carry poles,' he said. 'What kind of poles?' I persisted.
'Poles ... poles ... you know, spears. We carried 'em about fifteen years, and
den we changed to swords. But we kept callin' ousefs Pole Bearers. Man, we
was steppin' po' souls! Ever'time we come down the street, ever'thing stop
to watch us.'"[91] Although Olsson stayed with Lincoln Jackson for nearly a
month in 1971, he did not write all that much about fife and drum bands
in the area. In a March 1973 letter, he mentioned that the "Cordova band"
had played marches, just as the Broadnax band had.[92] In July, he was writing to David Evans that there was "possibly a complete fife and drum band
around Cordova,"[93] and in September, he wrote about a song by Mississippi
bluesman James McCoy called "Hold Up Sally" that he assumed might be
identical to a piece with similar words played by the Pole Bearers Society
No. 12 band.[94] Finally, in July of 1974, Olsson wrote the names of some
drummers from the IPB Society No. 12 band, mentioning drummer Will
Jones, drummer and fifer Clarence Wright, and drummer Arthur Fields,
noting that they "used to march through town," presumably the old town of

Cordova near the depot.[95] It is worth noting that one of the incorporators of the IPB Society in the Lenow community in January of 1893 was listed as "A. Feilds," which could well have been Arthur Fields.[96] Although Olsson suspected there was a rich fife and drum band tradition in the Mount Pisgah/Lenow/Cordova area, he left no recordings or other documentation of anything continuing in his day, and there is no information about where picnics were held. However, a former resident of the community named Billy Williams stated that the IPB Society No. 12 had a lodge hall behind Morris' Grocery at the corner of Pisgah and Macon Roads, and that he would see them out in front of it with their drummers.[97]

THE OWENS PICNIC AT OAKLAND, TENNESSEE

Strangely, Lincoln Jackson and his brother Steve did not say much to Olsson about fife and drum activity in the immediate vicinity of where they lived, but he had far more to say about picnics in Fayette County, particularly one called the Owens Picnic in Oakland:

> The one [picnic] in Oakland was called "The Owens' Picnic." There were also major picnics in Brunswick and Rossville (the L & N Picnic). Steve Jackson said the Oakland picnic would take place during the weekend corresponding to the first weekend in August. People came to picnics on horseback, in wagons and buggies, few came in cars. Beer, moonshine liquor, watermelons, barbecued hogs and goats, fried chicken. Frogs, cicadas, grasshoppers, fireflies, the wind blowing softly through the trees. Drinking, gambling and dancing themselves bowlegged to the music.
>
> Lincoln Jackson: "In them days we had what we used to call Moonlite Picnics. Last for three days straight! Out in the woods, you know, lots of shade, and ain't no one gonna bother you out there. The law's paid off to look the other way. At night we'd light rags with oil to get light. There'd be music everywhere, several different blues singers and little bands. Everyone was wild about that string music. Frank Stokes would be there—he had a good rhythm, you know. I'd second him most of the time he came out here. We was pretty close, he'd stay at my place every time he come around. Little Buddy Doyle would be there each and every year, Memphis Minnie once in a while. And we had drum and fife bands playing all them marches and stuff.[98]

Olsson eventually became aware of a reference to the Owens Picnic in an interview with Homesick James, whose father of course had played in a Fayette County fife and drum band. Both blues and fife and drum music seem to have been a feature of this picnic:

In an interview with Homesick James in Guitar Player 1993, James says he played with [Little Buddy] Doyle at a picnic outside of Oakland, out off Highway 64. Doyle, Stokes, John Estes, Jack Kelly were all among the regulars at the Oakland picnics, which were a big do, very, very popular. People came from far away to attend/be there. If there was one picnic not to be missed out on, many would have picked the one at Oakland. There might have been twenty or more separate guitar players and singers, in addition to piano players and a couple of drum and fife bands. The picnic season usually kicked off with the Fourth of July picnic. After that there were a number of larger or smaller ones, and the Labor Day weekend wound up the season, with maybe a couple of stray ones following.

"Honeyboy" Edwards: "I was at Oakland one time, they give a picnic there out in a pasture. They had killed a hog, had dug a hole in the ground, 'bout pretty close to 21 feet down, and put some pipe across down there and had some charcoal down there, put the whole hog on the pipes, and had two men sitting there to watch it. And when they start cooking that hog then that grease would come out him, it half put out the coal, but the coal would stay burning and smoke that meat. When the meat be done, you take a knife, cut the meat off there and put it on your sandwich. I played there with a piano player. They had a platform built in the pasture, and put the piano on the platform. And, man, about 9 o'clock at night, at that picnic they start fighting and a-shooting. We was gambling on some door come off a house, shoot dice good on it. Man, them guys started shooting them pistols, and goddamn, the pasture would light up just like electrical light! Pow! Pow! And I was so goddamn dumb, instead of trying to dive—I could have been killed, man!—I'm diving down there trying to get the money the n----rs had left on the table, I'm down there trying to get the money. Every time they shoot my hands light up. Man, I used to be through some hell of things!"[99]

The eastern part of Shelby County remains rural and has many points of connection with Fayette County to the east. Unfortunately, residents in the area seem suspicious of outsiders, and unwilling to talk about the old picnics and fife and drum bands.

OTHER FIFE AND DRUM BANDS IN WEST TENNESSEE

In addition to the better-known and better-documented fife and drum bands in Tennessee, there are numerous general and vague references to others throughout the region. Savannah Moore, a member of the Independent Pole Bearers No. 11 at Noahs Chapel AME Church on the Pleasant Ridge Road between Bartlett and Millington, described the members of her organization marching out of their lodge hall, dressed all in white, and marching to the picnic grounds to the music of a fife and drum band.[100] In July of 1974, Olsson gave some details about the musicians of IPB No. 11: "John Mitchell [snare/bass] & ? McKenzie [bass/snare] are around and there [are] supposed to be two more, but, sadly, no fife blower. Mitchell said he played in an old-time [Black] brass band with horns, tambourine and drums last year, but thought their songs—which he called ragtime—were too sinful. He, like everyone else, reckons 'Sally' is alright however. McKenzie says he started out as a drummer with the Jamestown Brass Band."[101] John Mitchell and his brother were the drummers that Lum Guffin took on his American Old Time Music Festival tour in 1976.

Blues musician Earl "Little Joe" Ayers, from Benton County, Mississippi, recalls a Fourth of July picnic in 1970 at Grand Junction in Hardeman County, at which he saw a fife and drum band perform.[102] However, the location of Grand Junction, two miles above the Mississippi state line and two miles east of the Fayette County line, means that we cannot be certain about the provenance of the band in question. It could have been a Fayette County band, or perhaps one from Mississippi. Bengt Olsson believed that this Grand Junction picnic was a Pole Bearers' picnic, but he offered no details about how he arrived at that conclusion.

Both Lum Guffin and Jessie James Smith were known to have played at a large picnic at Benjestown, southwest of Millington, near the present-day Meeman-Shelby State Forest, but it is unclear whether there was a fife and drum band based at Benjestown.

Middle Tennessee State University professor Charles Wolfe was quoted in 1981 in the *Jackson Sun* as saying that there had been a Black fife and drum band in Jackson, Tennessee, "just a few years ago."[103] But efforts to pursue this lead came up empty. Denmark, the predominantly Black town in western Madison County that would be the most likely location for such a band, had a brass band tradition, but neither the *Jackson Sun* nor the Big Black Creek Historical Society has any record of a fife and drum band there. There is a Charles Wolfe collection at MTSU, but it has no recordings of any fife and drum music, from Jackson or elsewhere. The Tennessee State Archives recorded a Black fife and drum group from Fayette County at Chickasaw State Park near Henderson, about thirty or so miles below Jackson, in 1980, and it is possible that Wolfe thought that the group in question was from Madison County. On the other hand, the existence of an organization called the Universal Aid Society, with six chapters, all in Madison County, suggests that the county had the kind of Black benevolent societies that threw picnics and hired fife and drum bands. So there could have been this kind of activity in Madison County.

Henning, in Lauderdale County, has also been suggested as a location for Black fife and drum bands. But in his unpublished manuscript, Bengt Olsson primarily refers to brass bands, and it would seem that Henning and Lauderdale County had a brass band tradition similar to that in Denmark in Madison County.[104] Although Olsson actually mentions fife and drum bands in connection with Henning, his specific information is only related to brass band musicians and brass bands, mainly in a quote from a local informant, Fred Montgomery:

> There was at least one permanent brass band in the area, headed by a man called "Reynolds." "Hambone" was still alive when we were there and played snare drum and "horn." Noah Lewis occasionally played at picnics with drum & brass bands—he could blow hard and strong, no doubt necessary to make his presence himself heard. The Henning Brass Band featured John Reynolds (clarinet), trumpet, trombone (Brad Henning and Jerome "Hambone" Manns), tambourine, 2 snare drums (Robert Goots) and a bass drum. Played at cafés and picnics. A band round here called the Henning Band, had them big old slide-horns, big drums. Now they were pretty popular. Sometimes we had a church picnic, we'd get them. Lot of them lived around here. And lot of the time they'd meet over at Orysa. At the church picnic they played church songs. They built a fire out there and fried up fish in them big black pans. And we had some fixing hot tamales. Had iced tea, some had a little corn whiskey there round the bend, you know.
>
> Brad Henning played that big thing (trombone), and then there was another Henning that played the kettle drum, Johnny he played a clarinet, there be 12–15 of them, and you would hear it all over the place! And they played mostly outdoor picnics and things.[105]

ED HARRIS, POSSIBLY THE LAST FIFE PLAYER IN TENNESSEE

Fife player Jeff Broadnax of the Broadnax Brothers band died in 1971, and his passing led a younger Fayette County man, Ed Harris, to pick up the fife, as he told interviewer Robert Jeffrey in August of 1980.[106] Harris already played the "lead drum" (snare), tenor drum, and bass drum. However, Ossie Broadnax soon became ill, and although he made some solo recordings for Bengt Olsson in 1971, his activities seem to have been curtailed thereafter due to poor health. He was not a participant in the 1974 recordings that Mark and Judy Mikolas made while they were in the Mason and Braden area.

Yet it would seem that Ed Harris tried to continue the Broadnax band as best he could, mentioning in an interview that he had played as recently as 1978 with a "Broadnax band," although it seems doubtful that Ossie was participating by then, and the question of who the members were by that time is very much a mystery. Possibly Hallie Manson of the old Fredonia band or Plez Rivers were still active during the early 1970s, but it is evident from Robert Jeffrey's interviews with Harris and with a local basket maker and singer named Emmanuel Dupree that there were still large rural picnics in Fayette County and that some of these had fife and drum bands. The best guess is that Harris was presiding over an aggregation of what was left of the Broadnax and Fredonia bands. What is not clear is how this last group of musicians came to the attention of the Tennessee State Park Folklife Project, a grant-funded proposal that put trained folklorists at state parks in each grand division of the state of Tennessee. The logical idea that Ed Harris and Emmanuel Dupree had been discovered by West Tennessee folklorist Robert Jeffrey is complicated by the fact that Jeffrey's interviews and photographs of these men are from July and August of 1980, yet they had performed at the Tennessee Folklife Festival at Chickasaw State Park in Chester County in May of that year. Of course, it is possible that they had already come to Jeffrey's attention before he interviewed them. Middle Tennessee State University professor Charles Wolfe's cryptic reference in 1981 to a fife and drum band in Jackson "a few years ago" may have been a misunderstanding of the home turf of Ed Harris's band, in which case it is possible that Wolfe first mentioned the band to Jeffrey. Yet it is also true that in the recorded interviews Jeffrey seems to be hearing about Ed Harris and his music for the first time. At any rate, a recording was made with Ed Harris and two unnamed drummers on May 6, 1980, at the West Tennessee Folklife Festival at Chickasaw State Park. An analysis of the recordings from that day shows that only one track includes fife and drums. It is unnamed, other than the designation "Fife and Drum," and is a fairly unstable effort.

The snare and bass drum attempt to play the same rhythms with each other, which is fairly unusual in fife and drum music, but they continue to get out of phase with each other as the tune develops. Harris's fife plays a number of arabesques and phrases in C major, but there is really no discernible melody as such, and the the whole tune seems destined to fall apart several times.[107] The other tunes are a mix of gospel songs and traditional blues songs, and for the most part they are sung a cappella, either by Harris alone, or on a couple of the songs with a female singer named Anna Marie Valentine and a male singer named Emmanuel Dupree. One track, "Train Train," features Harris playing the harmonica, an instrument that he considered to be similar to the fife, but otherwise singing dominates these recordings. It is also worth noting the extent to which the popular culture of recorded songs or broadcast radio seemed to pervade the culture of Fayette County by 1980. Harris's recorded choice of songs at Chickasaw State Park included both Bobbie Gentry's "Ode to Billie Joe" and McKinley Mitchell's "The End of the Rainbow," showing how recorded music gradually pushed out local and regional repertoire in rural Black communities.

Robert Jeffrey traveled to Fayette County in July and August of 1980 to conduct interviews with some of the folk artists and performers that had performed at the Chickasaw State Park festival in May, and he began by interviewing Emmanuel Dupree, a basketmaker and chair bottomer who had sung with Ed Harris at the festival and who could recall Black fife and drum bands and picnics in Fayette County. In a recorded interview on July 24, 1980, Dupree mentioned that fife and drum activity had gone on every year at something called the "Hall Picnic,"[108] and that Ed Harris was a "young man" who still played the fife, although most of the drummers were dead. He also discussed the drummers who had passed, one named Alf Moody and another whose last name was Wade. "They wouldn't have nothin' else but them drums and fife, and look at the rest of them playing ball. They'd have barbecue and stuff."[109] Dupree stated that the Hall Picnic still was going on, but that they no longer had fife and drum, or much live music at all. People danced to recorded music played on a tape deck or a record player. He said that 1970 was probably about the last year that the fife and drum musicians played at the Hall Picnic.[110]

On August 6, 1980, Robert Jeffrey interviewed Ed Harris, and in the interview, Harris stated that he had been influenced by hearing the Broadnax Brothers band, and that he picked up the fife after that band's fifer had died. He stated that it took him a year and a half of practice before he was ready to play with a band.[111] Asked by Jeffrey how important the drums were, Harris stated: "Very important. You could do without the fife blower, but you couldn't do without the drums. The drums were more important than the fife. . . . The band I played with had three drummers, a lead drummer, a tenor, and a bass. The drummers used to buy their drums, but the hall, out on the LaGrange Road, used to furnish drums for picnics."[112] Asked at what kind of picnics the bands played, Harris mentioned the Fourth of July and the 24th of August, but with regard to the latter, he did not know the significance, except that it was a picnic.[113] He stated that the last drummers he had seen in Fayette County had been at the Owens Picnic.[114]

The Tennessee State Archives referred to this discovery as "a Tennessee fife and drum band," but in reality, what Robert Jeffrey discovered was the remnants of a rapidly declining and disappearing tradition. Ed Harris had only been playing for a few years, but he did so as a response to the death of a fife player in the Broadnax band, and Harris had no band to speak of. Only one recorded track included drums, and the drummers were not even named in the field notes. The rest were solo fife tracks, or songs with handclapped accompaniment. Harris spoke of playing with the Broadnax band, but that had been a couple of years before, and whatever band he was putting together in 1980 had no real name. On the interview tape, he can be heard discussing "getting some drummers together" with the field researcher, so it is evident that what Jeffrey really discovered was just a fife player, and some old residents of Fayette County who could recall what had been going on up to a few short years before. With these recordings, the door seems to close on a Tennessee tradition of nearly two hundred years.

CONCLUSION

For more than seventy-five years, fife and drum music acted as a sort of soundtrack for Black communities in Tennessee. Its roots were in Black drumming for Southern militias prior to the Civil War, as well as perhaps the flutes and drums of a dimly remembered African past. It was reinforced by the use of Black fifers and drummers on both sides of the Civil War, and then became a rallying point for Black communities recently given freedom and political rights during the Reconstruction era.

It was at that point that the music became controversial. Whites in the South began to associate this tradition with Black political organizing, Black protest, and the assertion of Black independence, Black militancy, or Black self-sufficiency. There were soon attacks on Black fifers and drummers, and the instruments they played, especially drums. Larger cities, claiming that the music caused horses and mules to run away, began attempting to restrict fife and drum music with ordinances to prohibit such bands or restrict the parades and processions for which they played.

Contrary to the white opinion of fife and drum bands as a militant or military music, Black communities used this music in numerous ways, including for recreational activities such as picnics and dances. It also appeared in connection with labor organizing, Sunday school picnics, funerals, and even advertising, particularly in Nashville.

However, white opposition was not the only headwind facing the music. The growth of other kinds of ensembles, such as string bands and brass bands, began to crowd out fife and drum groups, particularly in the cities. Perhaps the fife and drum sound's association with the period immediately after the end of slavery, and with rural communities, made it something that increasingly sophisticated Black city residents preferred to replace with something newer or more "urban." City ordinances help push fife and drum music into rural areas, and so did the gradual reduction in Black political activity brought on by poll taxes and literacy tests.

By the dawn of the twentieth century, references to fife and drum bands in Black communities had largely disappeared from Tennessee newspapers, but it does not necessarily follow that Black fife and drum activity ceased.

It simply was occurring in remote, rural areas for the kind of Black picnics, anniversaries, and events that whites generally would not have known about or chosen to attend. The music would have likely remained hidden in rural Black communities had there not been a folk and blues revival in the years following World War II.

The efforts of musicologists, music researchers, writers, and folklorists in rural Black communities during the 1950s and '60s led to the discovery and rediscovery of many great rural Black musicians, and also the rediscovery of Black fife and drum bands, including those in Tennessee. The effort of these collectors brought them to the very remote Black communities where the fife and drum tradition had managed to hold on, and their interest in Black blues and folklore made them equipped to recognize the value in what they were seeing. They unfortunately could not prevent its dissolution, but they did manage to document what still existed while it was there.

So the obvious question is why Black fife and drum music died out in Tennessee, while it managed to hold on in north Mississippi for at least another generation. Although it is a good question, it is not one with a clear answer. Although Tate and Panola Counties in Mississippi, where fife and drum music has survived until the present era, were overwhelmingly Black and fairly rural, they were still only an hour from Memphis. Marshall County, Mississippi, was also a majority-Black county, but only a half hour from Memphis, and fife and drum bands did not survive there. DeSoto County, although not a majority-Black county, had a rich fife and drum tradition, which bluesman Kenny Brown recalled from his youth, but by 1970 it was largely gone. Fayette County, Tennessee, was once said to be one of the Blackest counties in America, but fife and drum music there did not survive. At least one factor seems to be distance from Memphis. The closer that a county was to Memphis (the big city), the more likely it seemed for the area to lose its fife and drum and other rural traditions. This could have been for many reasons—migration of Blacks to the city, the availability of modern radio and television, and the encroachment of new subdivisions and development on traditional Black communities, for example. As mentioned before, Lum Guffin told Bengt Olsson that the advent of life insurance companies was a factor in the decline of the societies, which in turn led to a decline in picnics and the fife and drum bands. Roy Brewer pointed out the growing problem of drugs and violence among young people, and Rev. Arthur Becton noted the changes in musical taste, and the electrification of rural Black communities, making DJs possible.

In short, it would seem that Bengt Olsson stumbled onto a Black fife and drum tradition in Tennessee that was much further in decline than the one that Alan Lomax and David Evans independently discovered in Tate and Panola Counties of Mississippi. In those areas, the bands and picnics had taken on an existence separate from the Black benevolent and burial societies, but that does not seem to have happened in Tennessee. By contrast, in Tennessee, the picnics were functions of the societies, and the bands were largely affiliated with the societies as well. As fared the societies, so fared the picnics and the bands, and as the societies began to be depleted of members in the 1960s and '70s, the musical style began to disappear. As the older musicians died, their children did not choose to continue the style of music.

Was Tennessee fife and drum music significantly different from that of Mississippi? If we were to judge from the extant recordings of Lum Guffin's United Sons and Daughters of Zion No. 9 Fife and Drum Band, we might certainly think so. Guffin's music was highly disciplined and showed a strong military influence; he preferred pentatonic melodies that seemed to have a bright, major tonality, and there was little blues influence, if any. But we also have reason to believe that Guffin's music was far from typical, even in Tennessee. He called his fellow fife and drum musician Hallie Manson's music "wild," and Manson, according to Bengt Olsson, tended to view Guffin's music as archaic and highly structured. The recordings made by the Tennessee Folklife Project in 1980 of the rump group headed by Ed Harris from Fayette County do not help us all that much, in that literally only one track has drums backing the fife. That one recording suggests a sound far more reminiscent of Othar Turner and other Mississippi fife and drum musicians. There are also recordings of Hallie Manson playing with Lum Guffin and Plez Rivers at Fredonia in 1974, and the drumming styles exhibited by Rivers and Manson in these recordings are highly syncopated and similar to the Mississippi style. At least one tune recorded by them ("When I Lay My Burdens Down") is also a standard of the Mississippi tradition.

The Tennessee Arts Council has been involved in recent years in efforts to reintroduce the Black fife and drum genre to West Tennessee, by having Kesha Burton in the region mentored by Mississippi fife and drum musicians, including R. L. Boyce and Willie Hurt. While arts organizations usually are engaged in preservation efforts, this is more of an effort at de-extinction. It seems a worthwhile effort, although, of course, we cannot be sure if the Tennessee style of fife and drum was the same as the Mississippi style. Nevertheless, it would be good to see this music reintroduced to Tennessee.

Advertisement for Robert Wardlow's band. *Daily Memphis Avalanche*, December 22, 1867.

Advertisement for Stephen Grayson's band. *Tri-Weekly Clarion* (Meridian, MS), October 14, 1869.

Order of the chief of police forbidding drum beating and street music in Memphis due to yellow fever. *Daily Memphis Avalanche*, October 8, 1873.

Advertisement for drums and fifes. *Public Ledger* (Memphis, TN), September 24, 1874.

H. G. Hollenberg's

MUSIC HOUSE.

MEMPHIS, TENN.   LITTLE ROCK, ARK.
OLD AND RELIABLE. THE BEST GOODS, LOWEST PRICES AND EASIEST TERMS. EMPORIUM FOR

Chickering, Sohmer and Hollenberg Pianos!

Burdette, Sterling and Bay-State Organs!

Drums and Fifes For Campaign Cheap,

Also General Agency for Mechanical Orguinette. Descriptive Catalogue free. Address— H. G. HOLLENBERG, 229 Main St., Memphis, Tenn.

Advertisement for drums and fifes from H. G. Hollenberg's Music House in Memphis. *West Tennessee Whig* (Jackson, TN), July 12, 1884.

DECORATION DAY.

The various colored societies of the city will visit the

NATIONAL CEMETERY

—ON—

Thursday, May 28, 1874

For the purpose of strewing flowers on the graves of the patriotic dead.

All classes of citizens are respectfully invited to participate in the ceremonies.

No booths or saloons will be allowed and persons are requested to have their dinners in baskets on the ground.
The societies will march from their various halls to the corner of Beal and Desoto streets, at 9½ o'clock a.m., where the line will be formed, and move up Beal to Main, and thence up Main to the Louisville depot, headed by the Pole Bearers brass and field band.
Trains will leave every hour during the day, commencing at 9 o'clock. Tickets for the round trip, 25 cents.

EXERCISES OF THE DAY.

The meeting will open with prayer by the Rev. Page Tyler, followed by addresses of prominent speakers. There will be present, Edward Shaw, General Patterson, Mr. Rankin, General Smith, Mr. Mitchel, L. E. Dyer, Col. Eaton, S. S. Garrett, W. S. Marsh, J. E. Thomas, Rev. Mr. Phillips, Rev. Mr. Henderson, and many others of our friends.
After speaking the procession will move into the cemetery and decorate the graves with flowers.

Committee of Arrangements.

A. Martin,   John Johnson,
Henry Shepard,   Robert Smith,
B. H. Smith,   Henry Gains,
A. Robertson,   James Boyde.
          Thomas Swan, Chairman.
J. WISEMAN, Grand Marshal of the day.
m22td

Advertisement for Decoration Day ceremonies at National Cemetery near Memphis on May 28, 1874. *Daily Memphis Avalanche*, May 23, 1874.

DECORATION DAY.

THE INDEPENDENT POLE BEARERS ASSOCIATION will visit the National Cemetery and Decorate the Graves of the Patriotic Dead on

FRIDAY, MAY 30.

The public exercises will open at 1 o'clock p.m., and consist of prayer by the Rev. Page Tyler, addresses by Rev. A. E. Baldwin, Hon. Barbour Lewis, and closing with the benediction by the Rev. W. H. Phillips.
All patriotic societies and citizens are cordially invited to join in the Decoration.
The very best order shall be maintained in and around the cemetery.
Special trains will run on the Memphis and Louisville Railroad. Fare for round trip, 25 Cents.
COMMITTEE OF ARRAGEMENTS.—Robert Pointer, Chairman; B. H. Smith, Wm. Herron, H. McGirt, John Johnson, F. Williams.
          THOMAS SWAN, President.
A. MARTIN, Secretary.
JOHN WISEMAN............GRAND MARSHAL

Advertisement for Decoration Day ceremonies at National Cemetery near Memphis on May 30, 1873. *Memphis Daily Appeal*, May 30, 1873.

This image of the Fredonia Fife and Drum Band was probably taken in the Douglass community of Haywood County, Tennessee, near Stanton, and was sent to me by Dorothy Grandberry. We have few details, but it is thought to have been taken in the 1950s. Courtesy of the Geneva Miller Historical Society.

Likely the Broadnax Brothers Fife and Drum Band, probably in the 1950s (picture of a picture taken by folklorist Robert Jeffrey at a home in Fayette County). Tennessee State Library and Archives, Fife and Drum Band, RG 59, Folder 80-CH-41, Negative #11/11A, Tennessee State Parks Folklife Project Collection, 1979–1984.

These photos of Lum Guffin were taken by Stephen Michelson in 1972; Michelson sent them to me by email. Michelson was a blues enthusiast and guitarist who recorded with Backwards Sam Firk in 1969 under the name Delta X. Although he has interview tapes with Lum Guffin, he could not locate them in time for me to use them in connection with the manuscript. He has spent the better part of his life as a political analyst and consultant.

Errol Harmon is the current president of the Independent Pallbearers Society No. 9 in Southeast Memphis. These five pictures were taken at one of the society's last picnics, possibly in 1975. The bass drummer, Jessie James Smith, is Harmon's grandfather. The location is believed to be a picnic ground called Faulkner's Grove, at the dead end of Faulkner Road near the intersection of Shelby Drive and Tchulahoma Road. Courtesy of Errol Harmon.

This image of Plez Rivers and his wife with their son Homesick James was taken in either 1975 or 1976 by blues researcher and record label owner Pete Lowry, in Fayette County, Tennessee, near Mason. Rivers was a snare drummer in the Broadnax Brothers Fife and Drum Band. The photo appeared on the back cover of Homesick James's album *Goin' Back Home*.

Image derived from a video of the United Sons and Daughters of Zion No. 9 Fife and Drum Band of Bartlett, Tennessee, in Seattle, Washington, for the American Old Time Music Festival on April 5, 1976. No still photos exist in the archive of this group; only this video, from which I created a still image. The Guffin family members were unable or perhaps unwilling to provide me with an image of Lum Guffin with his fife and drummers. Courtesy of University of Washington Ethnomusicology Archives.

Giambattista "Gianni" Marcucci is the owner of the Mbirafon record label in Italy, and a blues researcher who toured Mississippi and Tennessee in the early 1970s. On August 8, 1978, in conjunction with the filmmaker Tav Falco, he recorded Lum Guffin in his front yard in Bartlett, Tennessee. Guffin did not get out his fife or drums that day, but in response to my inquiries, Marcucci emailed this excellent picture of Lum, which he took that day.

Ed Harris, Fayette County, 1980. Tennessee State Library and Archives, Fife and Drum, #39899, Tennessee State Parks Folklife Project Collection, 1979–1984; taken by folklorist Robert Jeffrey.

Ed Harris, Fayette County, 1980. Tennessee State Library and Archives, Fife and Drum, #39900, Tennessee State Parks Folklife Project Collection, 1979–1984; taken by folklorist Robert Jeffrey.

Ed Harris Band, Fayette County, 1980. Tennessee State Library and Archives, "Fife and Drum Band Members Standing on Gas Station Porch," #39916, Tennessee State Parks Folklife Project Collection, 1979–1984; taken by folklorist Robert Jeffrey.

Independent Pallbearers Society No. 6
Lodge Hall, Brunswick, TN, July 16, 2017.
Taken by the author.

Independent Pallbearers Society No. 6 Lodge Hall sign, Brunswick,
TN, July 16, 2017. Taken by the author.

Grave of Thomas Swan, founder of the
Independent Pole Bearers, Zion Cemetery,
Memphis, Tennessee. Taken by the author.

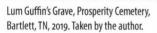

Lum Guffin's Grave, Prosperity Cemetery,
Bartlett, TN, 2019. Taken by the author.

Lum Guffin's House, Guffin Road, Bartlett,
TN, July 9, 2017. Taken by the author.

Fife and Drum Piece No. 2

Lum Guffin, Plez Rivers, Hallie Manson

Untitled March No. 1

Lum Guffin

NOTES

INTRODUCTION

1. David Evans, "Black Fife and Drum Music in Mississippi," *Mississippi Folklore Register* 6 (Fall 1972): 94–107.

2. Othar Turner's first name is often shortened to "Otha."

3. Lauren Joiner, "'Stuff You Gotta Watch': The Effect of Anglo-American Scholarship on North Mississippi Blues Fife and Drum" (MM thesis, Texas Tech University, 2009).

4. Carl Vermilyea, "The Otha Turner Picnic: Occupying Musical and Social Space in-between Saturday Night and Sunday Morning" (MM thesis, University of North Texas, 2011).

5. Kathleen Danser, "Representations of African-American Fife and Drum Music in North Mississippi" (MA thesis, University of Alberta, 2011).

6. Vermilyea, "The Otha Turner Picnic," 139–40.

7. Sylvester Oliver, "African-American Musical Traditions in Northeast Mississippi" (PhD diss., University of Memphis, 1996).

8. Evans, "Black Fife and Drum Music in Mississippi."

9. This was likely the Broadnax Brothers Fife and Drum Band from the Brewer community near Mason, Tennessee, or possibly the Fredonia Fife and Drum Band of Hallie Massey near Stanton. Neither was "just across the state line," but Fayette County did adjoin Marshall County's northern edge.

10. Georgia Writers Project, *Drums and Shadows: Survival Studies among the Georgia Coastal Negroes* (Athens: University of Georgia Press, 1986), 91–122.

11. Eileen Southern, *The Music of Black Americans* (New York: W. W. Norton, 1997); John Storm Roberts, *Black Music of Two Worlds: African, Caribbean, Latin, and African-American Traditions* (Belmont, CA: Wadsworth/Thomas Learning, 1998).

12. George Mitchell, *Blow My Blues Away* (Baton Rouge: Louisiana State University Press, 1971); William Ferris, *Give My Poor Heart Ease* (Chapel Hill: University of North Carolina Press, 2009), 69–76; Alan Lomax, *The Land Where the Blues Began* (New York: Pantheon Books, 1993), 314–57.

13. George Mitchell, *Mississippi Hill Country 1967* (Jackson: University Press of Mississippi, 2013), 32–49; Michael Ford, *North Mississippi Homeplace* (Athens: University of Georgia Press, 2019), 62–69.

14. *Afro-American Folk Song from Tate and Panola Counties, Mississippi* (Smithsonian Institution, Archive of Folk Song L67, 1978); *Traveling through the Jungle* (Testament 5017, 1973; reissued 1995).

15. *Gravel Springs Fife and Drum* (Memphis, TN: Center for Southern Folklore, 1971).

16. Bengt Olsson, *Memphis Blues* (London: November Books, 1970).

17. Bengt Olsson, unpublished manuscript materials (2006) for revision of *Memphis Blues* (London: November Books, 1970).

18. Bengt Olsson, liner notes to *On the Road Again* (UK: Flyright CD 58, 1997).

19. Judith Mikolas, letter to David Evans, April 7, 1975.

CHAPTER 1: "TO DRUM FOR THE FUN OF THE THING": AFRICAN AMERICAN DRUM-
MING AND FIFE AND DRUM MUSIC BEFORE AND DURING THE CIVIL WAR, 1776–1865

1. Southern, *The Music of Black Americans*, 41.

2. Joiner, "Stuff You Gotta Watch," 10.

3. Southern, *The Music of Black Americans*, 172.

4. Paul Alan Cimbala, "Fortunate Bondsmen: Black 'Musicianers' in the Antebellum Southern States" (MA thesis, Emory University, 1977), 27.

5. Cimbala, "Fortunate Bondsmen," 30.

6. *Mississippi Free Trader* (Natchez, MS), June 30, 1846.

7. The full name of the drummer is Jordan Bankston Noble (1800–1890). "Correspondence of the Tribune," *Weekly Marysville (OH) Tribune*, February 27, 1856.

8. *Tuskegee Republican*, September 15, 1853.

9. *Republican Banner* (Nashville, TN), May 22, 1858.

10. "Old Lun the Alabama Drummer," *Mississippi Free Trader* (Natchez, MS), January 28, 1861.

11. "Letter from Mississippi," *Alexandria (VA) Gazette*, April 10, 1861. Credit must be given to Dr. David Evans, who pointed out in an email to me that the Black drummers' choice of tune might not have been so "ignorant." The song contained the line "My master's gone away."

12. C. C. Henderson, "Murfreesboro and Rutherford County—A Historical Story," *Daily News-Journal* (Murfreesboro, TN), August 30, 1929.

13. Ancestry.com page for James Earthman, accessed August 10, 2019, https://www.ancestry .com/genealogy/records/james-earthman-24-2813trd.

14. Geni.com page for Dr. John M. Watson, accessed August 10, 2019, https://www.geni .com/people/Dr-John-M-Watson/6000000018776923442.

15. The Akan people had a tradition of naming children for days of the week, and Georgia informants mentioned Black people being named for months of the year. Georgia Writers Project, *Drums and Shadows*, 87

16. "Desultory Reminisces of the Olden Time," *Clarksville (TN) Weekly Chronicle*, January 22, 1887.

17. "Firemen's Annual Parade—Turnout of the Entire Force—Splendid Procession," *Memphis Daily Appeal*, May 14, 1859.

18. "Whangdoodle Convention," *Clarksville (TN) Chronicle*, July 20, 1860.

19. "Tennessee Intelligence," *Memphis Daily Appeal*, December 22, 1861.

20. "A Call To Arms—The Ringing Reply of the President of Forbes Bivouac," *Clarksville (TN) Leaf-Chronicle*, July 3, 1894.

21. "The Wars of the Factions—Attempted Assassination," *Nashville Union and American*, October 23, 1868.

22. "Home News—Gleanings from Our Country Exchanges," *Republican Banner* (Nashville, TN), October 24, 1868. Samuel Mayes Arnell was a candidate for Congress from Tennessee's Sixth District.

23. "Colored Fire Company," *Leaf-Chronicle* (Clarksville, TN), November 2, 1870.

24. "Criminal Court," *Leaf-Chronicle* (Clarksville, TN), June 21, 1876.

25. *Leaf-Chronicle* (Clarksville, TN), May 19, 1885.

26. GenealogyBank.com entry for Henry Rieves, accessed August 8, 2019, https://www
.genealogybank.com/doc/census/image/v2%3A16DABE9A383D710A%40GB3CENSUS
-16DABD455B77C4D0%402407716-16F470130605BF06%40/p_296380916.

27. "Volunteers for the Northwestern Railroad," *Nashville Daily Union*, October 4, 1863.

28. This phenomenon of Black fife and drum music as a form of advertising was particularly pronounced in the city of Nashville, where it continued far longer than anywhere else, being used to announce minor-league baseball games well into the 1920s.

29. *Nashville Daily Union*, October 10, 1863.

CHAPTER 2: "THE INEVITABLE FIFE AND DRUM": FIFE AND DRUM MUSIC,
BENEVOLENT SOCIETIES, AND BLACK POLITICAL ORGANIZING IN
TENNESSEE DURING RECONSTRUCTION, 1866–71

1. "The City Yesterday," *Memphis Daily Appeal*, January 2, 1866.

2. The Independent Pallbearers Society, usually abbreviated IPB, is a fraternal organization founded by Thomas Swan in Memphis in 1868 as the Independent Pole Bearers. Usually referred to as simply the "Pole Bearers," the organization was associated with Black political activity and militancy, despite its benevolent and social nature. Its name, the subject of much ridicule in the white community, was, in my opinion, not a misunderstanding of "pallbearers," but a reference to drilling to drums with poles or pikes.

3. Roy Brewer, interview by the author, March 27, 2018, Brunswick, TN.

4. Brian Daniel Page, "Local Matters: Race, Place and Community Politics after the Civil War" (PhD diss., Ohio State University, 2009), 123–24.

5. Phelemo Olifile Marumo, "Christianity and African Traditional Religion in Dialogue: An Ecological Future for Africa" (PhD diss., North West University [Mahikeng, South Africa], 2016), 80.

6. Page, "Local Matters," 133–41.

7. "Fling Out the Banner," *Nashville Daily Union*, March 29, 1866.

8. "The Sons of Ham And the Mayor," *Daily Memphis Avalanche*, May 27, 1866.

9. "The Sixth of June," *Public Ledger* (Memphis, TN), June 6, 1866. General Clinton Bowers Fisk was superintendent of the Freedmen's Bureau and the man for whom Fisk University in Nashville is named.

10. "Celebration by the Sons of Ham," *Nashville Union and American*, June 9, 1866.

11. Danny Barker and Jack V. Buerkle, *Bourbon Street Black* (London: Oxford University Press, 1973), 14.

12. Jerrilyn McGregory, *Downhome Gospel: African-American Spiritual Activism in Wiregrass Country* (Jackson: University Press of Mississippi, 2010), 12.

13. "Celebration of the Fourth," *Public Ledger* (Memphis, TN), July 5, 1866.

14. "Fort Gillem Affair," *Nashville Union and American*, July 7, 1866.

15. White Southerners in general ceased celebrating the Fourth of July with the onset of the Civil War, but definitively after the surrender in 1865. That Vicksburg had fallen on the Fourth of July in 1863 made it a day of mourning for many Southern whites (Joe Gray Taylor, letter to John Flower Taylor, March 4, 1984).

16. "The Fourth of July," *Nashville Union and American*, July 7, 1866.

17. "State News," *Nashville Union and American*, July 8, 1866.

18. "Colored Convention," *Nashville Union and American*, August 7, 1866.

19. "Demise of a Prominent Colored Man," *Republican Banner* (Nashville, TN), September 18, 1866.

20. "Max" is a reference to Emperor Maximilian, whom France had put on the throne of Mexico.

21. "River Matters," *Memphis Daily Appeal*, January 15, 1867.

22. "The Colored Convention," *Union Flag* (Jonesborough, TN), April 5, 1867.

23. "The Columbia Meeting," *Brownlow's Knoxville Whig*, May 1, 1867.

24. "From Old Marshall," *Republican Banner* (Nashville, TN), May 4, 1867.

25. "A Fizzle," *Republican Banner* (Nashville, TN), June 28, 1867.

26. "The Reign of Terror in Tennessee," *Nashville Union*, July 9, 1867.

27. "Riot at Franklin," *Republican Banner* (Nashville, TN), July 9, 1867.

28. "Statement of Joseph P. Williams," *Republican Banner* (Nashville, TN), July 9, 1867.

29. "Official History of the Affair," *Republican Banner* (Nashville, TN), July 9, 1867.

30. "Conservative Conciliation," *Brownlow's Knoxville Whig*, July 17, 1867.

31. "The Brownlow Riot at Franklin," *Nashville Union*, July 18, 1867.

32. "The Franklin Riot," *Republican Banner* (Nashville, TN), July 23, 1867.

33. "Off for the Front," *Republican Banner* (Nashville, TN), July 14, 1867.

34. Ben H. Severance, *Tennessee's Radical Army: The State Guard and Its Role in Reconstruction, 1867–1869* (Knoxville: University of Tennessee Press, 2005), 51.

35. "That Torchlight Procession," *Nashville Union and American*, July 28, 1867.

36. "River News," *Daily Memphis Avalanche*, December 6, 1867.

37. *Public Ledger* (Memphis, TN), December 6, 1867.

38. "An Intolerable Nuisance," *Daily Memphis Avalanche*, December 11, 1867.

39. "River Matters," *Memphis Daily Appeal*, December 14, 1867.

40. South Street was later renamed Calhoun Street and became an avenue in the early twentieth century, when a city ordinance made all east-west streets avenues. More recently it has been renamed for G. E. Patterson.

41. "Negro Procession," *Daily Memphis Avalanche*, December 14, 1867.

42. *Public Ledger* (Memphis, TN), December 17, 1867.

43. Transparencies were a kind of banner or artwork that were intended to be illuminated from behind with candles or torches so that their slogans could be clearly seen at night.

44. "The Mayoralty," *Memphis Daily Appeal*, December 27, 1867.

45. This seems to be the earliest instance of what would become the standard nonracial argument against fife and drum bands—that they tended to cause horse runaways. Most of the post-Reconstruction city ordinances against these bands were based on the desire to prevent runaways, which could cause damage to vehicles and buildings, and potential injury or loss of life.

46. "The K. K.," *Republican Banner* (Nashville, TN), December 28, 1867.

47. "Incidents of the Election," *Memphis Daily Appeal*, January 3, 1868.

48. *Merriam-Webster* defines a *hewgag* as "a toy pipe of especially the latter part of the 19th century resembling a kazoo."

49. "R. R. R.," *Nashville Union*, January 4, 1868.

50. *Home Journal* (Winchester, TN), March 12, 1868.

51. *Home Journal* (Winchester, TN), April 2, 1868.

52. *Home Journal* (Winchester, TN), April 2, 1868.

53. *Republican Banner* (Nashville, TN), April 4, 1868.

54. "Grand Celebration of the Fourth of July," *Memphis Post*, June 27, 1868.

55. "The 'Fourth' Yesterday," *Daily Memphis Avalanche*, July 5, 1868.

56. "Radical Politics," *Republican Banner* (Nashville, TN), July 15, 1868.

57. "The War of Races," *Nashville Union*, July 22, 1868.

58. "Panic at Slatetown," *Republican Banner* (Nashville, TN), July 22, 1868.

59. "Eclectic," *Republican Banner* (Nashville, TN), July 23, 1868.

60. "Meet Me by Moonlight Alone" was a song written by Joseph Augustine Wade and Franklin Peale. It was published in Philadelphia, Pennsylvania, in 1830, and was later recorded by the original Carter Family in 1928.

61. "Battle of the Buzzards," *Memphis Daily Appeal*, July 28, 1868.

62. "Set the Law at Defiance," *Memphis Daily Appeal*, August 6, 1868.

63. "Wardlow's Conservative Band," *Public Ledger* (Memphis, TN), August 8, 1868.

64. *Daily Memphis Avalanche*, August 13, 1868.

65. "Killing," *Daily Memphis Avalanche*, March 16, 1866.

66. "Again in Jail," *Public Ledger* (Memphis, TN), March 23, 1866.

67. "The Juvenile Thief and the Negro Receiver," *Public Ledger* (Memphis, TN), September 12, 1866.

68. "Nine Years' Imprisonment," *Public Ledger* (Memphis, TN), November 5, 1866.

69. "Penitentiary Visitors," *Public Ledger* (Memphis, TN), December 24, 1866.

70. "Criminal Court," *Public Ledger* (Memphis, TN), April 4, 1867.

71. "Meeting of Conservatives Last Night at the Courtroom," *Memphis Daily Appeal*, April 14, 1867.

72. "Conservative Meeting," *Public Ledger* (Memphis, TN), April 15, 1867.

73. "A Serenade," *Memphis Daily Appeal*, June 12, 1867.

74. "Criminal Court," *Memphis Daily Appeal*, June 19, 1867.

75. "Itemites," *Daily Memphis Avalanche*, June 19, 1867.

76. "Correspondence of the Appeal," *Memphis Daily Appeal*, July 31, 1867.

77. "Music for Balls or Parties," *Daily Memphis Avalanche*, December 22, 1867.

78. "Music," *Memphis Daily Appeal*, February 15, 1868.

79. While we might today tend to think of "watering place" as slang for a bar or tavern, Wardlow probably had in mind a summer resort such as Iuka, Mineral Wells, or Hot Springs.

80. "Bob Wardlow's Band," *Daily Memphis Avalanche*, May 27, 1868.

81. "Police Items," *Memphis Daily Appeal*, July 12, 1868.

82. "Funeral Notice," *Daily Memphis Avalanche*, August 23, 1868.

83. "Congestive chills" was an old name for malaria. It is possible that in a rural, remote place like Wythe Depot or LaGrange, Wardlow had been bitten by a mosquito that carried the disease, although the *Avalanche* stated that he had been in poor health for some time.

84. "News in Brief," *Daily Memphis Avalanche*, August 23, 1868.

85. "City Matters," *Memphis Daily Appeal*, August 24, 1868.

86. "The Prospective Militia," *Republican Banner* (Nashville, TN), August 8, 1868.

87. "The Rads in Council," *Memphis Daily Appeal*, August 21, 1868.

88. Again, a reference to West Indians in West Tennessee. There must have been a number of them who came to Tennessee at that time from the Caribbean, or perhaps the name was appropriated for the band to suggest a sort of exoticism.

89. "Democracy," *Memphis Daily Appeal*, September 13, 1868.

90. "The Barbecue," *Bolivar (TN) Bulletin*, September 26, 1868.

91. "Bolivar," *Daily Memphis Avalanche*, September 23, 1868.

92. "Stephen Grayson" seems the most correct form of his name and is the way he is listed in all Memphis city directories. However, the newspapers at various times called him "Steve Grayson," "Stephenson Grierson," and "Steve Greason."

93. "Steve Grayson," Shelby County Register of Deeds, Shelby County Death Records 1848–1967, accessed August 20, 2019, https://register.shelby.tn.us/index.php.

94. "Tennessee Marriages," Freedmen's Bureau Online, accessed August 20, 2019, https://www .freedmensbureau.com/tennessee/marriages/tennmarrg.htm.

95. *Halpin's Memphis Directory, 1867–1868* (Memphis, TN: Bulletin Publishing, 1867).

96. "Robbing a Country Darkey," *Public Ledger* (Memphis, TN), February 21, 1867.

97. "Serious Charges," *Memphis Daily Appeal*, September 26, 1867.

98. "A Pugnacious Negro," *Daily Memphis Avalanche*, September 26, 1867.

99. "The Courts," *Daily Memphis Avalanche*, February 7, 1868.

100. "City Items," *Memphis Daily Appeal*, July 22, 1868.

101. "The Cry Is Still They Come," *Daily Memphis Avalanche*, July 26, 1868.

102. "The Cry Is Still They Come," *Daily Memphis Avalanche*, July 26, 1868.

103. "A Card—Steve Grayson and the Democracy," *Memphis Post*, July 29, 1868.

104. "Tenth Ward," *Daily Memphis Avalanche*, August 11, 1868.

105. "Tenth Ward Democratic Colored Club," *Daily Memphis Avalanche*, August 20, 1868.

106. "Barbecue at Marion, Arkansas," *Memphis Daily Appeal*, August 3, 1868.

107. "Marion, Arkansas," *Daily Memphis Avalanche*, August 3, 1868.

108. "News in Brief, " *Daily Memphis Avalanche*, September 18, 1868.

109. "Jackson," *Daily Memphis Avalanche*, October 16, 1868.

110. "Shooting Affray Between Two Negroes," *Public Ledger* (Memphis, TN), November 28, 1868.

111. "News in Brief," *Daily Memphis Avalanche*, November 29, 1868.

112. "City Matters," *Memphis Daily Appeal*, December 1, 1868.

113. "City Matters," *Memphis Daily Appeal*, December 4, 1868.

114. "The Grayson-Tolliver Affray," *Daily Memphis Avalanche*, December 4, 1868.

115. "Court News," *Daily Memphis Avalanche*, January 15, 1869.

116. "City Matters," *Memphis Daily Appeal*, March 13, 1869.

117. "Run Down by a Hand-Cart," *Daily Memphis Avalanche*, March 14, 1869.

118. "Bully for Steve!," *Memphis Daily Appeal*, March 19, 1869.

119. "Fun: Meeting of the Factions," *Memphis Daily Appeal*, April 8, 1869.

120. "Local Paragraphs," *Memphis Daily Appeal*, July 28, 1869.

121. "City Matters," *Memphis Daily Appeal*, July 29, 1869.

122. Stokes was the Republican candidate.

123. "Odds and Ends, and Incidents of the Election," *Memphis Daily Appeal*, August 6, 1869.

124. "Local Brevities," *Public Ledger* (Memphis, TN), December 21, 1869.

125. "Local Paragraphs," *Memphis Daily Appeal*, January 6, 1870.

126. "Shooting Affray: Steve Grayson on the Rampage . . . He Shoots at a Crowd but Misses Them," *Memphis Daily Appeal*, January 31, 1870.

127. "Local Paragraphs," *Memphis Daily Appeal*, February 28, 1870.

128. "Local News," *Memphis Daily Appeal*, July 14, 1870.

129. "Brevities," *Public Ledger* (Memphis, TN), May 30, 1871.

130. "Decorating Federal Graves," *Memphis Daily Appeal*, May 31, 1871.

131. "The Candidates," *Memphis Daily Appeal*, January 15, 1874.

132. "Barbecue at Bartlett," *Memphis Daily Appeal*, July 26, 1878.

133. "Steve Grayson," Shelby County Death Records 1848–1967.

134. "Trade," *Memphis Daily Appeal*, October 14, 1868.

135. "Peace Signs," *Nashville Union*, October 29, 1868.

136. "Radical Pow-Wow," *Daily Memphis Avalanche*, February 24, 1869.

137. "The War: The Hunter-Shaw Embroglio," *Memphis Daily Appeal*, April 1, 1869.

138. "Fun: Meeting of the Factions," *Memphis Daily Appeal*, April 8, 1869.

139. *Daily Memphis Avalanche*, April 8, 1869.

140. "Radical Meeting Last Night," *Public Ledger* (Memphis, TN), April 8, 1869.

141. "The Raging Rads in Revolt," *Daily Memphis Avalanche*, April 9, 1869.

142. "The Radical Conventions," *Daily Memphis Avalanche*, April 18, 1869.

143. "Local Paragraphs," *Memphis Daily Appeal*, April 28, 1869.

144. "City News," *Memphis Daily Appeal*, April 29, 1869.

145. "News in Brief," *Daily Memphis Avalanche*, April 29, 1869.

146. "The Meeting of the Radicals Last Night," *Public Ledger* (Memphis, TN), May 6, 1869.

147. Peffer and Buck were Radical candidates for Montgomery County office.

148. "The Election—The Militia—Buck, Peffer, Bunker & Co," *Clarksville (TN) Chronicle*, June 5, 1869.

149. "B. L." refers to Barbour Lewis. "Local Paragraphs," *Memphis Daily Appeal*, July 4, 1869.

150. The location of White's Station occasions some confusion, as there were two places by that name in Shelby County in 1869. The White's Station on the Mississippi and Tennessee Railroad was named for that railroad's president, Col. Frank White, who lived near that station. It was later called Whitehaven. The other, on the Memphis and Charleston Railroad, was east of Memphis and west of Germantown, where White Station Road crossed the railroad. A later newspaper article about this event clarifies that the latter location is the one in question here.

151. Could this be an oblique reference to a fife and drum band?

152. *Public Ledger* (Memphis, TN), July 31, 1869.

153. "Local Paragraphs," *Memphis Daily Appeal*, August 3, 1869.

154. "Bloodless Riot at Santa Fe," *Columbia (TN) Herald*, August 13, 1869.

155. "Uneasy Sambo," *Republican Banner* (Nashville, TN), November 12, 1869.

156. "Uneasy Sambo."

157. "Sixth Anniversary," *Nashville Union*, January 2, 1870.

158. The *Appeal* was consistent in 1869–70 in using the term "moke" to refer to Black people. I could find no ready reference for this usage, but the *Oxford English Dictionary* lists the archaic "moke" as a reference to a "donkey" or "beast of burden." This is probably the etymology in question.

159. The description of these costumes and how they were made greatly resembles what we know of outfits worn by social aid and pleasure clubs in second lines. It suggests that this phenomenon is unique to New Orleans only to the extent that it still exists there, and that it once may have been found throughout the South.

160. It seems odd that the writer did not make the connection between "I.P.B." and the "Independent Order of Pole Bearers." This society is still referred to as IPB today in Shelby County.

161. The United Sons of Zion, a Black benevolent society, was the organization that Lum Guffin was later a member of in Bartlett. At some point its male and female sides merged into the United Sons and Daughters of Zion. Chapter No. 9 was the Bartlett chapter.

162. Undoubtedly, the Sons and Daughters of Zion were already fraternally associated, though perhaps they had not formally merged. A Daughters of Zion banner had been carried behind the Sons of Zion in this parade, and Sons of Zion were marching with the Daughters of Zion as well. This dynamic still exists in New Orleans. Although a second line might be sponsored by a female organization, such as the Lady Buckjumpers, plenty of men will take part in the parade.

163. "Africa Rampant," *Memphis Daily Appeal*, April 13, 1870.

164. "Anniversary Celebration," *Republican Banner* (Nashville, TN), April 13, 1870.

165. "The Radicals at Work," *Public Ledger* (Memphis, TN), May 21, 1870.

166. "T. S. Ayres, the Drummer Boy," *Public Ledger* (Memphis, TN), May 23, 1870.

167. "Colored S. S. Celebration," *Columbia (TN) Herald*, May 25, 1870.

168. "Organize," *Nashville Union and American*, July 21, 1870.

169. "Sidewalks Obstructed," *Nashville Union and American*, August 2, 1870.

170. "Local News," *Memphis Daily Appeal*, August 25, 1870.

171. "A Radical Can-Can," *Memphis Daily Appeal*, October 4, 1870.

172. "Our Candidates," *Public Ledger* (Memphis, TN), October 4, 1870.

173. "Brevities," *Public Ledger* (Memphis, TN), January 23, 1871.

174. Leo Touchet, *Rejoice When You Die: The New Orleans Jazz Funerals* (Baton Rouge: Louisiana State University Press, 1998), 22.

175. "Brevities," *Public Ledger* (Memphis, TN), May 30, 1871.

176. "Brevities," *Public Ledger* (Memphis, TN), August 9, 1871.

177. "Sons of Zion," *Herald and Tribune* (Greeneville, TN), August 10, 1871.

178. The Greek muse Euterpe was associated with flutes.

179. "Music and Politics," *Public Ledger* (Memphis, TN), September 8, 1871.

180. "City Paragraphs," *Memphis Daily Appeal*, September 30, 1871.

181. "Brevities," *Public Ledger* (Memphis, TN), September 30, 1871.

182. "Cat-gut" is possibly a reference to the fiddle, or alternately the snare drum. "City Paragraphs," *Memphis Daily Appeal*, November 9, 1871.

183. "The Purpose of the People," *Memphis Daily Appeal*, December 31, 1871.

CHAPTER 3: "THESE THINGS MUST HAVE THEIR DAY": FIFE AND DRUM MUSIC, BENEVOLENT SOCIETIES, AND BLACK POLITICAL ORGANIZING IN TENNESSEE, 1872–77

1. "Local Paragraphs," *Memphis Daily Appeal*, January 2, 1872.

2. "Riotous Conduct of Negroes," *Public Ledger* (Memphis, TN), January 2, 1872.

3. Matthew J. Mancini, *One Dies, Get Another: Convict Leasing in the American South, 1866–1928* (Columbia: University of South Carolina Press, 1996), 134–35.

4. Mancini, *One Dies, Get Another*, 134–35.

5. "Dyed in the Wool," *Memphis Daily Appeal*, May 11, 1872.

6. "Ratification," *Republican Banner* (Nashville, TN), June 8, 1872.

7. Horace Greeley was a former newspaper editor and the Liberal Republican nominee for the presidency.

8. "From Galloway's," *Memphis Daily Appeal*, June 14, 1872.

9. "Picnickers," *Memphis Daily Appeal*, June 23, 1872.

10. Curry and Wright were candidates for Shelby County sheriff.

11. *Memphis Daily Appeal*, July 2, 1872.

12. "Tennessee News," *Nashville Union and American*, July 3, 1872, quoted in the *Republican Banner* (Nashville, TN).

13. "Ninety-Sixth Anniversary," *Memphis Daily Appeal*, July 5, 1872.

14. Wythe Depot is now known as Arlington.

15. Mount Joyners is a church and cemetery on Tulane Road in the southern part of Shelby County, in what would now be considered Whitehaven. The Social Benevolent Society of Mount Joyners seemingly had four chapters in the Whitehaven area, quite apart from the other Social Benevolent Society chapters, for there was also a Social Benevolent Society No. 4 at Fullview Baptist Church at Bond's Station (Ellendale) near Bartlett. How the different

Social Benevolent Societies were related is unclear, but it appears that chapter numbers were not unique to locations. For example, there was both a Social Benevolent Society No. 1 in Memphis and a Social Benevolent Society No. 1 in Somerville.

16. "Forefathers' Day," *Daily Memphis Avalanche*, July 5, 1872.

17. "Forefathers' Day."

18. "The Fourth of July," *Public Ledger* (Memphis, TN), July 5, 1872.

19. "The County Court and Fortune of Shelby County," *Memphis Daily Appeal*, July 7, 1872.

20. "Clarksville," *Nashville Union and American*, July 7, 1872.

21. "Local Paragraphs," *Memphis Daily Appeal*, July 10, 1872.

22. "The Jailership," *Republican Banner* (Nashville, TN), July 11, 1872.

23. "County Election," *Memphis Daily Appeal*, August 2, 1872.

24. "Tennessee Colored Fair," *Nashville Union and American*, September 21, 1872.

25. "The Sons of Ham," *Nashville Union and American*, September 22, 1872.

26. "Memphis Colored People at the Tennessee Colored Fair," *Daily Memphis Avalanche*, September 25, 1872.

27. "Kercheval after the Battle," *Republican Banner* (Nashville, TN), September 29, 1872.

28. "Horace" refers to Horace Greeley.

29. "The Republican Rally Last Night," *Nashville Union and American*, October 16, 1872.

30. "Radical Failure," *Public Ledger* (Memphis, TN), October 17, 1872.

31. *Republican Banner* (Nashville, TN), October 20, 1872.

32. "Notes of the Election," *Memphis Daily Appeal*, November 6, 1872.

33. This was probably written backwards by the reporter. It seems more likely that the banner read "Liberal Republicans first cousins to Democrats."

34. "Cheering for Victory," *Daily Memphis Avalanche*, November 15, 1872.

35. "Cheering for Victory."

36. "News in Brief," *Daily Memphis Avalanche*, December 9, 1872.

37. "New Year's Day," *Memphis Daily Appeal*, January 2, 1873.

38. "Ten Years as Freemen," *Daily Memphis Avalanche*, January 2, 1873.

39. "Ten Years as Freemen."

40. "Miscellaneous," *Memphis Daily Appeal*, February 17, 1873.

41. "Local Paragraphs," *Memphis Daily Appeal*, March 14, 1873.

42. "Decoration Day," *Memphis Daily Appeal*, May 24, 1873.

43. This Peabody school was not the present institution located in the Cooper-Young neighborhood of Memphis, but rather a school in the South Memphis rail yards that was later converted to a Black school and renamed Kortrecht High School. It was replaced by Booker T. Washington High School in 1927.

44. "Local Paragraphs," *Memphis Daily Appeal*, June 16, 1873.

45. "Local Paragraphs," *Memphis Daily Appeal*, July 11, 1873.

46. "News in Brief," *Daily Memphis Avalanche*, July 11, 1873.

47. "Ledger Lines," *Public Ledger* (Memphis, TN), July 11, 1873.

48. "Mt. Pleasant Items," *Columbia (TN) Herald*, August 1, 1873.

49. "Ashwood Items," *Columbia (TN) Herald*, August 1, 1873.

50. "Frederick Douglass," *Republican Banner* (Nashville, TN), September 19, 1873.

51. "Special Order," *Daily Memphis Avalanche*, October 8, 1873.

52. "News in Brief," *Daily Memphis Avalanche*, October 29, 1873.

53. "The Tenth District in Arms," *Whig and Tribune* (Jackson, TN), December 13, 1873.

54. "More Disguised Men," *Whig and Tribune* (Jackson, TN), December 20, 1873.

55. "Ledger Lines," *Public Ledger* (Memphis, TN), January 26, 1874.

56. "Shelbyville," *Nashville Union and American*, January 28, 1874.

57. "Local Paragraphs," *Memphis Daily Appeal*, March 21, 1874.

58. "Sumner," *Memphis Daily Appeal*, March 23, 1874.

59. Greenwood was an early name for the neighborhood of South Memphis where Hamilton High School is located.

60. "The Dead," *Daily Memphis Avalanche*, March 23, 1874.

61. "The Dead."

62. "Ledger Lines," *Public Ledger* (Memphis, TN), May 16, 1874.

63. "Decoration Day," *Daily Memphis Avalanche*, May 23, 1874.

64. Springdale was presumably located where the current Springdale Elementary School is, near the intersection of Hollywood and Jackson Avenue in North Memphis.

65. A flying jenny was portable merry-go-round whose proprietor could take it to various events. They were recalled as being at the Independent Pole Bearers' picnics at Brunswick as late as the 1950s.

66. "Decoration Day," *Memphis Daily Appeal*, May 31, 1874.

67. "Decoration Day."

68. "Decoration Day," *Memphis Daily Appeal*, June 2, 1874.

69. "The Pole-Bearers' President in Trouble," *Daily Memphis Avalanche*, June 4, 1874.

70. "Important Arrests," *Public Ledger* (Memphis, TN), June 4, 1874.

71. "Local Paragraphs," *Memphis Daily Appeal*, June 6, 1874.

72. "The Pole-Bearers," *Memphis Daily Appeal*, June 9, 1874.

73. "The Pole-Bearers."

74. "The Pole-Bearers."

75. "A Social Rights Pow-Wow," *Daily Memphis Avalanche*, July 22, 1874.

76. "Where Was That Fife?," *Nashville Union and American*, July 25, 1874.

77. "All Over the City," *Nashville Union and American*, July 26, 1874.

78. "Les Miserables," *Nashville Union and American*, July 29, 1874.

79. *Republican Banner* (Nashville, TN), July 30, 1874.

80. "Heavy Skirmishing," *Nashville Union and American*, August 4, 1874.

81. Most snare drums had snares made of catgut. The use of goose quills seems unusual, to say the least.

82. "A Panicky Crowd," *Republican Banner* (Nashville, TN), August 5, 1874.

83. "Assassinated," *Republican Banner* (Nashville, TN), August 16, 1874.

84. *Fayetteville (TN) Observer*, September 10, 1874.

85. "Stop It," *Memphis Daily Appeal*, September 11, 1874, 2.

86. There had been a riot and mass lynching in Gibson County during the summer.

87. "Stop It."

88. "For Sale—Drums and Fifes," *Public Ledger* (Memphis, TN), September 24, 1874.

89. "Died," *Memphis Daily Appeal*, November 1, 1874.

90. "News in Brief," *Daily Memphis Avalanche*, November 1, 1874.

91. "Descent upon a Colored Dance-House," *Memphis Post*, August 10, 1866.

92. "Death of Tom Swan," *Public Ledger* (Memphis, TN), November 2, 1874.

93. "Thomas Swan," *Daily Memphis Avalanche*, November 3, 1874.

94. "Thomas Swan."

95. "Ledger Lines," *Public Ledger* (Memphis, TN), August 24, 1875.

96. "Dedication of the Monument of the Late Thomas Swan," *Memphis Daily Appeal*, June 13, 1880.

97. "Emancipation Day," *Daily Memphis Avalanche*, January 2, 1875.

98. "Ledger Lines," *Public Ledger* (Memphis, TN), January 2, 1875.

99. "Ledger Lines," *Public Ledger* (Memphis, TN), May 15, 1875.

100. "National Decoration Day," *Public Ledger* (Memphis, TN), May 26, 1875.

101. "Local Paragraphs," *Memphis Daily Appeal*, June 16, 1875.

102. "Ledger Lines, " *Public Ledger* (Memphis, TN), June 28, 1875.

103. "To The Pole-Bearers," *Memphis Daily Appeal*, July 1, 1875.

104. "Celebration of the Fourth of July," *Daily Memphis Avalanche*, July 1, 1875.

105. "Notice," *Memphis Daily Appeal*, July 3, 1875.

106. I have labored under the assumption that this was Montgomery Park, the racetrack that later became the Fairgrounds that we know in Memphis today. The excursion trains to the festival being on the Charleston (Southern) Railroad, which runs past the current Fairgrounds, would seem to bolster my assumption. But the issue is far from certain, and I can find nothing to confirm or deny it.

107. "The Fourth," *Memphis Daily Appeal*, July 6, 1875.

108. "America's Natal Day," *Daily Memphis Avalanche*, July 6, 1875.

109. "A Curious Case," *Public Ledger* (Memphis, TN), July 9, 1875.

110. "Ledger Lines," *Public Ledger* (Memphis, TN), August 4, 1875.

111. "Ledger Lines," *Public Ledger* (Memphis, TN), August 5, 1875.

112. "News in Brief," *Daily Memphis Avalanche*, August 7, 1875.

113. "Bartlett," *Memphis Daily Appeal*, August 13, 1875.

114. "Wilson in Spots," *Daily American* (Nashville, TN), August 31, 1875.

115. "Local Paragraphs," *Memphis Daily Appeal*, September 7, 1875.

116. "Boisterous Sovereigns, " *Daily American* (Nashville, TN), September 16, 1875.

117. "Municipal Politics," *Daily Memphis Avalanche*, January 12, 1876.

118. "4345," *Memphis Daily Appeal*, January 14, 1876.

119. "Ledger Lines," *Public Ledger* (Memphis, TN), March 14, 1876.

120. *Home Journal* (Winchester, TN), March 16, 1876.

121. "Ledger Lines," *Public Ledger* (Memphis, TN), July 19, 1876.

122. "Among the Boisterous Sovereigns," *Nashville American*, August 2, 1876.

123. "Ledger Lines," *Public Ledger* (Memphis, TN), August 21, 1876.

124. *Daily American* (Nashville, TN), September 15, 1876.

125. *Knoxville Daily Tribune*, November 4, 1876.

126. "Yesterday and Last Night," *Knoxville Daily Tribune*, November 7, 1876.

127. "McClellan Guards," *Daily Memphis Avalanche*, June 6, 1877.

128. "The Glorious Fourth," *Memphis Evening Herald*, July 5, 1877.

129. "The Fourth," *Memphis Daily Appeal*, July 6, 1877.

130. "The Fourth," *Bristol (TN) News*, July 10, 1877.

131. "City Politics," *Daily American* (Nashville, TN), August 16, 1877.

132. "Murder," *Memphis Daily Appeal*, August 24, 1877, 4.

133. "A Desperado at Bay," *Daily Memphis Avalanche*, August 26, 1877.

134. "The Big Creek Killing," *Memphis Daily Appeal*, August 30, 1877.

135. "Shelby County Lawlessness," *Memphis Evening Herald*, October 3, 1877.

136. "A Wounded Negro," *Daily Memphis Avalanche*, October 4, 1877.

137. "The Mack Williams Gang," *Public Ledger* (Memphis, TN), October 4, 1877.

138. "The Sheriff's Posse," *Memphis Daily Appeal*, November 5, 1877.

139. "Herald Notes," *Memphis Evening Herald*, November 8, 1877.

140. "More Shooting Near Raleigh," *Public Ledger* (Memphis, TN), November 12, 1877.

141. "Odds and Ends," *Chattanooga Daily Dispatch*, November 15, 1877.

142. "The Flippin Meeting," *Memphis Daily Appeal*, December 14, 1877.

143. "Local Paragraphs," *Memphis Daily Appeal*, December 14, 1877.

144. *Memphis Evening Herald*, December 14, 1877.

CHAPTER 4: "SO IMPORTANT A PART OF THE MACHINERY":
BLACK FIFE AND DRUM MUSIC IN TENNESSEE DURING REDEMPTION, 1878–92

1. "Local Paragraphs," *Memphis Daily Appeal*, January 1, 1878.

2. "Local Paragraphs," *Memphis Daily Appeal*, January 4, 1878.

3. Anderson was the mayoral candidate of the Workingmen's Party.

4. "Ninth Ward," *Public Ledger* (Memphis, TN), January 9, 1878.

5. "News in Brief," *Daily Memphis Avalanche*, January 10, 1878.

6. "Spare Us the Infliction," *Daily American* (Nashville, TN), June 15, 1878.

7. "Local Paragraphs," *Memphis Daily Appeal*, July 7, 1878.

8. "Grand Democratic Rally," *Memphis Daily Appeal*, July 12, 1878.

9. "Democratic," *Memphis Evening Herald*, July 12, 1878.

10. "Slightly Apathetic," *Daily Memphis Avalanche*, July 13, 1878.

11. "News in Brief," *Daily Memphis Avalanche*, July 14, 1878.

12. "Talking for Votes," *Daily Memphis Avalanche*, July 17, 1878.

13. "Local Paragraphs," *Memphis Daily Appeal*, July 18, 1878.

14. "News in Brief," *Daily Memphis Avalanche*, July 20, 1878.

15. "Political," *Memphis Daily Appeal*, July 26, 1878.

16. "Local Paragraphs," *Memphis Daily Appeal*, July 27, 1878.

17. "Local Paragraphs."

18. "Statement of the Pole-Bearers No. 1 of Memphis, Tennessee, during the Great Epidemic from August 1 to November 1, 1878," *Memphis Daily Appeal*, November 3, 1878.

19. "Ledger Lines," *Public Ledger* (Memphis, TN), November 29, 1878.

20. "To Whom It May Concern," *Daily Memphis Avalanche*, May 21, 1879.

21. "Independence Day," *Memphis Daily Appeal*, July 5, 1879.

22. "Local Paragraphs," *Memphis Daily Appeal*, October 2, 1879.

23. "Jubilee Day," *Daily American* (Nashville, TN), October 7, 1879.

24. "Local Paragraphs," *Memphis Daily Appeal*, December 20, 1879.

25. "The News" is a reference to the *Bartlett News*, which the *Avalanche* quotes elsewhere in 1880. No copies are extant.

26. "News in Brief," *Daily Memphis Avalanche*, February 3, 1880.

27. "Getting Up Steam," *Daily Memphis Avalanche*, June 13, 1880.

28. "Getting Up Steam."

29. "More Politics," *Public Ledger* (Memphis, TN), July 2, 1880.

30. "Local Paragraphs," *Memphis Daily Appeal*, July 6, 1880.

31. "Local Paragraphs."

32. "Local Paragraphs," *Memphis Daily Appeal*, July 28, 1880.

33. "Local Paragraphs."

34. "The Speaking Last Night on the Bluff," *Public Ledger* (Memphis, TN), July 28, 1880.

35. "Miscellaneous," *Public Ledger* (Memphis, TN), July 29, 1880.

36. "Collierville," *Daily Memphis Avalanche*, August 3, 1880.

37. "An Expiring Effort," *Daily Memphis Avalanche*, August 3, 1880.

38. "Memphis," *Memphis Daily Appeal*, September 23, 1880.

39. The Hannibal Guards were another Black militia in Memphis.

40. "Memphis," *Memphis Daily Appeal*, September 23, 1880.

41. "Memphis."

42. "Local Paragraphs," *Memphis Daily Appeal*, October 5, 1880.

43. "Colored Democrats," *Daily Memphis Avalanche*, October 6, 1880.

44. "From a Dry Goods Box," *Daily American* (Nashville, TN), October 15, 1880.

45. "Ledger Lines," *Public Ledger* (Memphis, TN), June 15, 1881.

46. "Amusements," *Memphis Daily Appeal*, July 5, 1881.

47. "Ledger Lines," *Public Ledger* (Memphis, TN), July 21, 1881.

48. "City Legislation," *Daily American* (Nashville, TN), August 2, 1881.

49. "Ledger Lines," *Public Ledger* (Memphis, TN), January 3, 1882.

50. The word *senegambian* was used routinely to refer to Blacks in this era. Although the evidence is clear that a lot of Black Tennesseans were in fact descended from people that were kidnapped from the Senegambia region, it is not at all clear that the newspaper editors of the day knew that to be the case. The choice of term was probably viewed as poetic rather than scientific or accurate.

51. "The High Tax Republican Wing," *Public Ledger* (Memphis, TN), July 15, 1882.

52. "They Say," *Daily Memphis Avalanche*, July 16, 1882.

53. "Chattanooga," *Daily American* (Nashville, TN), September 15, 1882.

54. "News in Brief," *Daily Memphis Avalanche*, October 12, 1882.

55. "The Workingmen," *Daily Memphis Avalanche*, October 12, 1882.

56. Hook was a Republican candidate for Shelby County sheriff.

57. "The Workingmen," *Daily Memphis Avalanche*, October 12, 1882.

58. "Ledger Lines," *Public Ledger* (Memphis, TN), October 12, 1882.

59. "Ledger Lines," *Public Ledger* (Memphis, TN), October 13, 1882.

60. "They Say," *Daily Memphis Avalanche*, October 15, 1882.

61. "Fussell Demonstration that Sine Die-d," *Public Ledger* (Memphis, TN), October 23, 1882.

62. "Local Paragraphs," *Memphis Daily Appeal*, October 25, 1882.

63. "Local Paragraphs," *Memphis Daily Appeal*, October 31, 1882.

64. "Covington, Tenn.," *Memphis Daily Appeal*, July 8, 1883.

65. "A Fife and Drum Surfeit," *Daily American* (Nashville, TN), October 13, 1883.

66. "Flem, the Fiddler," *Daily American* (Nashville, TN), March 1, 1884.

67. "They Say," *Daily Memphis Avalanche*, May 4, 1884.

68. "H. G. Hollenberg's Music House," *West Tennessee Whig* (Jackson, TN), July 12, 1884.

69. "They Say," *Daily Memphis Avalanche*, July 20, 1884.

70. "Brownsville," *Daily American* (Nashville, TN), July 26, 1884.

71. "A Week Off," *Memphis Daily Appeal*, August 1, 1884.

72. "Chattanooga," *Daily American* (Nashville, TN), August 3, 1884.

73. "The Republican Rally," *Daily American* (Nashville, TN), August 13, 1884.

74. "Local Politics," *Daily Memphis Avalanche*, October 2, 1884.

75. "A Sufferer's Complaint," *Daily American* (Nashville, TN), October 4, 1884.

76. "City Officials," *Daily Memphis Avalanche*, October 10, 1884.

77. "Local Paragraphs," *Memphis Daily* Appeal, November 5, 1884.

78. "The City's Interests," *Daily Memphis Avalanche*, November 14, 1884.

79. "The Great Jollification," *Daily American* (Nashville, TN), November 14, 1884.

80. "To-Night's Procession," *Daily American* (Nashville, TN), November 15, 1884.

81. "Forty-Fourth General Assembly," *Daily American* (Nashville, TN), March 11, 1885.

82. "A Kercheval Campfire," *Daily American* (Nashville, TN), October 8, 1885.

83. "News in Brief," *Daily Memphis Avalanche*, January 1, 1886.

84. *Daily American* (Nashville, TN), June 29, 1886.

85. "Base Ball Yesterday," *Chattanooga Commercial*, July 13, 1886.

86. "Their Armor On," *Daily American* (Nashville, TN), August 4, 1886.

87. The reference is to David Parks Hadden, president of the taxing district from 1882 to 1891. He was a reform-minded leader of Memphis, popular with the Black community.

88. "News in Brief," *Daily Memphis Avalanche*, August 24, 1886.

89. "At Rest in Olivet," *Daily American* (Nashville, TN), September 7, 1886.

90. "Bob Is Here," *Daily American* (Nashville, TN), October 17, 1886.

91. "To-Day," *Daily American* (Nashville, TN), October 31, 1886.

92. "By the Way," *Daily American* (Nashville, TN), July 16, 1887.

93. This was likely the baseball stadium that became known as Sulphur Dell. Fife and drum activity had been mentioned there earlier in connection with a political rally at Sulphur Springs, and would be a continuing feature there well into the twentieth century.

94. I.O.I. is a reference to the Independent Order of Immaculates, a Black fraternal order.

95. Interestingly, the terminology would suggest that this "foot ball" was a game of soccer rather than the American game we know today. In addition, the teams only had nine members, which would also preclude the eleven-man teams of American football.

96. "The Langston Rifles," *Daily American* (Nashville, TN), September 13, 1887.

97. "The State at Large," *Daily American* (Nashville, TN), September 29, 1887.

98. "Brownsville," *Daily American* (Nashville, TN), September 29, 1887.

99. "The Day in Lebanon," *Daily American* (Nashville, TN), September 30, 1887.

100. "The Reception," *Chattanooga Commercial*, October 13, 1887.

101. "Order of Procession," *Daily Memphis Avalanche*, October 14, 1887.

102. "Memphis Mourns," *Public Ledger* (Memphis, TN), October 18, 1887.

103. "The Banner Bearer Stabbed," *Memphis Daily Appeal*, January 4, 1888.

104. The author seems to use "latter day saints" as a derisive reference to carpetbagger politicians. It is not clear why he does, but he almost certainly does not mean that any Mormons were running for office in Fayette County.

105. "No. 15 News and Notes," *Fayette Falcon* (Somerville, TN), July 25, 1888.

106. Although there is a better-known Shakerag near Millington in modern Shelby County, this Shakerag was an old name for Oakville along the Pigeon Roost Road. "Shakerag" referred to a kind of rag or flag that could be used to flag down a train: in other words, a community that was not a regular station or stop. Oakville and Capleville would remain centers of fife and drum activity into the 1970s.

107. "The Shakerag Scrape," *Daily Memphis Avalanche*, August 16, 1888.

108. "Another Election Affray," *Public Ledger* (Memphis, TN), August 14, 1888.

109. "Caught on the Fly," *Public Ledger* (Memphis, TN), August 30, 1888.

110. This is a reference to General James Ronald Chalmers, a Civil War general who had taken part in the Fort Pillow massacre but had subsequently joined the Republican Party in 1884.

111. *Memphis Daily Appeal*, October 27, 1888.

112. "Houk and Taylor," *Daily American* (Nashville, TN), October 28, 1888.

113. "News in Brief," *Daily Memphis Avalanche*, October 29, 1888.

114. "Decoration Day," *Memphis Daily Appeal*, June 3, 1889.

115. "Maj. Edgington Speech," *Memphis Daily Appeal*, June 4, 1889.

116. "The Negro Should Move," *Memphis Daily Appeal*, June 4, 1889.

117. "A Nuisance and an Outrage," *Public Ledger* (Memphis, TN), June 10, 1889.

118. "Police Court," *Public Ledger* (Memphis, TN), June 11, 1889.

119. "Local Brevities," *Public Ledger* (Memphis, TN), June 11, 1889.

120. "Local Jottings," *Reporter and Falcon* (Somerville, TN), August 7, 1889.

121. "News in Brief," *Daily Memphis Avalanche*, November 24, 1889.

122. A later newspaper article indicates that Cornelius Gowdey was a flautist, so it seems likely that his drum corps included a fife. "Easter Services," *Nashville American*, April 13, 1895.

123. "A Big Celebration," *Daily American* (Nashville, TN), January 2, 1890.

124. "A Big Celebration."

125. "A Wind Artist," *Daily American* (Nashville, TN), August 3, 1890.

126. "The Prohibition Rally," *Daily American* (Nashville, TN), August 7, 1890.

127. "Harrison Condemned," *Daily American* (Nashville, TN), January 2, 1891.

128. "Harrison Condemned."

129. Some have questioned these yards belonging to the Chesapeake and Ohio Railroad. Certainly that railroad did not build them, but a check of 1892 maps shows them labeled "C & O."

130. Preston Lauterbach, *Beale Street Dynasty* (New York: W. W. Norton, 2015), 101–7

131. Lauterbach, *Beale Street Dynasty*, 103.

132. "Local and Personal News," *Camden (TN) Chronicle*, July 22, 1892.

133. "Meeting of Citizens," *Daily American* (Nashville, TN), August 21, 1892.

134. While most Nashville accounts of fife and drum ensembles are of Black bands, we cannot be sure that the band referenced here was a Black one. However, it does seem likely.

135. "Labor Day," *Daily American* (Nashville, TN), September 4, 1892.

136. The Populites were adherents of the Peoples' Party, the new party formed by the Farmers' and Laborers' Alliance in the wake of the mass meeting at Ocala, Florida, in 1892.

137. "Only Eight Days," *Columbia (TN) Herald*, November 1, 1892.

138. "Bedford Celebrates," *Daily American* (Nashville, TN), November 13, 1892.

CHAPTER 5: "NERVE-TORTURERS AND WHOLESALE DISPENSERS OF DISCORD":
BLACK FIFE AND DRUM MUSIC IN TENNESSEE DURING THE NADIR AND
SEGREGATION, 1893–1941

1. "Ren Mulford's Musings," *Nashville American*, October 5, 1901.

2. "Conduit System up in Council," *Nashville American*, April 25, 1902.

3. "City Officials on Telephones," *Nashville American*, May 9, 1902.

4. "City Officials on Telephones."

5. *Nashville American*, May 10, 1902.

6. *Nashville American*, May 24, 1902.

7. *Nashville American*, May 25, 1902.

8. "Letters from the People," *Nashville American*, March 26, 1903.

9. "Letters from the People."

10. "Indorses 'Sufferer's' Protest," *Nashville American*, March 28, 1903.

11. "Letters to the Editor," *Nashville American*, March 27, 1904.

12. *Nashville American*, August 27, 1904.

13. "The Drums and Fifes," *Nashville American*, June 10, 1908.

14. Nashville's minor-league baseball club was eventually named the Volunteers, which is somewhat confusing, given that the University of Tennessee team was also the Volunteers.

15. *Nashville American*, April 3, 1909.

16. "Detectives Get Relief," *Nashville American*, June 2, 1909.

17. Formerly on the site of Sulphur Springs, where Black fife and drum bands had played during Reconstruction, Sulphur Dell was the name of Nashville's longtime minor-league baseball park. It was demolished in 1967.

18. *Nashville American*, March 31, 1910.

19. "Detroit Arrives Today," *Tennessean* (Nashville, TN), April 4, 1910.

20. Vols and Lookouts Stage Big Parade," *Tennessean* (Nashville, TN), April 14, 1915.

21. "Make Plea for Equal Suffrage," *Tennesean* (Nashville, TN), October 24, 1916.

22. "Registered Men in Ninth Ward Busy," *Tennessean* (Nashville, TN), June 8, 1917.

23. "Main Body of Local Delegation Leaves," *Tennessean* (Nashville, TN), June 18, 1917.

24. "District Governor Allison Makes Report," *Tennessean* (Nashville, TN), June 19, 1917.

25. "Nashvillians Made Hit on Stunt Night," *Tennessean* (Nashville, TN), June 21, 1917.

26. *Tennessean* (Nashville, TN), September 19, 1917.

27. "Victorious Vols Face Barons in Dell Today," *Tennessean* (Nashville, TN), April 16, 1920.

28. The meaning of "Rippydedee's" was doubtless familiar to Nashvillians of the era but is not something I could decipher.

29. "Vols Drop First Road Game in Ten Innings," *Tennessean* (Nashville, TN), April 15, 1927.

30. *Tennessean* (Nashville, TN), April 19, 1927.

31. "On a State's Warrant," *Nashville American*, April 5, 1896.

32. "Marriage Licenses," *Nashville American*, March 12, 1899.

33. "Negro Woman Dead," *Nashville American*, July 22, 1899.

34. GenealogyBank.com page for "Yeatman Milam," accessed October 19, 2019, https://www .genealogybank.com/doc/census/image/v2%3A16DABE9A383D710A%40GB3CENSUS -16DABD57666AC338%402415021-16FA0D06D55C1417%40/p_57647216.

35. "Bijou Theatre, Nashville, Tenn.," *Nashville Globe*, December 6, 1918.

36. "Colored Death Notices," *Tennessean* (Nashville, TN), November 28, 1947.

37. "Vols to Play Brewers in Sulphur Dell This Afternoon," *Tennessean* (Nashville, TN), April 11, 1929.

38. "Memos at Random," *Tennessean* (Nashville, TN), January 14, 1948.

CHAPTER 6: "LIKE A MUFFLED, RUMBLING HEARTBEAT": THE REDISCOVERY AND DISAPPEARANCE OF BLACK FIFE AND DRUM MUSIC IN TENNESSEE, 1942–84

1. Dr. David Evans believes, with some good reason, that Lomax was likely mistaken about the name of this picnic grounds. "Po Whore's Kingdom" doesn't sound like the name of a picnic grounds. But it could have been the owner's nickname, or an informal name for a place whose formal name was something else. Furthermore, of course, there was a Po Monkey's Lounge in Merigold, so similar names can be found. But "Po Whore" would have been pronounced "Po Ho," and Lomax may have misunderstood what they were saying.

2. Alan Lomax, *The Land Where the Blues Began*, 314–26.

3. Alan Lomax, *The Land Where the Blues Began*, 327–33.

4. "Tennessee Artists Make Big Hit at Smithsonian," *Tennessean* (Nashville, TN), July 14, 1968.

5. "10 From Tennessee in Folklore Meet," *Tennessean* (Nashville, TN), June 29, 1968.

6. "Bill Barth: Carpetbagging Savior of the Blues," Mount Zion Memorial Fund, December 19, 2017, https://www.mtzionmemorialfund.org/2017/12/bill-barth.html.

7. Jon Pareles, "Robert Palmer Is Dead at 52; Critic Covered Rock and Blues," *New York Times*, November 21, 1997.

8. "Something Old, Something New in Shell's Blues," *Commercial Appeal* (Memphis, TN), July 5, 1968.

9. "Folk Festival Fails to Excite at Newport," *Harvard Crimson* (Cambridge, MA), July 29, 1966.

10. *1968 Memphis Country Blues Festival*, Sire Records SES 97003 (1968).

11. *Memphis Swamp Jam*, Blue Thumb Records BTS 6000 (1969).

12. Dr. David Evans believes it likely that Napolean Strickland, Johnny Woods, and Otha Turner did play at the Memphis Country Blues Festival in 1968, and were the "Southern Fife and Drum Corps" in question. He seems to base that at least in part on their inclusion in the *Memphis Swamp Jam* recording. Weighing against his theory is the fact that the Southern Fife and Drum Corps name seems to have exclusively been used by the Youngs. On the other hand, I have found nobody who was present at the festival who remembers a fife and drum band playing there at all.

13. Robert Jennings, "Wayne Newton Makes Sept. 26 Fair Date," *Commercial Appeal* (Memphis, TN), May 21, 1969.

14. Eugene Chadbourne, "Folk Artists Mix Music with History," *Calgary (AB) Herald*, April 1, 1976.

15. "Grassroots Days Evoke 'Down Home' Feeling," *Tennessean* (Nashville, TN), September 9, 1977.

16. Bengt Olsson, "Drum and Fife," in unpublished manuscript materials for revision of *Memphis Blues*.

17. Annie Humphrey, interview by the author, June 13, 2019, Fredonia, TN.

18. Ed Harris, interview by Robert Jeffrey, August 6, 1980, Somerville, TN.

19. Anonymous, interview by the author, October 13, 2018, Mason, TN.

20. Anonymous, interview by the author, October 13, 2018, Mason, TN.

21. Bengt Olsson seems to have misunderstood the name of this community as Bruels, possibly from the way Ossie Broadnax or Plez Rivers pronounced the name.

22. Joe Gray Taylor, letter to John Flowers Taylor, February 4, 1984.

23. Olsson, "Drum and Fife."

24. Myles Wilson, interview by the author, October 10, 2018, Somerville, TN.

25. This tantalizing reference to a recording of the Broadnax Brothers has not yet yielded any information about what became of this recording.

26. Olsson, "Drum and Fife."

27. Olsson, "Drum and Fife."

28. In August of 2020, a group of men at the dead end of Brewer Road pointed across the road to a concrete slab foundation and stated that this was the location of the Dew Drop Inn.

29. Olsson, "Drum and Fife."

30. Ceremonial swords were mentioned in regard to the benevolent societies in Memphis newspaper articles of the 1870s.

31. Olsson, "Drum and Fife."

32. Bengt Olsson, letter to David Evans, July 12, 1974.

33. Bengt Olsson, letter to David Evans, July 12, 1974.

34. Bengt Olsson, letter to David Evans, July 12, 1974.

35. Mark Mikolas, email to the author, June 21, 2019.

36. But that was from her perspective in 2019. From a 1975 letter she sent to David Evans, it would seem that there were five hours of film footage and fifteen hours of interviews. It's hard to imagine that Plez Rivers was not in some of the footage.

37. Bengt Olsson, letter to David Evans, March 27, 1972.

38. Dr. Dorothy Granberry, "The Fredonia AF—AM Lodge Drum and Fife Band," *Brownsville (TN) Press*, December 2, 2015.

39. Granberry, "The Fredonia AF—AM Lodge Drum and Fife Band."

40. Olsson's information about this community of Oak Grove in Fayette County is somewhat confusing. There was a community called Oak Grove in eastern Shelby County along Highway 64 near Bartlett, and an Oak Grove chapter of the Independent Pole Bearers Society, which was No. 2. But Hallie Manson did not live in Shelby County, and this was probably not the community in question. There is today no Oak Grove community in Fayette County, but there is an Oak Grove Gin Company on Highway 222 between Somerville and Stanton in Fayette, which suggests that there once might have been a community by that name in northwestern Fayette County. It is also possible that there was an IPB Society No. 3 there, but there is nothing to suggest this other than Olsson's manuscript.

41. Annie Humphrey, interview by the author, June 13, 2019, Fredonia, TN.

42. Dr. David Evans had a fifteen-track listing for what was likely a seamless reel of tape, but when he burned a CD-R of it for me, the resulting disc only had seven tracks. I used his fifteen-track list in compiling the contents of the seven tracks.

43. Olsson, "Drum and Fife."

44. Comments on the recording suggest that this may in fact have been the house of Annie Humphrey, whom I interviewed in the summer of 2019. A woman's voice can be heard, and one of the drummers refers to Bennie Thompson as "her daddy."

45. Judith Mikolas, letter to David Evans, May 13, 1974.

46. Mount Olive Missionary Baptist Church is along the LaGrange Road southeast of Somerville in Fayette County.

47. Union Hill Missionary Baptist Church is on Highway 179 near Whiteville in Hardeman County. Bledsoe was a Fayette County pastor who seems to have been active in civil rights activity there during the 1960s. He seems to have lived near Mason.

48. "Fredonia Church Fife and Drum Band, March 15, 1974," reel of tape in possession of Dr. David Evans.

49. Bengt Olsson, letter to David Evans, July 12, 1974.

50. This was likely Tucker's Mill, a place just to the north of Somerville along what is now Highways 76 and 59.

51. Bengt Olsson, letter to David Evans, July 12, 1974.

52. David Evans, "Black Fife and Drum in Mississippi," *Mississippi Folklore Register* 6 (Fall 1972): 94–107.

53. "Local Paragraphs," *Memphis Daily Appeal*, November 19, 1882.

54. Bill Barth, liner notes to Lum Guffin, *Walking Victrola* (UK: Flyright LP 503, 1973).

55. Bengt Olsson, "Fayette_Shelby County," in unpublished manuscript materials for revision of *Memphis Blues*.

56. Bill Barth, liner notes to *Walking Victrola*.

57. Olsson, "Fayette_Shelby County."

58. Bill Barth, liner notes to *Walking Victrola*.

59. Olsson, "Fayette_Shelby County." Although the picture and clipping mentioned were undoubtedly real, they do not appear in any microfilmed Memphis newspapers from 1969. Although there were multiple editions of the *Commercial Appeal* each day, only one was microfilmed for preservation. Although the University of Memphis has acquired the *Appeal*'s morgue, the collection has not been processed and is not yet available for research.

60. Stephan Michelson, email to the author, July 22, 2019.

61. The paragraphs on the album's back cover are attributed to Bill Barth, but they also appear in Bengt Olsson's unpublished manuscript of the revised *Memphis Blues* from around the time of Olsson's death in 2006. While the paragraphs do not read particularly differently from the rest of Olsson's manuscript, the fact is that Barth was also a writer. At the time of Barth's death, excerpts from his autobiography, *Confessions of a Psychedelic Carpetbagger*, had appeared online. I have chosen to consider Barth the author, as the album attribution to him in 1973 is the older reference.

62. Barth, liner notes to *Walking Victrola*.

63. IPB Society No. 5 was actually the Bridgewater chapter. The Oak Grove chapter was IPB Society No. 2.

64. Rev. Arthur Becton, interview by the author, February 3, 2018, Bartlett, TN.

65. E. Davies Rogers, *The Holy Innocents* (Brunswick, TN: Plantation Press, 1966), 345.

66. Rogers, *The Holy Innocents*, 345.

67. Roy Brewer, interview by the author, March 27, 2018, Brunswick, TN.

68. Bengt Olsson, liner notes to *On the Road Again*, Flyright 58 (1997).

69. Olsson, liner notes to *On the Road Again*.

70. Bengt Olsson, "Drum_Fife."

71. Olsson, liner notes to *On the Road Again*.

72. "Old Time Music Festival Coming to U of C," *Calgary (AB) Herald*, March 26, 1976.

73. Seven years before 1976 would be 1969, which raises the interesting question of whether Chadbourne was in Overton Park at the Memphis Country Blues Festival. I am not aware of any other public fife and drum band performance that year. The Como Fife and Drum Band played the inaugural New Orleans Jazz and Heritage Festival in Congo Square the next year, 1970, but that would not have been seven years before.

74. Eugene Chadbourne, "Folk Artists Mix Music with History."

75. Helen Lacko, "Old Time Fest Provided Unique Blendings," *Daily Utah Chronicle* (Salt Lake City), April 5, 1976.

76. Philip Elwood, "Old Time Music Delights Faithful," *San Francisco Examiner*, April 12, 1976.

77. University of Washington Ethnomusicology Archives, "Robert Garfias Recordings: Sons & Daughters of Zion #9; J. Jackson, 1976–04–05," accessed October 24, 2019, http://archiveswest.orbiscascade.org/ark:/80444/xv78097/pdf.

78. The original film in question is held by the Robert Garfias Collection at the Ethnomusicology Archives at the University of Washington in Seattle, which graciously provided MP4 files of it for my research.

79. "Week End Wraparound," *Tennessean* (Nashville, TN), October 15, 1976.

80. Bengt Olsson, letter to David Evans, July 12, 1974.

81. Stephan Wirz, "Lum Guffin Discography," accessed October 24, 2019, https://www.wirz.de/music/guffin.htm.

82. Steve James, email to the author, March 28, 2018.

83. James Chisum, "Burial Customs Rooted in Ex-Slaves' Pride," *Commercial Appeal* (Memphis, TN), November 30, 1976.

84. This would seem to be Faulkner Grove, a picnic ground at the dead end of Faulkner Road off of Getwell Road, south of Shelby Drive. Incredibly, as of 2019, this picnic grove still exists and has been improved, with a deck and patio, a stage for performers, and a small building that would seem to be used as a bar.

85. "Chicken" George Walker, interview by David Evans, March 7, 1984, Memphis, TN.

86. Sandra Stepton, interview by the author, May 16, 2019, Memphis, TN.

87. There is a Jackson Pit Road in that neighborhood.

88. Elizabeth Harmon, interview by the author, May 16, 2019, Memphis, TN.

89. Olsson, "Fayette_Shelby County."

90. Olsson, "Drum_Fife."

91. Olsson, "Drum_Fife."

92. Bengt Olsson, letter to David Evans, March 30, 1973.

93. Bengt Olsson, letter to David Evans, July 3, 1973.

94. Bengt Olsson, letter to David Evans, September 3, 1973.

95. Bengt Olsson, letter to David Evans, July 12, 1974.

96. "None Signed Their Names," *Commercial Appeal* (Memphis, TN), January 29, 1893.

97. Billy Williams, Facebook message to John Shaw, January 16, 2020.

98. Bengt Olsson, "Little Buddy Doyle_Hattie Bolten," in unpublished manuscript materials for revision of *Memphis Blues*.

99. Olsson, "Little Buddy Doyle_Hattie Bolten."

100. Savannah Moore, phone interview by the author, March 2018.

101. Bengt Olsson, letter to David Evans, July 12, 1974. Jamestown was a community in Tipton County near the Mississippi River.

102. Little Joe Ayers, phone interview by the author, June 2018.

103. Dan Brown, "Eephing: Fancy Hiccup Is West Tennessee's Gift to the World," *Jackson (TN) Sun*, May 28, 1981.

104. Bengt Olsson, "Lauderdale_Haywood County," in unpublished manuscript materials for revision of *Memphis Blues*.

105. Olsson, "Lauderdale_Haywood County."

106. Ed Harris, interview by Robert Jeffries, August 6, 1980 (notes and recording held by the Tennessee State Archives).

107. I originally intended to transcribe this track as I did two others from other sets of Tennessee fife and drum band recordings. Ultimately, I decided it was so tentative and out of sync with itself as to defy transcription.

108. Emmanuel Dupree, interview by Robert Jeffrey, July 24, 1980 (notes and recording held by the Tennessee State Archives).

109. Dupree, interview by Robert Jeffrey, July 24, 1980.

110. Dupree, interview by Robert Jeffrey, July 24, 1980.

111. Ed Harris, interview by Robert Jeffrey, August 6, 1980 (notes and recording held by the Tennessee State Archives).

112. Harris, interview by Robert Jeffrey, August 6, 1980.

113. There seems to have been a tradition in Fayette County of celebrating Emancipation in August. That could have been the occasion for the August 24th celebration.

114. Ed Harris, interview by Robert Jeffrey, August 6, 1980 (notes and recording held by the Tennessee State Archives).

BIBLIOGRAPHY

Barker, Danny, and Jack V. Buerkle. *Bourbon Street Black*. London: Oxford University Press, 1973.

Cimbala, Paul Alan. "Fortunate Bondsmen: Black 'Musicianers' in the Antebellum Southern States." MA thesis, Emory University, 1977.

Danser, Kathleen. "Representations of African-American Fife and Drum Music in North Mississippi." MA thesis, University of Alberta, 2011.

Davies-Rogers, E. *The Holy Innocents*. Brunswick, TN: Plantation Press, 1966.

Evans, David. "Black Fife and Drum in Mississippi." *Mississippi Folklore Register* (Fall 1972): 94–107.

Ferris, William. *Give My Poor Heart Ease*. Chapel Hill: University of North Carolina Press, 2009.

Ford, Michael. *North Mississippi Homeplace*. Athens: University of Georgia Press, 2019.

Georgia Writers Project. *Drums and Shadows: Survival Studies among the Georgia Coastal Negroes*. Athens: University of Georgia Press, 1986. First published 1940.

Hay, Fred J. *Goin' Back to Sweet Memphis: Conversations With the Blues*. Athens: University of Georgia Press, 2001.

Jenkins, Earnestine Lovelle. *Race, Representation and Photography in 19th-Century Memphis*. Burlington, VT: Ashgate, 2016.

Joiner, Lauren. "'Stuff You Gotta Watch': The Effect of Anglo-American Scholarship on North Mississippi Blues Fife and Drum." MM thesis, Texas Tech University, 2009.

Lauterbach, Preston. *Beale Street Dynasty*. New York: W.W. Norton, 2015.

Lomax, Alan. *The Land Where the Blues Began*. New York: Pantheon Books, 1993.

Mancini, Matthew G. *One Dies, Get Another: Convict Leasing in the American South, 1866–1928*. Columbia: University of South Carolina Press, 1996.

Marumo, Phelemo Olifile. "Christianity and African Traditional Religion in Dialogue: An Ecological Future for Africa." PhD diss., North West University, Mahikeng, South Africa, 2016.

Massie, James William. *America: The Origin of Her Present Conflict*. London: John Snow, 1864.

McGregory, Jerrilyn. *Downhome Gospel: African-American Spiritual Activism in Wiregrass Country*. Jackson: University Press of Mississippi, 2010.

Mitchell, George. *Blow My Blues Away*. Baton Rouge: Louisiana State University Press, 1971.

Mitchell, George. *Mississippi Hill Country 1967*. Jackson: University Press of Mississippi, 2013.

Oliver, Sylvester. "African-American Musical Traditions in Northeast Mississippi." PhD diss., University of Memphis, 1996.

Olsson, Bengt. *Memphis Blues*. London: November Books, 1970.

Olsson, Bengt. Unpublished manuscript materials (2006) for revision of *Memphis Blues* (London: November Books, 1970). Used with permission of the author's widow, Suzette Moser.

Page, Brian Daniel. "Local Matters: Race, Place and Community Politics after the Civil War." PhD diss., Ohio State University, 2009.

Roberts, John Storm. *Black Music of Two Worlds: African, Caribbean, Latin and African-American Traditions*. Belmont, CA: Wadsworth/Thomas Learning, 1998.

Severance, Ben H. *Tennessee's Radical Army: The Tennessee State Guard and Its Role in Reconstruction, 1867–1869*. Knoxville: University of Tennessee Press, 2005.

Southern, Eileen. *The Music of Black Americans*. New York: W. W. Norton, 1997.

Touchet, Leo. *Rejoice When You Die: The New Orleans Jazz Funerals*. Baton Rouge: Louisiana State University Press, 1998.

Vermilyea, Carl. "The Otha Turner Picnic: Occupying Musical and Social Space in-between Saturday Night and Sunday Morning." MM thesis, University of North Texas, 2011.

Wells-Barnett, Ida B. *The Memphis Diaries of Ida B. Wells*. Boston: Beacon Press, 1995.

AUDIO RECORDINGS

1968 Memphis Country Blues Festival. Sire Records SES 97003, 1968.

Afro-American Folk Song from Tate and Panola Counties, Mississippi. Archive of Folk Song L67, 1978.

Ed Harris, James Tatum, Emanuel Dupree. Performance recording, Chickasaw Folklife Festival, Henderson, TN, May 6, 1980. Tape held by the Tennessee State Archives in Nashville.

"Fredonia Church Fife and Drum Band, March 15, 1974." Reel of tape in possession of Dr. David Evans.

Memphis Swamp Jam. Blue Thumb BTS 6000, 1969.

Old Country Blues, Field Recordings, 1969–1974. Flyright (UK) 553, 1979.

On the Road Again. Flyright (UK) CD 58, 1997.

Traveling Through the Jungle. Testament 5017, 1995 (reissue of 1973 album).

FILMS

Gravel Springs Fife and Drum. Memphis, TN: Center for Southern Folklore, 1972.

"Lum Guffin Fife and Drum Band." April 5, 1976. Robert Garfias Collection, Ethnomusicology Archives, University of Washington, Seattle.

INDEX

ABOUT THE AUTHOR

John M. Shaw is a musicologist, musician, writer, and blogger, currently pursuing a doctorate at the University of Memphis. He contributed an essay to *Shreveport Sounds in Black and White*, published by University Press of Mississippi.

9 781496 839558